WOOD ENERGY
A Practical Guide
to
Heating with Wood

by

Mary Twitchell

Illustrations by Cathy Baker

Garden Way Publishing
Charlotte, Vermont 05445

Printed in the United States
Second printing, January 1979
First printing, November 1978
ISBN 0-88266-145-0

Table of Contents

Introduction

The January wind whistles around the home, its cold fingers testing each door and window, each possible crack for ways to cool this building. Cold plus wind mean heating units work their hardest, but in this home, there's no hum of an oil burner at work, no meters spinning wildly to clock the use of energy.

This house is wood-heated with heat radiating out from an airtight stove, a stove that in the winter draws family members close to its side. Near the stove, too, is a woodbox, heaped with a two-day supply of wood that's dry and warm, ideal for burning. Outside there's a roomy woodshed. All members of this family like to look at it and sense again the warm satisfaction that comes from helping to cut, split, and stack those ten cords that will heat their home for this winter and part of next.

That wind may carry snow that blocks the highway; snows and wind, too, can snap wires and fell poles. This family may worry about the storm but won't suffer from the cold. They aren't dependent for heat on the arrival of the oil truck, or the continued flow of electricity through those wires. As long as the family feeds the fire, that stove will radiate its heat.

That's one side of heating with wood: the independence ten cords of dry wood can give you; the money you can save, particularly if you have a woodlot of your own; and the good feeling of ac-

complishment a family gets if wood heat is a family project.

There's another side, of course. Burning wood requires a degree of work and participation undreamed of by the family whose heat consists of setting the thermostat and writing the check for the fuel. There's wood to be cut, stacked, and dried, and carried into the home on a very regular basis. There's the stove to be set up in the fall and taken down in the spring, and cleaned of its ashes on a regular basis. There's stove tending and tinkering and feeding, and good is the man or woman who can mind the stove no more frequently than every six hours. This means no weekend trips, if you depend solely on wood heat, unless you have a fire-sitter.

Joan Wells, writing in her **Downwind from Nobody** about the people who try homesteading and succeed or fail, says, "Seen at a distance, it isn't so much events that make the difference between surmounting and going under, and sheer luck is too rare to consider. At the bottom, it's attitude."

And so it is with burning wood in the home. Some try it, hate it, and go back to what may be more expensive but is worth it to them.

For others, there's a deep satisfaction in burning wood, in its rituals and chores.

For those who have turned to wood and enjoy it, the choice was made, and was a satisfying one. On some day in the future, all of us will have to

1

face decisions about alternate methods of heating. Estimates of world reserves of fossil fuels vary with the year and the reporter, but they emphasize that the sun is setting on the day of cheap petroleum products.

Our country has changed fuels before. In 1850 wood provided 90 percent of our energy needs, with coal supplying a mere 10 percent. By 1895 coal accounted for 65 percent of the energy pie. With the discovery of oil, the use of coal decreased as the era of easy oil and natural gas began.

Figures for 1970 illustrate our reliance on fossil fuels:

Coal	20%	Hydroelectric	4%
Petroleum	41%	Miscellaneous	2%
Natural Gas	33%		

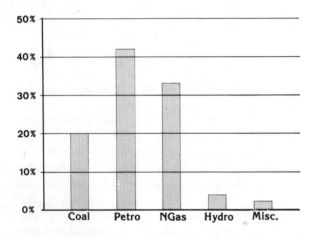

The supply of fossil fuels is finite. Some people are optimistic about coal, particularly since the United States possesses considerable coal reserves. But at some point it will cost more energy to recover coal than the coal can produce. There are also recovery difficulties with coal: deep mining presents well-documented health hazards; strip mining, although cheaper, can be extremely damaging to the ecology; and the burning of coal is a severe pollution problem.

The Economic Research and Development Association (ERDA), the branch of the government which deals with energy matters, has allocated 40 percent of its current budget to nuclear energy. Clearly this is the government's hope. With a combination of nuclear power plants and breeder reactors which will reprocess the spent uranium ore, we can potentially have unlimited power. However, nuclear energy presently meets only 5 percent of America's energy demand. By the year 2000 this figure is predicted to rise to 30–40 percent. What will provide the rest?

Not only will nuclear energy be unable to bridge this gap, but the industry is plagued with problems. The technology is still rudimentary, construction costs have risen, safety standards have become more stringent, radioactive waste is accumulating with no fail-safe method of storage, and the concern of environmental groups for the safety of plant, animal and human life is growing steadily. The government worries about national security and sabotage, for plutonium, easily made into bombs, could fall into the wrong hands. While the breeder reactor program (a program which will make more fuel than it uses) remains on the drawing boards, radioactive spent ore is accumulating, and our supplies of uranium are dwindling.

The nuclear industry may even price itself out of the market. With escalating costs, mandatory safety standards, shutdowns, etc., the cost per kilowatt hour (from nuclear energy) could surpass that for coal.

There are other alternatives. Geothermal (heat from within the earth) and tidal power have been suggested, but neither would be of much significance on a large scale.

Solar energy reaches the earth at 100–120° F., ideal for home heating, and concentrating lenses can be used to multiply these temperatures for other uses. Solar energy is versatile, but collectors are costly, and in many parts of the country it remains economically unfeasible to attempt to meet all heating-cooling needs with solar collectors.

Solar energy can be used in other forms such as water, wind, biofuels, or wood. The alternative to low-cost oil may not be one source of energy, but many. Thus harnessing sunlight may become commonplace in the sunny Southwest; wind stations located off the coast may furnish power for much of the East; hydroelectric installations may be depended on for electricity where such installations can be used; and in areas where there is a generous wood supply, such as New England and the Northwest, wood heat may be generally accepted.

Possibly one-third of the United States might be heated with wood, with use of wood expanding from the present stoves to wood-burning furnaces in common use, and gigantic amounts of wood refuse being ground up and fed into furnaces for the generation of electrical power.

Such a move may bring with it an improvement in one of our most valuable natural resources, our forests. If we made no effort to manage our forests but removed only what the forest turned over naturally, we could have some 200 million cords of wood annually without diminishing the forests at all. But we could go further. Undesirable trees now abound. As we improve the forest land by taking cull trees for fuel, trees that produce better sawlogs get an opportunity to grow. And we could go still further. If the forests were well managed, their productivity could be doubled. Finland and Germany have increased forest output through intensive woodlot management. In addition, lumber companies in this country utilize only 27 percent of the available tree material. The remainder is perfectly acceptable for fuel.

Wood

Wood as a heating fuel has many advantages. It is in good supply in areas remote from energy pipelines. This makes it an attractive hedge against disaster, be it national, regional, or personal (were the furnace to fail, leaving the pipes in danger of freezing). Relying on local resources would reassert a regional sense of security and independence now threatened as all parts of the country tie into one-grid or one-fuel systems.

Fuel transportation costs are cut when wood locally available is burned. Pollution problems are reduced, too, since there's little difference in emissions between wood burned and wood left to rot on the forest floor. When compared with other fuels, wood has almost no sulphur or ash content.

There are disadvantages. Wood will never be as convenient to burn as oil or gas. Wood is bulkier and less efficient, providing almost one-third of the heat of oil per pound, and half that of coal.

Oil can be pumped into an unobtrusive cellar tank, or unseen outdoor and underground tank, but wood requires at least five times the space oil demands for a winter's supply.

Heating with wood may be fun the first year, but it can become tiring, dull, and demanding, since, like babies, wood stoves must be fed on a regular schedule. In the spring and summer, trees must be felled, bucked, split, hauled, stacked, stored, dried, carried; the stove must be installed, stoked, cleaned, reassembled, stoked again and again. Ash pans must be dumped; dampers must be pampered. To heat with wood is a part-time, underpaid occupation.

Most people who enjoy heating with wood like saving money, or enjoy the independence it permits them, or simply want to be more self-sufficient, and so heating with wood is a part of a lifestyle that includes raising their own food, making their own clothing, and finding deep satisfaction from all of these.

There's no question but that money can be saved, in most areas. If your per-gallon cost for oil is more than 50¢ and if you can buy good wood for burning for $60 or less a cord, the wood is a less expensive fuel.

Wood-burning may become even more attractive. If oil prices rise, more and more homeowners will turn to wood for economic reasons alone. Too, the technology of wood-burning is still developing. Stoves and furnaces will be designed to burn more efficiently. We may soon see automatic feeding systems which will relieve the homeowner of the constant stoking and vigilance.

But it is time to stop dreaming of the future and confront the present. You're thinking of burning wood, or perhaps you've already installed a stove or a furnace, or want to get some extra heat out of that fireplace. Let's get at those practical questions.

Fireplaces

What homeowner isn't indignant when he reads that his fireplace, the traditional focal point of family activity, is zero percent efficient as a heating unit? Many of us bought homes specifically because of the fireplace—the memory of childhood, Christmas, popcorn, fragrant smells, fantasy, and warmth. But with the wood stove craze, fireplaces are taking a beating. What, we ask, would be left of Dickens's **CHRISTMAS CAROL** were the Cratchet family huddled in the cellar around the oil jet for Christmas? But science, whether we want them or not, always provides figures to shatter the best of dreams.

Heating efficiencies are stated in percentages that tell you what amount of the total chemical energy in the wood is converted into useful heat. Quite simply, they tell you what you are getting for what you are putting in. Chemical energy is measured in BTU's or British Thermal Units. One BTU is the amount of heat required to raise one pound (or one pint) of water 1 °F. (A BTU is roughly

the heat produced by a kitchen match; the human body produces about 400 BTU's per hour; and it takes approximately 20,000 BTU's per hour to heat an average room.) Hence if I can calculate the BTU content of the wood which I am burning (about 8600 BTU's per hour per pound of wood) as well as the BTU's which the stove or fireplace is providing as useful heat to the room, I can calculate the efficiency of the unit I am using. Efficiencies can vary tremendously. If a fireplace draws poorly or the fire has been laid sloppily, it's obvious that little heat is being radiated.

Generally, a fireplace is 15 percent efficient; antique stoves (including modern replicas of the Franklin, pot belly and parlor stoves) are 30 percent efficient, while modern airtight stoves are 45–65 percent efficient. This means that the fireplace uses more than three times as much wood as a modern wood stove to generate the same amount of heat. Fireplaces are the Cadillacs of the wood heating industry. They have outrageous class!

Fireplace Inefficiency

Wood needs oxygen to burn. Therefore to reap even a modicum of heat, fireplaces, because of their voracious appetites for wood, need large infusions of oxygen. For every pound of air the fire consumes in combustion, a pound of air must enter, and this is generally drawn through cracks around windows and door openings. Cold air then is replacing warm air which is sucked in by the fire, rises across the flames to the shelf back and soon is lost up the chimney. With a fireplace there is no way to control the rate of burn. Use of the damper, which provides minimal control if partially shut, can lead to smoking out the fire's most ardent devotées.

If the house thermostat is in the same room as the fireplace, the heat from the fireplace will raise the room temperature a few degrees, just enough to keep the furnace off. At this point the rest of the house cools, rather dramatically if it is a cold, windy night.

Since even a smoldering fire gives off noxious gases, the damper must be left open, usually all night. During the night the furnace goes on, and air heated by the furnace begins escaping up the chimney. At this point the fireplace is zero percent efficient.

However, the picture need not be as bleak if fireplaces are used judiciously. The longer you are comfortable without the furnace on, the greater the savings in fuel. With a long continuous burn, you may be able to keep the furnace off all day and still be comfortable. This is easily accomplished on calm, mild days or in the spring and fall when there is no danger of frozen pipes.

Mid-winter use of a fireplace on an exterior wall is impractical. But if the chimney is contained within the house, the masonry will gradually warm, so that, when the fire dies down, heat will still radiate from the stone or brick.

Fireplaces in today's homes are not designed to be central heating systems, but you may be able to prolong the seasonal use of a fireplace if you are willing to live with lower temperatures in other rooms. Many times because of the fireplace location (in a den, for example), it is possible (by closing doors to the fireplace room) to keep that room warm enough even for sedentary activities such as reading and watching TV. Bedrooms and basements never needed 70°F. temperatures. With caulked windows, thermal curtains and plenty of blankets, puffs, flannel sheets and warm pajamas, bedrooms can be left unheated practically all winter. The kitchen generally provides its own heat. Hot water left in the bathtub will increase both the heat and the humidity of the house if the door is left open, and extra clothes are cheaper than oil bills. Such a system for zoning one's house will afford savings sufficient to offset the cost of wood.

Remember that fires can be regulated to some degree by the damper. Study your damper when there's no fire in your fireplace. It should have two or three notches, permitting it to be partially closed. Start your fire with the damper wide open, then partially close it. This will decrease the oxygen intake of the fire, and result in more heat in the room.

None of these readjustments is worth a nickel unless they spell the difference between turning the furnace on or leaving it off. Certainly the mid-winter fire built for those enchanted by the ballet of flames is worthless if you are hoping to cut your fuel bill.

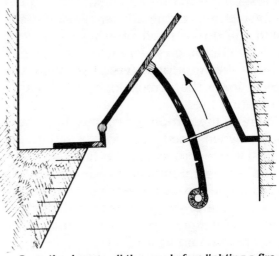

Open the damper all the way before lighting a fire.

FIREPLACE DEVICES

Since one out of every five houses and apartments has a fireplace, there's a tremendous market for devices which will make the fireplace more efficient. Most of the devices such as fireplace grates, metal reflectors, and blowers attempt to direct into the room some of that heat normally lost up the chimney. Glass doors and metal shields are designed to prevent furnace-warmed air from escaping up the chimney.

Reflectors

Metal heat reflectors are simple to make. Anything which provides a reflective surface will do—heavy foil, aluminum flashing, sheet metal, or ready-made firebacks of black iron. Holes should be drilled or punched (depending on which material you use) through the fireback and into the masonry with a masonry bit. The shield is then attached to the back wall of the fireplace with lag bolts.

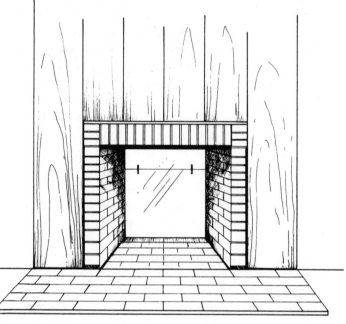

Reflector

Fireplace Shields

A fireproof fireplace cover can be made to block off the hearth opening at night when the fire dies out, so that furnace-heated air is not lost up the chimney all night. The tighter the fit the greater the efficiency. Any metal shield will do—a sheet of asbestos, ¼-inch stove-board, ⅛-inch sheet metal, or even better, tight-fitting heavy steel plate doors. Be sure to leave the damper open even with a smoldering fire.

There is the remote possibility that these shields when used on exterior chimneys could be dangerous. As the fire cools, the natural updraft diminishes and should it be reversed, the fire would be reactivated and/or cause smoke or noxious gases to enter the room. The danger is less with interior chimneys which retain heat longer.

Fireproof shields are somewhat inconvenient, but cheap.

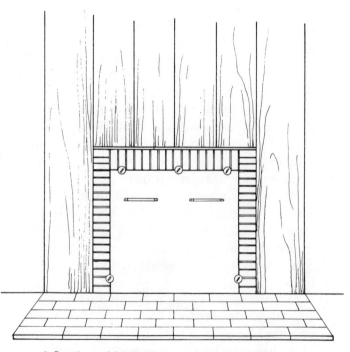

A fireplace shield will prevent the loss of furnace-heated air at night.

Glass Doors

Door units of tempered glass provide even more control. With the doors closed you still have the enjoyment of watching the fire while being able to regulate the amount of oxygen entering the fireplace. There are air inlets in the bottom of the unit which, once you have the fire going, can be opened or closed according to how much oxygen the fire needs. Since glass loses its temper at 600°F., there is a second air inlet at the top of the doors which sets up a draft pattern down the doors to prevent them from cracking.

By enclosing the fire, glass doors make the fireplace function much like a wood stove. Control over the combustion of a fire means a longer, hotter fire. However large quantities of the warm infrared radiation are absorbed by the glass. With the doors closed the amount of direct radiation is decreased by as much as 65 percent, even though the firebox temperatures are at least 200–300°

hotter. There is some value in this if you have an interior chimney, but with an exterior chimney, heating the masonry is heating the outdoors.

The only way to use glass doors efficiently is to leave them open except when the fire is almost out or at night to prevent losing furnace-warmed heat, in which case a tight-fitting metal shield is cheaper and just as effective.

Glass doors

Glass door Thermogate Fireplace Heater combines glass doors with the convection type forced hot air heat of the tube grate.

7

Heat Chambers

Heat chambers which project out from the top of the fireplace opening capture heat generated by the fire. When the fireplace heat reaches a designated temperature, a blower, which can be plugged into normal household current, is automatically switched on to circulate the excess heat. These units will fit most fireplace openings. You need only measure the width, the depth of the fireplace at the top, and the width at the rear of the firebox. To the cost of firewood, you now must add the cost of the unit, plus electricity.

Conventional andirons lose heat up the chimney.

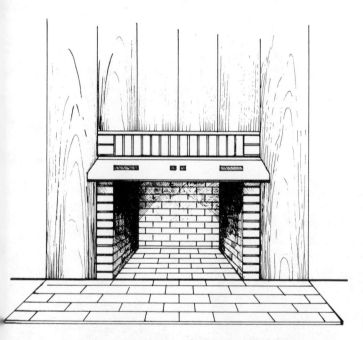

Heat chambers recover fireplace heat ordinarily lost up the chimney.

Fireplace Grates

Recently there has been a great deal of interest in redesigning fireplace grates. Traditionally fires are built with newspaper and kindling placed between the andirons on a bed of ashes. The larger logs rest on but are at right angles to the andirons. Since fire burns the exterior of the logs and since the hottest part of the fire is between the bottom two logs, the faces of the logs closest to the flame are the ones to burn first. This means the log closer to the room is shielding the room from the most intense heat.

To increase heat flow into the room, grates have been designed to shield the flame from the chimney and thereby encourage radiation outward. The fire is still built in the traditional manner. Newspaper and kindling are arranged on what's left of the andirons with air space enough for the fire to ignite the newspaper and kindling. Larger logs are stacked on the diagonal frame before the fire is lit. These logs will char but never burn with flame intensity. What the back support does is to slow down the passage of oxygen and heat out the chimney. Since the fire burns above instead of under the grate, the oxygen can be fed through the ash pit door if it is left ajar. As a result the fire burns more slowly without taking room air and radiates more of its heat into the room.

8

By changing the grate design more heat is radiated into the room.

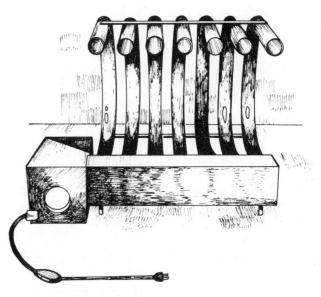

Tubular fireplace grate

Tube Grates

Tube grates require almost no assembly or installation and will fit almost any fireplace size. (It is important that they be sized accurately to fit your fireplace opening.) If the pipes are too long, they can be cut with a hacksaw, and if too short, extensions are available.

The tube grate is a C-shaped series of steel tubes, providing its own grate and designed to follow the lines of the firebox. The tubes should be flush with the upper face of the fireplace. If the tubes are too low, set the legs on firebricks. Position the tubes one or two inches behind the upper fireplace edge, being sure that the unit sits well back in the fireplace. If you obstruct the draft, smoke will wander the wrong way. Next adjust the tubes so that heat will be blown in all directions.

Some tube grates work on natural convection alone. Cold air enters the pipes near the hearth, is gradually heated, rises, and exits from the top of the pipes. To make this system at all effective, the pipes have to be of a sizeable diameter, and ones of this diameter may pull in ashes and soot which are then circulated around the room.

A substantial gain (3–20 percent increased efficiency over a fireplace) is achieved when a fan is added. The fan is attached to a manifold by a flexible piece of pipe. When the fire has produced a bed of hot coals (10–15 minutes), the blower is turned on. Air is pulled out of the room, warmed, then circulated back into the room.

Manufacturers of some of these units claim they will heat 7,000–8,000 cubic feet, 5–6 rooms, and produce between 25,000–50,000 BTU's per hour (a normal fireplace produces 6,000–8,000 BTU's per hour), but these estimates depend on house layout. Large rambling farmhouses are the worst to heat because it is difficult to move heat from room to room. A tube grate generally provides heat only to the room in which it is located unless other provisions are made. A small fan or ceiling registers to help the natural air flow would increase heat circulation.

The problem with some fireplace heaters has been the pipes which because they are subjected to intense heat have burned out in less than a year's time. As a result some companies now use stainless steel which will last longer. Other units are designed with extra steel plates to protect the pipes or are of double wall construction. Should the outer pipe burn through, it can be slipped off and replaced.

In buying a tube grate, pay attention to the construction. You want heavy duty design, indicated by the weight of the unit and the thickness of the pipes. Lightweight units of thin metal, unless of stainless steel, may burn through. Ask if the unit is guaranteed and whether the parts are replaceable.

Turn on the fan. Blowers above 100 cubic feet per minute are noisy; below 60 cfm are ineffective. You should not have a roaring fire without turning on the blower or you may damage the pipes.

A good tube grate costs from $100 to $200. If the unit is very expensive, it will take many fires to recover the investment. The problem of heat loss during the night still exists with tube grates. Some units can be used with glass doors, but that of course means an additional expense.

Tube grates demand no maintenance, but the blower should be oiled periodically.

Pre-Fabricated Fireplaces

The two basic types of pre-fabricated fireplaces are zero-clearance and free-standing. Both come in assembled kits. You must install the stovepipe and chimney, and the most difficult part of that procedure is cutting the hole in the roof. The do-it-yourselfer can install one easily in a single day. No foundation or floor supports are required since the units are lightweight (200–500 pounds). They cost about one-third as much as a masonry fireplace.

Zero clearance means just that. The fireplace can be installed directly against house walls on three sides because the fire chamber is of multiple-wall construction. Between the fireplace walls is either air space or insulation which protects the house walls from heat.

In installing the unit follow the manufacturer's instructions carefully. Do not, for example, increase or decrease the flue sizes. Floor protection of 3/8-inch thickness in front of the firebox should be provided. Whether you decide to use brick, tile, stoveboard or another non-combustible, the hearth should extend sixteen inches into the room and twelve inches to each side beyond

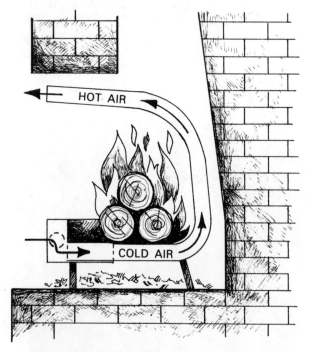

The blower on a tube grate draws in cool air, heats it, and then recirculates it back into the room.

the unit. A combustible mantle should be at least twelve inches from the unit.

Free-standing fireplaces come in all sizes and shapes with a decorative exterior, generally of baked enamel, and with factory installed firebox, hearth, and damper. They can be placed anywhere, but preferably in the center of a room. Since they throw off heat in all directions, they are more efficient than a conventional fireplace. Single wall smokepipe, which can be used from the free-standing fireplace to eighteen inches away from the ceiling, will increase heat radiation.

Both units are of metal, which lacks the heat storage capacity of masonry. Therefore they heat up quickly, but also cool quickly. Free-standing ceramic stoves work the opposite way. They take time to warm up but will still be radiating heat twelve hours after the fire has gone out.

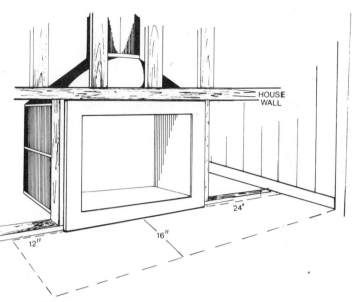

Minimal clearance distances for zero clearance fireplaces.

Free-standing fireplace

Malm Fireplaces

11

Circulating Fireplaces

Still further designs include heat-circulating units which are built into the masonry fireplace. They don't change the appearance of the fireplace except that instead of the firebox being lined with brick, it is of double wall metal construction. Heat passes through the metal, warming the air in the ducts to either side. This sets up a natural draft pattern. Air is drawn in through the cold air returns; hot air is emitted above the fire chamber. Some of these fireplace units include tube grates as well as fans to increase the flow of air.

Metal transfers heat very quickly. Circulator fireplaces therefore sacrifice the heat storage capacity which refractory brick in a masonry fireplace would provide, but much of this heat is often wasted anyway.

Heat circulating units will increase efficiency, but at some point the metal will corrode and the unit will have to be replaced —no easy job.

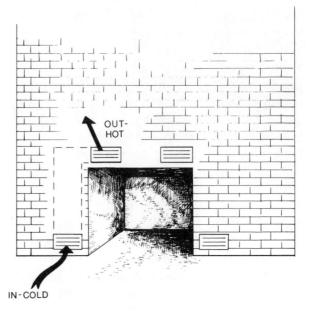

Air flow in circulating fireplace.

Thriftchanger

Thriftchanger

The "Thriftchanger" is a fireplace heat exchanger which requires no auxiliary power to reclaim extra heat from the chimney, resulting in a dramatic increase in fireplace efficiency. It must be incorporated into the original fireplace design since it involves the placement of a rotary damper 16 inches higher than the traditional position and the addition of two pieces of smokepipe ducting the gases from the fireplace to the exchanger and back into the flue above the damper.

The "Thriftchanger" unit also has glass doors which allow fire watching and prevent the loss of room heat.

The firebox is lined with refractory brick which because of its capacity to hold heat increases the firebox temperature. The damper is opened; the fire is lit, and after about ten minutes the damper is closed forcing the hot fumes to pass through the stovepipe from the firebox into the heat exchanger. Here the fumes travel through 64 vertical tubes and are united to pass through the stovepipe and back into the masonry chimney. Heat is conducted through the tubes to a duct located behind the tubes. Natural convection sets up a draft pattern of hot room air moving up the duct to the ceiling above, displacing that air and setting up a circular movement of air throughout the room.

Such a system has the advantages of high combustion temperatures, therefore more complete burning, as well as high heat recovery. Periodically the "Thriftchanger" will have to be cleaned which is done with a special brush provided with the unit.

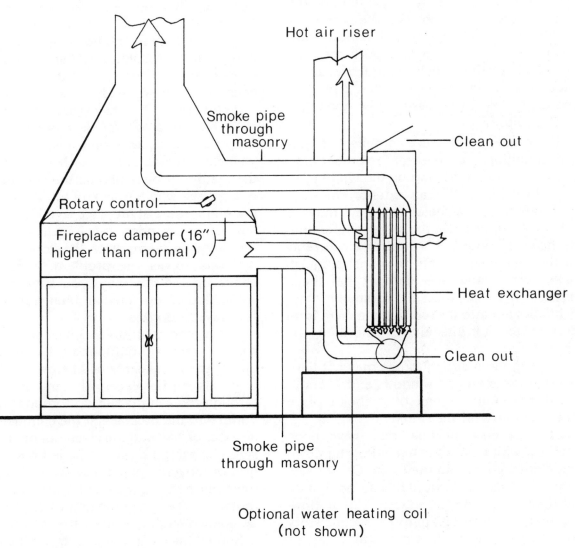

Thriftchanger for making fireplaces more efficient.

TROUBLESHOOTING

Fireplaces, the homeowner soon learns, have their own idiosyncrasies, usually reserved for that formal dinner party when a cozy fireside chat suddenly becomes mayhem in a smoke-filled house. If the host is lucky he finds he simply forgot to open the damper, and quickly corrects the problem.

Or perhaps he built the fire too far forward in the fire chamber. He can push the andirons back so they touch the fireback, and if necessary nudge the fire in that direction, and the smoking will cease. Green wood may be the culprit.

The cause can be more complicated. Several conditions may prevent the proper draft pattern of smoke flowing up the chimney.

1. In cold weather an exterior chimney, and particularly a metal chimney, may be filled with air at about the same temperature as the air outdoors. There are no air currents in the chimney, or only the most sluggish ones, even after the damper has been opened. When the fire is lit, the smoke simply billows out into the room, since there is no current to pull the air up and into the chimney.

2. A modern airtight home may not have enough leaks around windows and doors to provide the huge volume of air the fireplace needs to carry off the smoke.

3. A reverse air flow may have been created, with cold air actually flowing down the chimney and into the room. One or several conditions may cause this. Condition #2 (airtight home) may be a factor. Hot air flowing up to, then escaping from a second story (due to an open window, major air leaks, or poor insulation) will reduce the ground-floor air pressure, and pull in air from the outside, even down the chimney. Exhaust fans in a kitchen or bath will push out air, and the air pulled in by this drop in pressure may come down the chimney.

To learn whether there is a downdraft, veteran Boy or Girl Scouts will wet a finger and hold it in the fireplace throat, learning the direction of the air flow by which side of the finger is cooled. Those with less training will light a match, hold it well into the throat, and see whether the direction of the flame remains up.

The easiest way to establish the proper draft pattern is to wad up a newspaper, light it, then thrust it as high into the chimney as possible. This will warm the air in the chimney, the warm air will rise, and a pattern in the right direction will have been created. If condition #1 was your problem, it is solved. It may be necessary to heat the chimney air each time you are ready to light a new fire.

If condition #2 or #3 exists, some method must be found to provide more air for the fireplace—preferably unheated air so that you are not heating air with your furnace, then letting it be pulled up the chimney and out. To see whether lack of air (or relatively low air pressure at fireplace level) is the problem, open a window a few inches, either in the fireplace room, or on the floor below.

If this solves the problem, and smoke heads up the chimney, you should install some kind of regulated air intake. Here are a few ways to do this.

In new construction air inlets can link the hearth directly to outdoor air, incorporating one of the ideas explained below.

In existing fireplaces, air can be supplied through the ash pit and up through the ash dump into the fireplace. If the chimney is on an exterior wall and the clean-out door is outside, the ash pit door can be left open and a grill or louvered panel inserted to keep animals out and decrease snow and rain accumulation. The ash dump in the hearth should be opened slightly while a fire is burning.

Should the clean-out door be on the inside of the house, the same procedure can be used, although this means that air heated by the furnace will be drawn through the fireplace. An unused dryer vent and hose near the clean-out can provide unheated air by linking the hose from the vent to the fire-

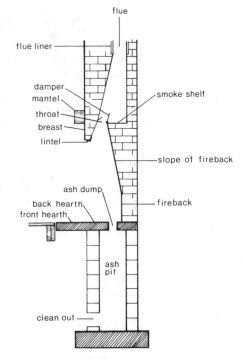

flue

flue liner

damper

mantel

throat

breast

lintel

smoke shelf

slope of fireback

ash dump

back hearth

front hearth

fireback

ash pit

clean out

Fireplace in cross section.

Other systems can be devised. If the exterior chimney has an ash pit (which insures an opening below the fireplace), a brick can be removed and a "ventilating brick" or grill installed leading into the pit. Use a hammer and cold chisel to remove the mortar. Remember to leave the ash dump cover slightly ajar when you have a fire.

Tinkering with the ash dump may have quite the reverse effect. Instead of pulling smoke up the chimney, it may push it into the room. Before making any investment in hardware, be sure this system will work.

If your fireplace lacks an ash pit, the same procedure can be followed, but with the opening made into the fireplace itself, through the fireback and as near the hearth or fireplace floor as possible. A draft regulator that can be closed when the fireplace is not in use should be installed.

You may prefer to leave the bricks and mortar alone but make the opening in an exterior wall of the room, close to the fireplace. In this case a draft regulator should be added. You can also install a dampered floor register in front of the front hearth and connect it to an outside duct in the basement. These methods have several things in common. All of them provide outside and therefore unheated air to the fireplace, and all can be closed when the fireplace is not being used.

place via the ash pit. Another variation is to disconnect the hose and insert a draft regulator in the vent that leads outdoors. This regulator will open only when air is needed, and will permit air to be pulled from outdoors in, then through the ash pit, into the fireplace, and up the chimney.

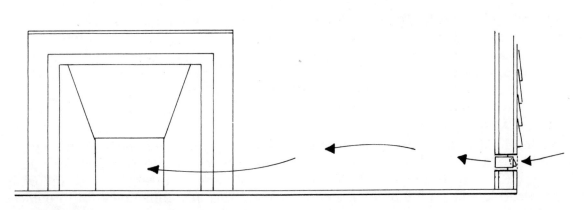

Air can reach the fire through a louvred panel.

A system for using outdoor air should be advantageous. It reduces drafts from around doors and windows where cold air leaks in. The problem of maintaining adequate humidity in your home is lessened. In a tight, well-insulated house, it may be the only way to avoid a smoking fireplace. But there are disadvantages. Outside air fed directly to the fire robs the homeowner of the freshness of infiltrating air. Also outdoor air, which is cooler than house air, will lower combustion temperatures, thereby increasing creosote and soot.

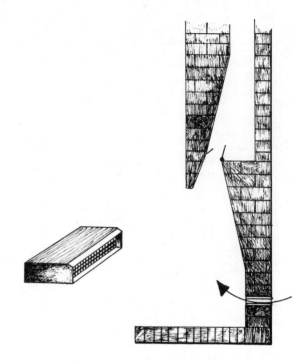

An air inlet can be built into the firebox.

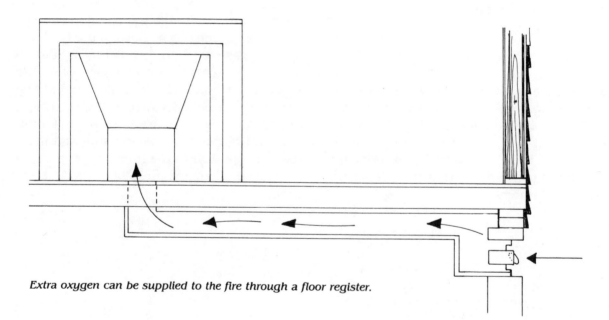

Extra oxygen can be supplied to the fire through a floor register.

A Numbers' Game

Is the design of your fireplace the cause of its smoking?

Since the time of Count Rumford (a hero recently resurrected by wood-burning enthusiasts), fireplace design has become a science of juggling numbers. Measure your fireplace height and depth, and the flue opening. Check them against the following dimensions recommended for fireplaces by the USDA.

Size of fireplace opening						Size of flue lining required	
Width	Height	Depth	Minimum width of back wall	Height of vertical back wall	Height of inclined back wall	Standard rectangular (outside dimensions)	Standard round (inside diameter)
Inches	Inches	Inches	Inches	Inches	Inches	Inches	Inches
24	24	16–18	24	14	16	8½ × 8½	10
28	24	16–18	24	14	16	8½ × 8½	10
30	24	16–18	16	14	18	8½ × 13	10
36	24	20	24	14	18	8½ × 13	12
42	24	20	28	14	18	8½ × 18	12
48	25½	21	32	14	20	13 × 13	15
54	30	22	36	14	24	13 × 18	15
60	30	24	44	14	24	13 × 18	15
54	40	20–22	36	17	29	13 × 18	15
60	40	26	40	17	30	18 × 18	18
66	40	26	44	17	30	18 × 18	18
72	40	22–28	48	17	30	18 × 18	18

Recommended dimensions for fireplaces and size of flue lining required

Your flue may be incorrectly sized for the dimensions of your fireplace opening. A cross-section of the flue liner should be $\frac{1}{10}$–$\frac{1}{12}$ the area of the firebox opening. For example, if your flue liners are 8×12 (or 96 square inches) and your fireplace opening is 30×32 (or 960 square inches), your flue liners have been properly sized. However, if your flue opening is less than $\frac{1}{12}$ of the fireplace opening, you're likely to have a smoky fireplace. To adjust the flue size is impossible. To decrease the fireplace opening is relatively simple.

Once you have gone through the calculations, you should know how much to reduce the fireplace opening. A quick double-check can be done by holding a sheet of plywood above the opening, then lowering it until no smoke escapes into the room. Measure the amount by which the opening must be reduced. When the fire is out and the hearth cleaned, a more permanent solution can be fabricated. You can either raise the hearth or lower the lintel.

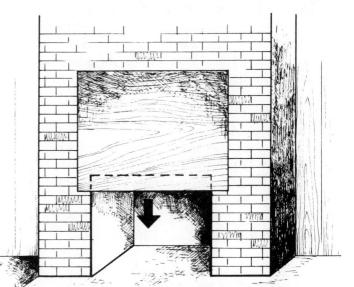

Decrease fireplace opening until smoke no longer escapes into the room.

Raising the Hearth

The hearth can be raised by using a fire basket, putting the andirons on firebrick, or covering the entire back hearth with firebrick. If you intend the latter, first lay the bricks without mortar to be sure it will work. If it does, mortar the bricks in place, splitting them where necessary to get a snug fit against the slanted walls. As many as three layers of bricks can be added. Firebrick can be added to the sides and the fireback if the fireplace opening hasn't been reduced sufficiently. Experiment before cementing them in place.

Lowering the Lintel

Another possibility is to lower the fireplace lintel. A piece of sheet metal can be cut to the width of the fireplace opening plus four inches, and to the height desired plus four inches.

Remove a two-inch square from each of the four corners with tin snips. Mark where the masonry nails or lag bolts will go through the sheet metal. Before bending the sides which will attach to the bricks, punch these holes with a nail to make assembly easier. Bend the sheet metal by placing it on a 2 × 4 with the two-inch lip extending beyond the 2 × 4, and bend the lip with a hammer. Use a masonry bit to drill the holes in the masonry. Then fasten the unit to the fireplace.

A more complicated but more permanent method is to drop the lintel. This means adding a steel lintel and filling the space between the first and second lintel with bricks and mortar. Decide how far down the lintel will come on the brick jambs and chip out the mortar between the bricks on either side.

After the lintel has been set in place, forms will have to be built to give the bricks and mortar support while drying. Using brick-like tiles of ½-inch thickness will simplify the process. Concrete can be troweled into the forms and the brick tiles set in place.

The Damper

The damper, which should be eight to ten inches above the fireplace lintel, may cause a fireplace to smoke. Sometimes dampers have been installed incorrectly so that the damper doubles as the lintel. Smoke traveling up the fireback should be deflected off the breast and up the flue but will find your living room much easier egress if the damper is placed too low. A metal shield or hood may solve this problem. Otherwise the chimney must be rebuilt—a lengthy, costly procedure.

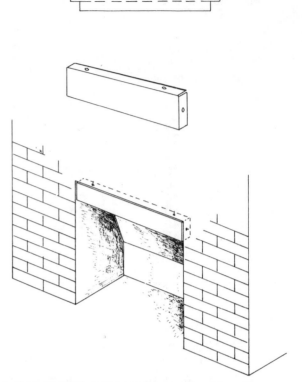

A piece of sheet metal can be used to reduce the size of the fireplace opening.

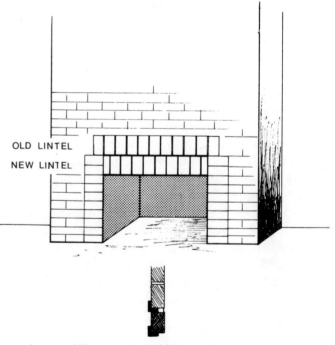

OLD LINTEL
NEW LINTEL

A second lintel can be added and the intervening space filled with bricks and mortar.

18

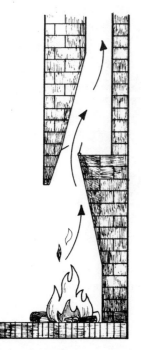

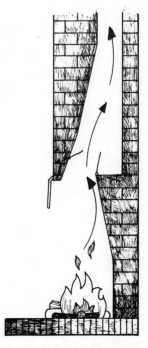

Correct placement of damper.

When the damper is too low, smoke may enter the room.

A metal hood will direct the smoke up the chimney.

Chimney Height

Smoking can be caused by insufficient stack height. For reasons of draft and safety, fire regulations recommend that the chimney extend three feet above the highest point where it passes through the roof and be at least two feet higher than any part of the building within ten feet. But other things can affect the draft. Roofs (including your own) may be too close, or the chimney may be affected by the topography (a house built at the bottom of a knoll, etc.). The overall height of your chimney may not be sufficient (twenty feet for masonry and twenty-four feet for furnace boiler stacks). All these things can cause air to move down the chimney causing smoke from the fire to fill the room.

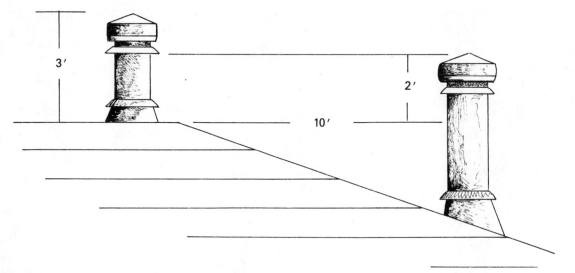

The chimney should extend three feet above the highest point where it passes through the roof and be at least two feet higher than any part of the building within ten feet.

Extending the Flue

Flues work like a siphon—the greater the height the stronger the lifting force. Sometimes extending the chimney will eliminate smoke problems. While there is a small fire in the fireplace, go up on the roof. Place another section of flue liner or metal smoke-pipe on top of the existing flue. If this increases the draft, the flue should be extended permanently. (There is no point in extending the chimney beyond the point where it is of benefit. The stack will just gather more creosote, and in a high wind it may topple over.)

The extension can be of flue tile, factory-built pipe or heavy metal pipe. Insulated, factory-built pipe will cause less creosote build-up than metal pipe, but is heavier and more expensive. You will need an **anchor plate** which is made specifically for attaching insulated pipe to masonry chimneys. The anchor plate covers the flue and has a short, threaded section of pipe to which the factory-built pipe can be twist-locked. The plate should be bolted into the masonry, using the pre-drilled holes of the unit. If the extension is over six feet tall, it should be supported with metal braces or guy wires. Tubular roof braces with a chimney band can be bought

and are adjustable to between five and eight feet. Be sure to apply roofing cement to the screw heads to prevent leaking.

Flues also can be extended by adding a section of flue tile liner. Using a cold chisel and hammer, chip off the bevelled cement cap which binds the masonry to the existing flue tile liner. In buying extra bricks, try to match them for size and color with those of

20

your chimney. Masonry suppliers carry used brick. Follow the pattern of your existing chimney. It may have two layers of brick or cement block faced with brick. Begin with the outside layer and lay each course from the corners inward. The height you go will be determined by the length of flue tile you install (usually in one-foot or two-foot sections). If necessary, the tile liners can be cut with a masonry saw blade. The tile should project four inches above the bricks, so stop the brick some six inches below the final height.

Mortar the tile in place, and trowel mortar into any spaces between the layers of masonry. When the cracks are filled, a mound of mortar should be made. Be sure it is bevelled (the cap should slope from the tile to the brick) to shed water and direct outdoor currents to pull gases out the chimney. Wait a couple of days before lighting a fire, and make the first fires small ones.

Sealing Flue Tile Joints

Chimneys with more than one flue may have poorly sealed joints between the tiles, in which case gases from one flue may be sucked into the second. The possibility of such a leak is increased when the flues are placed side by side and is even more likely if the joints between the flue liner haven't been staggered. A trouble light on an extension cord should illuminate this problem.

Work involved in the cure may be frustrating. Fill a canvas bag with sand or use a weighted bag full of hay. The bag must tightly fill the chimney flue. Attach the bag to a strong rope and lower it down the flue to a level just below the joints which need repair. Secure the rope to the chimney. Pour thin mortar on top of the bag, preferably close to the edges. Now pull the bag up and down to work the mortar into the leaky joint.

The rope, of course, can break, or the mortar can slip by the bag to land on the smoke shelf and obstruct the damper. Even if you avoid these mishaps, you may be left with a messy joint. Jagged edges between flue tiles will interrupt the draft, creating a gathering place for creosote. This method is better than ripping down the chimney, but it must be done with care and patience.

Chimney Hoods

Intermittent smoke problems may be caused by the wind. If the wind causing the problems blows consistently from a certain direction, you may wish to install a hood. Leave the hood open to the prevailing winds. If, for example, the prevailing winds are from the west, extend the brickwork on the north and south sides of the chimney. Be sure the total area left open is at least equal to a cross-section area of the flue.

Two Flues

Two flues in the same chimney may cause smoky fires if the flues are of equal height. An updraft in the unused flue can descend into the fireplace flue, causing the fire to smoke. If blocking off the top of the culprit flue increases the fireplace draft, a hood should be added. Extend the brickwork on two sides with a central brick wythe to prevent one flue from affecting the other.

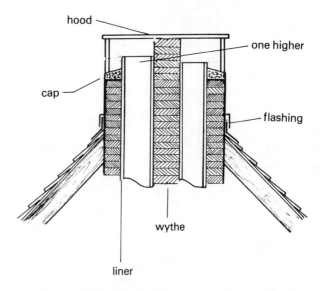

The problem of smoke being pulled down an adjoining, unused flue will be lessened if the flues are built to different heights above the masonry.

Chimney hoods do mitigate the vagaries of the wind, thereby reducing wind disruption to the fire. They also reduce the flow of chimney gases, which increases chimney temperatures and helps to maintain a more stable flow of air. On the other hand, hoods can be a hindrance, particularly if the draft is weak. They may reduce the velocity of air moving through the chimney enough to create a smoking problem.

Spark Arresters

Spark arresters are rounded cone structures of wire mesh. They fit over the chimney top, but do not interfere with the flow of gases. Install them if you fear sparks may set fires in nearby wooded areas. They're also helpful in preventing squirrels and birds from nesting in the chimney.

Check Your Chimney

Whether you burn wood in a fireplace or stove, you face problems with chimneys. Are they built properly? Are they safe? Have they deteriorated? Do they need cleaning? To avoid repetition, we have printed this information, valuable to fireplace owners as well as stove owners, in the chapter titled "Operating the Stove."

Ten causes of chimney troubles and their cures.

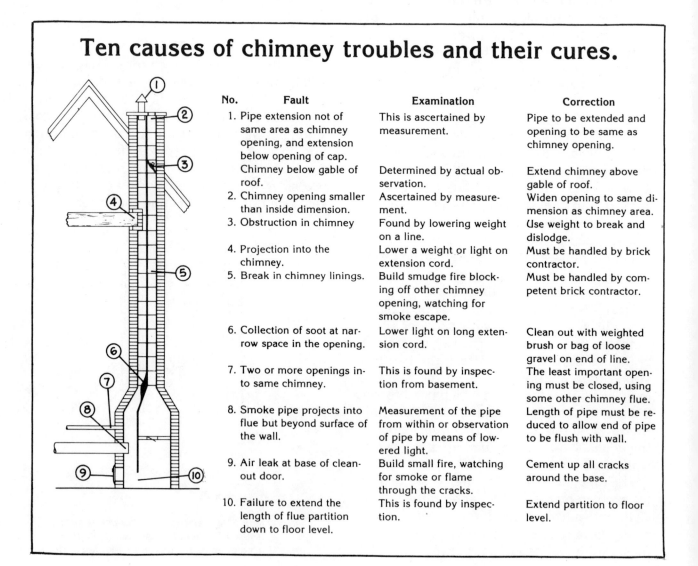

No. Fault	Examination	Correction
1. Pipe extension not of same area as chimney opening, and extension below opening of cap.	This is ascertained by measurement.	Pipe to be extended and opening to be same as chimney opening.
Chimney below gable of roof.	Determined by actual observation.	Extend chimney above gable of roof.
2. Chimney opening smaller than inside dimension.	Ascertained by measurement.	Widen opening to same dimension as chimney area.
3. Obstruction in chimney	Found by lowering weight on a line.	Use weight to break and dislodge.
4. Projection into the chimney.	Lower a weight or light on extension cord.	Must be handled by brick contractor.
5. Break in chimney linings.	Build smudge fire blocking off other chimney opening, watching for smoke escape.	Must be handled by competent brick contractor.
6. Collection of soot at narrow space in the opening.	Lower light on long extension cord.	Clean out with weighted brush or bag of loose gravel on end of line.
7. Two or more openings into same chimney.	This is found by inspection from basement.	The least important opening must be closed, using some other chimney flue.
8. Smoke pipe projects into flue but beyond surface of the wall.	Measurement of the pipe from within or observation of pipe by means of lowered light.	Length of pipe must be reduced to allow end of pipe to be flush with wall.
9. Air leak at base of cleanout door.	Build small fire, watching for smoke or flame through the cracks.	Cement up all cracks around the base.
10. Failure to extend the length of flue partition down to floor level.	This is found by inspection.	Extend partition to floor level.

Wood Stoves – Old & New

Before you buy your stove—old or new—you should understand how combustion works. In that way you will be better able to judge how the stove you are considering attempts to cope with the varied problems that are a part of wood combustion.

The burning of wood is a three-stage process:

1. When dry, wood is composed of water, volatile gases (carbon dioxide, carbon monoxide, methane, hydrogen, etc.) and, after the other two have been removed by heat, charcoal. When green or wet, the water content of wood can be more than 50 percent. Even dried, wood is rarely less than 20 percent unless it is oven-dried.

In the first stage of combustion, the wood temperature stays below the boiling point (212°F.) until the moisture is evaporated. You will hear a hissing sound as the temperature in the firebox rises. The more moisture in the wood, the more heat is required to vaporize the water. For this reason, it may take some time before a fire catches when wet wood is used.

At 300°–400°F. the wood begins to give off volatile gases, some of which will burn. The other gases are diluted with carbon dioxide and water vapor. The gases carry them out of the fire zone, appearing from the chimney as smoke. At 400°F. the smoking ceases.

2. Wood begins to burn at 600°F. At this point the fire is self-sustaining. But not until temperatures reach 1100°F. will all the gases burn, and then only if there is a sufficient supply of oxygen. With the right amount of air and heat, the gases will be forced into flame, providing heat and greater combustion efficiencies.

3. Charcoal, mostly carbon, is what's left after the gases burn. It contains about half the wood's heat potential. The bed of coals begins to form at 1000°F. and for maximum heat should flame, not glow. The coals provide slow and even heat. Incomplete combustion produces carbon monoxide, hydrocarbons, and other gases. Complete combustion occurs at temperatures well above 1000°F (preferably around 3000°F.) with plenty of oxygen, and produces only water vapor, carbon dioxide and a little carbon monoxide. It is difficult for present-day wood-burning appliances to reach these temperatures.

As the fire burns and another log is added, some of the same process will be repeated because the firebox temperature has suddenly been lowered. The only difference is that instead of the moisture being evaporated by the intense heat of kindling and newspapers, it will be driven off by direct contact with the flames, burning gases or radiant heat from the coals, flames or interior surfaces of the firebox. When the fire is established, temperatures in the entire firebox will have risen considerably. The radiant heat will dry the wood much more quickly than the more localized flame of a beginning fire. Consequently it is much easier to keep a fire going than to start one.

Roughly 50 percent of wood's heat value is in the charcoal, but charcoal doesn't move and therefore presents no problem. The rest of the heat is in the gases. The trick is to get them to burn, but since all three stages of combustion are going on simultaneously, this isn't easy. The gases are extremely agile. They can exit too soon or rise too rapidly.

Old stoves, Franklins, and potbellies, because they leak excess air to the fire, create uncontrollable updrafts which prevent the gases from burning. To insure that the gases are completely burned, temperatures must be held above 1100°F. and the gases contained in the combustion zone or pulled back through the combustion zone, or forced to a part of the stove where temperatures are at least 1100°F.

If the gases are released while the water is evaporating, they will be trapped in the water vapor and travel, unburned, out of the fire zone. If you've just lit the fire, the stack is still cold. Since these gases condense when the temperature falls to around 250°F., they will be deposited in the form of creosote somewhere en route up the chimney.

If the gases are released when the temperature is much higher so that water vapor isn't a problem, they are quite hot and will rise rapidly out of the fire zone and will leave the firebox unburned. To avoid this loss, many stoves have features designed specifically to move the gases in predetermined ways so they will be burned.

Oxygen

Oxygen intake is also related to combustion. The oxygen necessary for expelling trapped moisture (Phase #1) should enter either at the base or **below** the load of wood (primary air inlet), whereas oxygen to ignite the gases (Phase #2) must enter the stove **above** the coals (secondary air inlet). Of the air reaching the stove, 20 percent should enter below the fuel and 80 percent above.

The problems for wood stove designers as well as wood stove owners are many. A well-designed stove can be operated so as to maximize its efficiency. But even with a skilled operator and an efficient stove, the problem of regulating the draft still remains. Oxygen must enter the stove; spent gases must exit. When the fire is dampened too much (i.e., too little oxygen), the gases fail to reach the ignition point and condense on the flue walls. If the damper is wide open (too much oxygen), the fire blazes and the unburned gases will be exhausted out the flue. For wood heat to be efficient, the rate of combustion must be carefully controlled, with a second infusion of oxygen coming at the right time, temperature, and location.

This is only the beginning. Once you've gotten the most heat out of the wood, you must get it into the room—and this isn't easy.

OLD STOVES

Second only to the romance of a fireplace is that of old stoves. At auctions the stoves draw the crowds. Every auctioneer or antique dealer has his favorite. If you're lucky, he'll take you out back where hidden under a tarp is his Round Oak, a gem whose tarnish serious woodburners can see through. But if a stove is up front on the auction block, take a long and careful look before you begin the financial ascent. All is not gold. . . . Stoves can be blacked, polished, and temporarily pieced together for quick sale. The disaster may occur just loading it in the truck or later with the first fire.

Stoves made in the great woodburning boom of the nineteenth century were fired long and hard. If that didn't destroy them, they went on to further toil when coal became the fuel. With the introduction of central heating many of these stoves were dismantled and carted to attics, basements, or barns where in some adjunct shed offering minimal shelter, they withstood the seasons for generations. But once you've seen one of those beauties that was not abused and is in working order, it's hard to believe the stove for which you just bid $800 isn't going to be the same. Watch out! You may get burned.

Get to the auction early so that you can investigate the stove carefully. Shine a flashlight inside the stove and try to see the light outside, going over every inch to locate cracks. Pinhole and minor cracks can be filled with furnace cement, but cracks which run along the firebox can be dangerous. Even if the crack is welded or brazed (as in the case with cast iron), the stove may crack again, probably resoundingly so with the first hot fire.

Since metal gradually oxidizes, it may not be possible to get a good bond between the metals. To circumvent this problem, plates can be made (within reason) and bolted to the stove to bridge a crack.

Bridging a crack with steel plating

Check to see that all the parts are there. The grates if warped or cracked can be replaced or improvised. If you think you can locate new parts, check your stove before ordering to be sure that the original size will still fit. Stoves may warp with age, in which case you will need to have the piece custommade.

You should be able to locate replacements of the same diameter for missing plates, or a local metal shop can make them to order. Missing legs can be fashioned from heavy pipe or taken from old bathtubs. Door handles, knobs, slide-type vents can be fabricated by a welding shop unless you have the equipment and know-how to do it yourself. Parts can be nickel-plated, and rust can be removed with elbow grease and steel wool.

The following companies carry stove parts:

Portland Stove Foundry
57 Kennebec St.
Portland, ME 04104

Portland Stove Company carries parts for its stoves, Clarions made by Wood and Bishop of Bangor, and Kineos made by Noyes and Nutter of Bangor.

Brewer Atlantic Clarion Stove Company
Brewer, ME 04412

Brewer sells parts for Atlantic and Clarion stoves.

Empire Furnace and Stove Repair
793 Broadway
Albany, NY 12207

Aetna Stove Company, Inc.
S.E. Cor. 2nd & Arch Streets
Philadelphia, PA 19106

Inspect used stoves carefully before buying

Provide the company with the following information: the name and model number of the stove; the name of the manufacturer; a careful description of the part requested which may necessitate sending either the old part or a rough sketch with dimensions, and a description of the casting marks.

Not to dampen your enthusiasm, but an old stove, even one in good condition, has a lower heating efficiency than the modern airtights. No matter how rigorously you caulk, air will leak in around the doors, lids, and draft openings where it is detrimental to efficient stove operation. Old stoves tend to burn more like fireplaces. Fires which are difficult to control burn hotter and quicker, require more stoking, are less efficient in burning volatile gases, and usually can't be coaxed into maintaining an overnight fire. A damper in the first section of stovepipe is essential to increase control of the fire.

Summing up: If you're starting out on wood burning, start out with a new stove. You may pass up the antique bargain of the year, of course, or you may avoid a lot of problems.

Pipe makes a good replacement leg

NEW STOVES

With an estimated half-million stoves of many models manufactured in 1977–1978 alone, it's no easy task to choose a new stove. The would-be buyer need only pick up a copy of **Yankee, Country Journal, Mother Earth News** or **Wood Burning Quarterly** to be inundated by stove advertisements all promising more heat for less money. To compound the problem of selection, stoves can be bought at lawnmower shops, fireplace shops, lumberyards, craft stores, sporting goods stores, hardware and general stores, chain stores, and **stove** stores. Shopping for oil was never like this! Before subjecting yourself to the senseless task of opening and closing doors just to check whether there is a fuel box, consider your needs as you investigate the following options.

Materials

Stoves can be made of ceramic, tile, or soapstone, but generally they are made of cast iron or sheet metal. Ceramic, tile, or soapstone stoves have very low thermal conductivity. This means the heat passes through the stove material very slowly. Perhaps the ultimate in this system is the European tile stove which has massive amounts of masonry. Some of the modern ceramic stoves have an open flame so that as the fire heats up, some radiant energy will pass from the fire directly to the room. But since this opening is usually quite small, the heat will be felt only within a very small radius. Even with a roaring fire, the mass remains cool for a number of hours. Slowly it begins to warm so that as the fire dies down and then is extinguished, heat from the fire which has been stored in the walls is gradually released. This doesn't mean these stoves give off less heat than others. It means only that they provide a lower level of heat for a much longer period of time.

Cast iron and sheet metal of the same weight and thickness have the same heat transfer characteristics. However, because they are different materials, they have different properties which should be considered in buying a stove.

Sheet steel is molten steel which has been rolled into sheets of between $\frac{1}{64}$ "–$\frac{1}{4}$ " thickness. **Sheet metal** usually refers to sheets up to $\frac{3}{16}$ ". Sheets of $\frac{3}{16}$ " or thicker are called **plate steel.** Within these categories, you will find many terms, each trying to sound tougher than the next, but what is crucial is the thickness (or gauge) of the steel.

The metal for steel stoves is bought in large sheets and cut to shape with a torch—much like cutting out a dress pattern. The joints are then subjected to extreme heat which melts the metal on either side as well as the filler rod which is slowly fed into the joint. Because steel can be rolled and worked

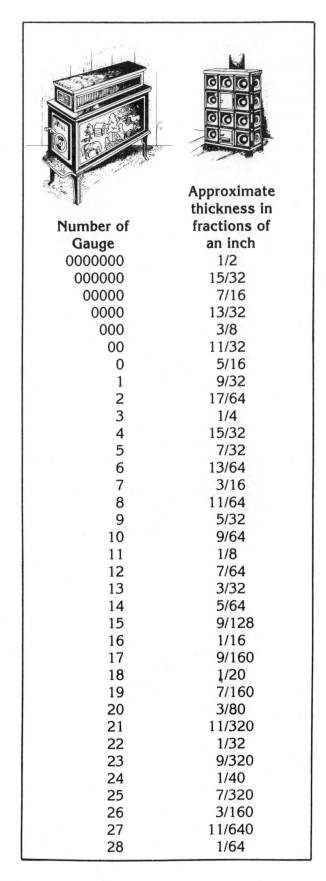

Number of Gauge	Approximate thickness in fractions of an inch
0000000	1/2
000000	15/32
00000	7/16
0000	13/32
000	3/8
00	11/32
0	5/16
1	9/32
2	17/64
3	1/4
4	15/64
5	7/32
6	13/64
7	3/16
8	11/64
9	5/32
10	9/64
11	1/8
12	7/64
13	3/32
14	5/64
15	9/128
16	1/16
17	9/160
18	1/20
19	7/160
20	3/80
21	11/320
22	1/32
23	9/320
24	1/40
25	7/320
26	3/160
27	11/640
28	1/64

at very thin thicknesses, stoves of sheet steel often are lighter and lower in cost ($150–$400) than cast-iron stoves ($200–$1,000), but the thinner the metal, the more likely it is to burn through. The lighter sheet steel provides a more immediate first surge of heat but is less capable of spreading the heat laterally through itself than cast iron. Consequently under the continued stress of heating and cooling, the steel may bend or warp.

Warping is a problem. Though the operation of the stove may not be affected, the warping can be unsightly unless the stove is designed to make the warping visually acceptable. Warping in circular stove designs is less offensive than in rectangular stoves.

Warping usually occurs in stoves built with sheet metal of $\frac{1}{16}$" or less. If the warping occurs around the door, it may permit unwanted, uncontrollable air to enter. To decrease this likelihood, most sheet-steel stoves have cast-iron doors to help retain the stove's airtightness, but even these aren't foolproof. Though the door won't warp, the sheet steel against which it fits may. Other stoves are made of such heavy gauge metal that the manufacturers feel so certain they won't warp that they have included that claim in their advertising.

The efficiency of a stove depends on its airtightness. Therefore look for sheet-metal stoves with cast-iron doors, cast-iron door frames and asbestos gaskets, as well as cast-iron grates and liners.

The lighter the sheet metal, the more essential that the stove have metal or **firebrick liners.** Liners not only protect the outer surface from warping and from the intensity of the heat, but will help maintain high firebox temperatures for more complete combustion.

Stoves usually come with liners if they will need them. However, if you have a thin sheet-metal stove made-to-order by a local welder, be sure it is lined on both sides and bottom with firebrick before the first fire is lit. Building bricks can also be used, but they will have to be replaced more frequently. Only firebrick can withstand the extreme changes in temperature.

Firebrick can be purchased at masonry supply houses and is easy to install. It can be laid down or the bricks mortared together. If some of the bricks eventually crack, it may be a little more difficult to remove and replace cemented bricks, but they offer better protection. Firebrick also is cast in circular designs for cylindrical stoves and should be used to line a do-it-yourself barrel stove.

Firebrick provides another heat-absorbing material which, though it raises the temperature in the firebox, slows down the heat transfer of the stove. This is of benefit if you want long, continuous, even heat, but, while protecting your stove, it does reduce the "instant warmth" value of the thin sheet-metal stoves.

The thinner the walls, the faster the heat transfer. In stoves of thin double-wall construction, the outer lining protects the stove from being a fire hazard. However, the inner wall, which may be quite thin, must be examined periodically. In time it will burn out. Your distributor or the factory can replace the inner lining.

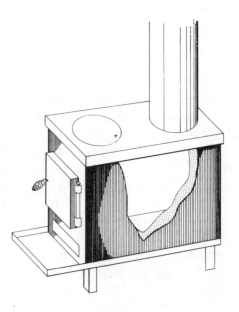

Double wall construction.

Sheet-metal stoves should not be fired so hot that the walls become red hot. These stoves are less durable, do not hold heat as long, but are cheaper and easier to repair than cast-iron stoves. In buying, check the quality of the welds (which should be continuous) and the door seal (which should have a gap no greater than paper thickness). Look for sheet-metal stoves designed in combination with other materials to make them airtight and more durable.

Cast iron is an alloy of iron ore, carbon, and silicon. It is melted, then poured into molds designed for a particular stove. These pieces are individually machined by hand to create a tight fit, then assembled, bolted together, sanded and painted, and the joints caulked with furnace cement. The seams of cast-iron stoves are molded so that the sides overlap. Sparks shouldn't pass through the corners, but for further safety and airtightness these should be caulked each year with furnace cement.

Furnace cement can be bought in pint- or quart-sized cans at hardware stores. Dab the cement on with a stick. Let it dry for twenty-four hours before lighting a fire.

Cast iron usually lasts longer than sheet metal. Because the stove parts are cast, they are thicker, sturdier, heavier and retain heat longer. The heavier the stove the longer it will stay warm after the fire is out, but the longer it will take to heat.

To move even the smallest of the cast-iron stoves will tax the strength of one person; the larger ones can tax an entire neighborhood. In choosing a stove, you should consider whether you will want to dismantle it during the summer. This may be the case if the stove is centrally located in a heavily trafficked area. To move a heavy, cast-iron stove to the cellar is a task most of us want to avoid. Be sure you have sufficient space, summer and winter, to sacrifice to your stove installation if you intend to buy a medium-large, cast-iron stove.

Since cast iron is not easily repaired, great care should be taken when lighting a fire in a

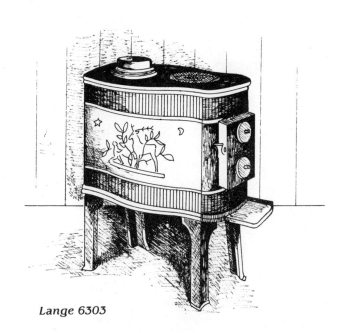

Lange 6303

new stove. Begin with small fires for a week to season the metal. Care should always be taken when reloading a cast-iron stove for it is particularly sensitive to sudden changes in temperature and severe blows which can crack the metal. When reloading, don't whack the back or sides of the stove with the wood, and don't bring in an ice-laden log and place it directly on the fire. Likewise don't remove the baffles and place them on a cold hearth if they are still warm.

Cast iron is brittle. Though it shouldn't warp or crack under normal conditions, it should be treated with care.

There are a number of shoddy cast-iron stoves now on the market. Such stoves are crudely bolted together and lack adequate furnace cement to seal the joints. The cast iron may be of varying thicknesses and may be porous or badly pitted. When buying a stove, scrutinize all parts and joints carefully with a flashlight. Check the door and lids, particularly, for tight seals. Check for thin spots in the side panels. These panels may have ribs and/or designs. The unevenness allows for greater surface heat radiation but is more difficult to cast. Therefore check to be sure panelled sides are of uniform thickness. Also be sure all stove parts are included.

MODERN STOVE DESIGN

Wood stoves are an investment, potentially a substantial and continuous investment of time and money. So before buying one, consider when you intend to use the stove, how many rooms you want it to heat, and for how long. Unless you are convinced you have a **use** for a stove, that money might be better spent in weather stripping and insulation.

Wood stoves can be for the occasional "take the nip out of the air," supplemental or total heat, emergencies, or for cooking. But no stove is ideal for all purposes.

If your stove is for emergencies (no doubt, to save the plumbing in sub-zero weather), then you may want lots of heat fast. For this you may have to sacrifice aesthetics and complete combustion of the gases.

Units for occasional or supplemental heat probably will be located in the living room or den. With a stove on display, aesthetics and low, continuous heat may be important. But for this, you may have to wait twenty to thirty minutes while the stove warms up. Knowing that stoves generally involve some kind of trade-off means you will have to wend your way slowly through decisions about what you want and what you are willing to sacrifice.

CIRCULATING STOVES

Heat is delivered by radiation, conduction, or convection. **Conducted** heat passes through a material, moving from the hotter to colder area. It takes only a cup of hot coffee, a plastic spoon and a silver spoon to prove that heat travels at different rates through different materials. Cast iron and steel, the materials out of which most stoves are made, conduct heat at almost the same rate if of the same thickness; ceramic, tile,

soapstone and masonry conduct heat much more slowly; insulation conducts very little heat.

The furnace is a good example of **convected** heat. The oil burner generates intense heat of 3000 °F. The heat is then transferred to a heat-carrying medium—air or water—which transports the warmth through hot air ducts or radiators.

Radiant energy exists in the form of wavelengths. Infrared radiation is not actually heat but energy which becomes sensible heat when it is absorbed by surfaces. We can feel perfectly warm out-of-doors on a cold wintery day if we are standing in the sun so that the infrared radiation of the sun can be absorbed by the skin. If there is snow on the ground, we can be even warmer because the sun's radiant energy hits the snow and is re-radiated.

All three principles are used in wood stove designs. Most stoves give off heat by radiation, although there is a small group (circulating heaters) which convect the heat. Radiant heaters work like fireplaces except that the heat passes through the metal before it is radiated.

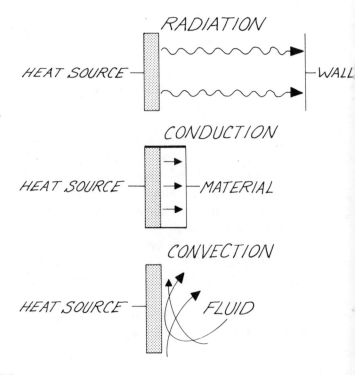

30

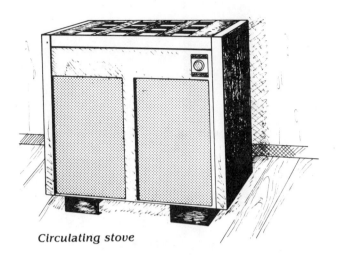

Circulating stove

Circulating heaters are radiating units that have been encased in louvered or perforated grill enclosures, usually of enameled sheet metal. They are of a double-wall, box construction with a two- to five-inch air space between the firebox and the outer jacket. Heat passes through the metal of the firebox by conduction and is picked up by the circulating air; the heat is then moved by convection in a doughnut-shaped pattern throughout the room. Cold air is pulled in from the floor as the heated air rises, thus establishing a circulating draft pattern.

The cabinets look like oversized humidifiers, and often are criticized because they lack the homey appeal of other wood stoves. They are easy to care for and should be kept rust-free to prolong the life of the stove. Often the cabinet tops can be lifted for limited cooking.

Circulating heaters used in old, drafty houses may just be heating the outdoors. Since the flow of convected air travels to the ceilings and walls, it may escape before it comes to you. For such buildings radiant heaters make more sense. You need only intercept the heat before it reaches the walls to be perfectly warm.

Circulators work well on the main floor of a well-insulated house where the desired pattern of air movement can be established. In such cases, circulators may be more satisfactory than radiant heaters.

The heat given off by a radiant unit varies greatly during a burn cycle. You may begin by huddling next to the stove, then find yourself backing off in a half-hour, then moving closer again as the fire dies down. A circulator gives much gentler, more even heat. Another big advantage of the circulator: The jacket remains relatively cool. This is particularly important if there are children in the home. A child is most likely to be badly burned with a sheet-steel stove; least likely with a circulating heater.

The principle of circulating stoves could be adapted to a radiant stove if, for example, you require more heat in rooms above the stove. With a plenum around the stove, and ceiling registers installed over the stove, heated air will flow to the next floor. Walls of soapstone built into the design of the stove as side panels will allow more heat to circulate, the unit to remain much cooler, and the soapstone, because it conducts heat so slowly, to release this heat long after the fire has gone out.

Check the heaters carefully. Doors should close tightly, grates and liners should be heavy and well constructed, thermostats should be dependable. There are cheap models on the market. Some are of inferior construction with spot welding, aluminum door handles which conduct heat, very thin grates, and leaky doors.

RADIANT HEATERS

There is a vast difference in design among radiant heaters.

Box Stoves (parlor, pot belly, box)

Some box stoves can be operated with the doors opened, and thus provide the emotional advantages of an open fire. But all of them are inefficient and demand frequent attention, and most have small fuel capacities. The joints around the seams and the doors tend to let unwanted air seep into the fire, resulting in less efficiency. And because there may be no air-tight regulation of the draft, the stove may around 3 a.m. begin to burn out of control. Dampers are essential to the efficiency of these stoves, and should be installed. Usually there is no secondary air inlet, so the gases escape unburned. At best these stoves may heat a single room, but they are relatively cheap ($90–$175).

Pot belly stoves usually are of cast iron with ornate design and trim. They have such small fireboxes that the wood fuel has to be cut to very small dimensions.

Parlor stoves also are of an older, traditional design with double wall or steel jacket construction.

Box stoves are long rectangles, square in cross-section and come in many sizes. Since they lack grates, the wood sits on a bed of ashes or two inches of sand. Box stoves are fed from the top or front and because of their shape can take big logs. The stoves are extremely utilitarian.

Franklins

The Franklin, a combination fireplace-stove, has retained its traditional-looking design of the 1800's. Its charm has always been that it could be operated with the firebox opened or closed. Even when a Franklin is operated with the doors closed, air leaks in around the loose-fitting doors, making the stove about 30 percent efficient. Unless the damper is used to regulate the fire, the Franklin is as inefficient as a fireplace. It has a small fuel capacity, requires frequent reloading, may not hold a fire overnight, and demands vigilance to damping the fire once it is under way.

RADIANT AIRTIGHT HEATERS

If a stove is well designed, it should be airtight. Airtight doesn't mean that with the drafts closed no air can enter the stove. Were that true, a fire dampened way down would go out. But airtights are virtually airtight. Air reaches the fire only through air inlets and not from around the edges of poorly fitting doors or lids. If unwanted oxygen enters the stove, the fire burns hotter with much of the heat escaping up the chimney. Airtight stoves will burn longer at an even temperature and burn one-fourth to one-half as much wood for the same amount of heat output as a Franklin.

Primary and Secondary Combustion

Both primary and secondary combustion take place under ideal burning conditions. Just a primary air inlet, theoretically, isn't sufficient because air must enter the stove in much larger quantities and in a different location to burn the hot gases, which is the secondary combustion.

In practice, it is very difficult to provide the conditions for secondary combustion, since it means keeping the firebox temperature well above the 1100°F. needed to burn the gases, while adding cooler air. Adding preheated air should help keep the higher firebox temperatures, but in the Ashley design the air temperature probably is raised no more than 50°, hardly enough to make a difference. Thus secondary combustion may not occur even though there is a secondary air inlet. On the Ashley design, for example, the secondary air inlet is so far from the in-

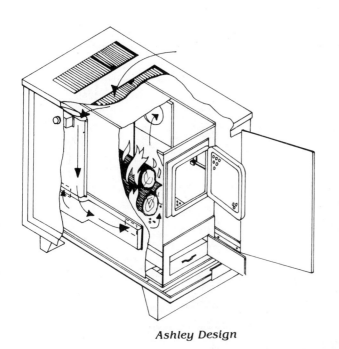

Ashley Design

The Ashley Design (Ashley, Shenandoah)

The Ashley stove design won great popularity during the early days of the wood-burning movement because it was far more efficient than the pot bellies, Franklins, and other models available at that time.

The Ashley has two air inlets. The primary air inlet is thermostatically controlled and permits air to enter at the bottom of the stove, usually below where the wood is burning. When the air inlet is open, air is sucked in and down between the outer shell of the stove and fire chamber where, because the shell is warm, the air is pre-heated before it reaches the wood load. As the wood burns, the volatile gases are released. As they rise, air is admitted through the secondary air inlet to aid in burning the gases before they can exit.

When the fire overheats, the primary air inlet closes; when the fire cools, air is again admitted to the firebox.

tensity of the fire that temperatures at that point are probably too low for any further combustion of the gases.

In small stoves secondary combustion is of less concern because firebox temperatures are high enough to burn most of the volatiles, and the air inlet provides more air than is required for the primary combustion, so there is extra oxygen for secondary combustion.

Thermostat

Some stoves have an automatic thermostat which controls the primary air inlet to regulate the rate of combustion. It is a coil of two strips of different metals which are fused together. Since the two metals expand and contract at different rates, the coil bends one way or the other depending on the temperature. A lightweight chain is attached to the coil to use this movement of the coil to open or close the inlet. Some thermostats permit a gradual opening or closing of the inlet; others provide only open-shut control. When the air inlet is opened, air is allowed to enter the firebox which increases the intensity of the fire. When the temperature reaches the thermostat setting, the inlet is closed.

Thermostats readjust the draft automatically. They are helpful in maintaining even temperatures and in controlling the rate of burn if the stove is left unattended. But thermostats can become stuck, and if stuck in the "open" position can produce a runaway fire. The thermostat on the Ashley models without cabinets can cause such fires because the thermostat is so close to the air intake. A rapidly burning fire may cause a sudden inrush of air that, instead of closing the damper, will open it wider because the rush of cool air has lowered the thermostat. On Riteways the thermostats are more effective. They have an Off/On setting which means when the damper is "open," temperatures are high and complete combustion occurs with little creosote accumulation. However when the damper is shut, temperatures and burning efficiency fall off rapidly because of the large firebox.

The thermostat should be checked periodically and cleaned at least once a year to insure that it doesn't become stuck. Blow out the thermostat with a vacuum cleaner or a tire pump.

Base Burners (Riteway, Defiant)

To get more heat from wood and to solve the problems of creosote build-up, many stove designers have attempted to make the secondary air inlet more efficient in burning the gases. Most of the base-burning stoves and downdrafters preheat both the secondary and primary air so that they don't cool the volatiles as they enter the combustion chamber.

The Defiant because of the baffles in the firebox forces these gases to follow a horizontal path, while the Riteway, because the exit chamber is located below the load of wood, forces the gases down through the fire zone. Consequently in both stoves the volatile gases are burned.

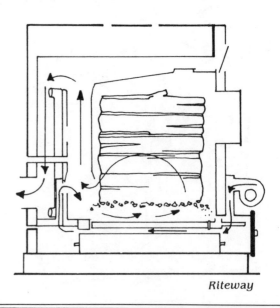

Riteway

Ash Pans

Ash pans make fire-tending a cleaner, easier chore. As the wood burns the ashes drop through a grate into a metal pan which can be removed and dumped even while the fire is burning. The owner of a stove without an ash pan must wait until the fire has died out completely before removing the ashes.

And, now that we have sold you on the worth of the ash pan, we must alert you to the cold facts of reality: many wood stoves don't have ash pans.

In the small Scandinavian models or in models which aren't airtight, this isn't much of a problem. The fire goes out during the night, and the ashes are removed before the fire is rebuilt. On models which will burn through the night, getting the ashes out is more difficult.

If your stove lacks an ash pan, the ashes can be shoveled into a coal scuttle, metal pan, or bucket. Be sure to use fire-resistant equipment. Do not shovel even the deadest ashes into a plastic or paper bag. People have left such bags near the stove only to return to a hole in the living room floor and a mess in the cellar.

After you've emptied the stove, take the ashes immediately outdoors where they can be added to a compost pile, then shoveled onto the garden in spring. If you don't want them to leach, they can be stored in a metal container.

The ash accumulation in wood stoves depends to some extent on the completeness of the burn. In some stoves much of the residual fly ash exits with the smoke. In stoves without grates, the fire is built directly on the accumulating ashes. This packs down the ashes so frequent removal is not necessary. Ask your dealer how often the ashes must be removed.

Also check the ash lip on stoves. If there is no ash lip or if it is quite small, loading the stove and removing the ashes may be hazardous.

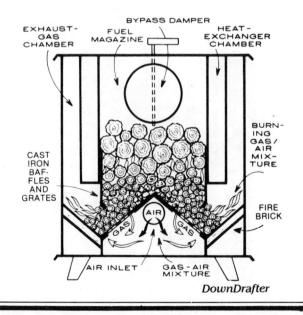

DownDrafter

Down Draft Stoves (DownDrafter)

Down draft stoves, as the name implies, force the gases down through the coals. As primary air enters above the load of wood, the volatile gases are forced down through the coal bed where they meet air from the secondary air inlet, located below the V-shaped grate on which the fire is built. Air and gases mix in passing around a stainless steel baffle plate.

Loading Door

Stoves can be top, side, or front loaders. **Top loaders** are easy to load with wood because there's no bending to put in the wood. But for this ease, you may have to confront smoke and gases.

These stoves are designed so that a good draft will maintain the pull of the smoke out of the stove even when the lid is opened to add wood. The gases become a problem only when adverse weather conditions affect the draft, or when the stove has been loaded with green or wet wood which isn't burning properly.

Before adding wood, wait until the fire dies down so that the fire is smoke-free and all the gases have been burned. Infrequently, backflashes can occur when gases are very hot and suddenly are given a large amount of oxygen as when the top of the stove is opened.

Side or **front loaders** are usually preferred. The wood is less likely to jam, and can be more easily fed into the fire, and there is less trouble with smoke.

As you look at various stoves, remember the intimate relationship between the size of that stove door and the amount of work you must do if you split your own wood. If the door is tiny, you will do much more splitting than if your stove has a roomy door that permits loading a long-burning chunk. Check too on how firmly the door closes. If a burning chunk moves and knocks against that door, will it swing open, permitting burning embers to spill out?

Front and side-loading Defiant

Scandinavian Stoves

Scandinavian stoves, finding very little quality competition, were the first to flood the American wood-burning market. The stoves are attractive, airtight, efficient, and of high quality.

In general Scandinavian stoves have ribs and intricate relief side panels. The parts are finely machined and have asbestos rope gaskets to insure tight-fitting fuel doors. Door latches remain cool enough so that doors can be opened and closed without a glove. The stoves come with a black finish which will need to be stove-blacked every year; stoves in attractive enamel colors are also available at slightly higher prices, but the enamel has been known to crack or chip.

The bottom of the firebox is ribbed. Before the first fire is lit, two inches of sand should

Lange

Baffles

In stoves without baffles, the oxygen travels in an updraft pattern, causing the fire to burn hotter and quicker. Baffles slow down the passage of air by lengthening the flame path. This produces more heat because the baffles create more radiating surface. A longer flame path means the increased possibility that the volatiles will burn because the gases are forced to remain for longer periods of time in the fire zone. In small stoves baffles aren't as necessary. The firebox is so small that the fire is close to all radiating surfaces, but the lighter and/or larger the stove, the more effective the baffles will be. In the larger stoves, the volatiles can move to a cooler part of the fire zone if not forced by baffles to remain close to the most intense heat and in contact with radiating surfaces.

Most Scandinavian stoves have some kind of baffling system. Many have top as well as side baffle plates. The side baffles protect the walls of the stove from intense heat, as well as maintaining higher firebox temperatures and re-radiating heat as the fire dies down.

The top baffle plate prevents the usual updraft. The gases can exit only after they have travelled in an "S" pattern back through the combustion zone. This results in more complete combustion, greater heat transfer, less creosote, and evener heat.

Baffles can also be vertical as in the Riteway and DownDrafter. While the vertical baffles on the Riteway force the gases down before they exit, the DownDrafter actually forces them through the fire zone and below stainless steel grates where the secondary air enters for additional burn.

Baffles work best in large stoves, with plenty of wood, and burned with the draft fairly wide open.

be placed in the bottom to protect the cast iron from the intensity of the fire. Ashes can be removed only after the fire is out. This is an inconvenience if you intend to use the stove for continuous heat.

The Scandinavian stoves provide still another approach to combustion. The stoves are designed to burn from front to back in "cigar fashion." To burn properly, the coals must be raked to the front before the stove is reloaded. The draft disk in front controls the primary and secondary air. Because the stoves are so airtight, a stovepipe damper is unnecessary. Remember on Scandinavian stoves the draft should never be closed entirely or creosote will form rapidly.

As the fire burns, gases are released. They rise and move horizontally over the coals along the baffle plate toward the front of the stove where they come in contact with the secondary air and burn.

These stoves need no thermostat. With the baffles and "S" draft pattern, a much evener, longer, slower heat is given off, and complete combustion occurs if the stove is properly operated.

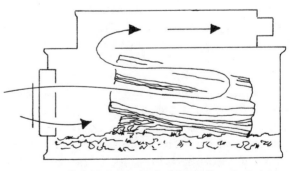

"S" draft pattern typical of Scandinavian stoves

Will Your Stove Last?

Durability is related to the safety of your stove. If the castings are poor or the sheet metal paper thin, you may have instant problems. Some stoves are potential fire hazards. The lowest priced stoves are junk, and should be junked. An exception is the unpretentious do-it-yourself barrel stoves which cost about $50–$60. In other low-priced stoves the liners and grates are thin, the door gaskets are cheap and unreliable, the "should-be-porcelain" finish is paint, and seams have been spot welded.

Durability is directly related to weight; weight is related to price; price is related to quality. You get what you pay for. Generally sheet-metal stoves are lighter than and won't last as long as cast-iron ones, but they are cheaper. Usually the thicker the metal, the longer the life.

The heavier the stove the greater its mass and therefore the greater its ability to retain heat. This means you are more likely to have higher firebox temperatures and a better chance that the volatiles will burn. And if the stove is airtight, you have control over the rate of burn. Both these advantages mean that the stove will burn less wood. If you are buying wood, this is an additional expenditure which you will have to calculate. The dollars you save by buying a cheap, lightweight stove may be spent in firewood.

Sizing A Stove

Choose the right size stove for a given location, remembering that a large stove dampened down to a smoking fire will generate creosote, and a small stove overfired will be unsafe and inefficient. To determine the size of stove you need, first count the rooms you intend to heat and decide whether you want to keep the fire going overnight.

Stove capacity is usually listed in cubic feet or BTU's. The latter is a far more accurate estimate of the stove's capacity, but the former is quoted more often. Capacity given in terms of cubic feet of living space is not at all exact since there is no provision for the insulation of the house, the outdoor temperature, the number of windows, house airtightness, wind velocity, location of house on south or north slope, air circulation, Maine or Florida location, etc.

If the stove is listed by BTU's, 20,000 BTU's will heat an average room. BTU's, however, depend also on such variables as chimney height, moisture content in the wood, and the draft of the stack.

Another rough estimate is by weight. A 15×18 foot room can be heated with a 125-pound cast-iron stove and for every additional 100 pounds, another room can be heated. You also can calculate by the size of the firebox. Generally each cubic foot of firebox in a cast-iron stove will hold enough wood to heat one room for eight to twelve hours.

The smaller stoves aren't designed to burn overnight, and there are disadvantages to damping down a small stove. To do so you must fill the firebox full of wood, let it catch, and before going to bed close the draft completely. When all air intake is cut off, the fire will begin to smoulder, producing creosote. In larger stoves which have room for a large bed of coals, firebox temperatures can be kept hotter, longer, hence less creosote will be produced.

Keeping a fire overnight has its temptations. It's easier to rekindle the fire in the morning. In addition there has been some heat output from the stove during the night. But there are dangers in holding the fire. Sparks can escape through the draft opening; the door if not latched completely can be opened by logs shifting in the firebox against a poorly latched door; and with the thermostatic stoves, the damper might get stuck in the "open" position. There also is the possibility of a flow reversal in the chimney especially during a slow-burning fire. Air could backpuff, depositing sparks and smoke in the room. If you intend to keep a fire overnight, it would be a good idea to install a smoke detector (see pp. 116-17).

A stove which is too large has one advantage: larger pieces of wood can be burned, and the stove will have to be filled less often. The problem with stoves too large for the job is that they are filled with wood, put out too much heat, then are damped down and begin producing creosote. A large stove is difficult to maintain at a low heat output.

Try to buy a stove designed to fill your needs. Whatever you choose, it's best to operate the stove close to but not beyond its ability. The stove should be sized slightly larger than the space in which it will be located. Providing heat for more than that room means distributing the heat. Floor registers or fans will help move extra heat to adjacent rooms.

To determine the space you want to heat, multiply the length times the height times the width to find out the number of cubic feet. Keep in mind that heat rises, and to get heat to travel horizontally and around corners may be nearly impossible, particularly in a rambling old farmhouse. Some heat can be moved laterally either with fans or through passages cut in the walls with small fans inserted. Also decide whether there are portions of the house which really don't need to be heated (bedrooms, for example).

More Heat

If there are no insulating materials in the firebox, such as firebrick, heat is transferred almost instantaneously. Still other ways to increase heat transfer include the choice of stove color. The darker the color (black being the best), the greater the radiation. If the surface area of the stove is increased, more heat will be transferred. This can be done by increasing the size of the firebox chamber, or by adding baffles or an arch to a stove design.

Many stoves have internal baffles; the following have models with an arch or heat chamber: Shaker, Jøtul, Morsø, Lange, Styria, SEVCA.

Lange

BARREL STOVES

Barrel stoves can be purchased, barrel and all for $55–$75. Even cheaper are the barrel stove kits. Barrel stoves are short-lived (one to two years if you don't burn coal), but the cast-iron conversion kits are cheap ($20–$65) and can be moved from barrel to barrel as your stoves wear out. Barrel stoves make sense for occasional heat in a garage, camp, shop, or deer hunting cabin; installing a $25 barrel stove in a $40,000 house is too risky.

Barrel stoves have no baffles which means they put out a lot of heat very quickly but they will not carry much of a fire overnight.

Even the mechanically inept can assemble a barrel stove in a couple of hours. If you are an amateur welder, you can even fashion the doors and legs yourself. However, the doors for barrel kits are of cast iron. Unlike plate steel doors, cast-iron ones won't warp, and can be used again and again on different barrels.

The kits usually include a front door frame, a cast-iron door assembly with draft controls, an ash door, legs, knobs for the doors, and a cast-iron stovepipe flange.

To put the kit together you will need:

saber saw with metal cutting blade
adjustable wrench
pliers
screwdriver
file
electric drill and bits

And, of course, a barrel.

Barrels can be located in the "Yellow Pages" under "Drums and Barrels" or from waste metal junk yards, gas stations, bakeries, laundries, or cleaners, health food stores, auto body repair shops, or feed stores. Stovepipe can be bought at hardware stores or wood stove stores.

Barrels come in 55-, 30-, and 15-gallon sizes. The 55-gallon barrel is the easiest to find but is impractical for heating purposes. It is too big and if fully stoked will make the room uncomfortably warm. The 30-gallon is a more practical size, with the 15-gallon best for heating a small room. Never use a barrel that has previously contained flammable materials (such as gas, naphtha, lacquer thinner, etc.). Fumes from these liquids may cause an explosion.

Conversion kits offer various extras such as pyrex glass doors for fire viewing, grates, and cooking tops.

Check the barrel to be sure the face without the bung and/or vent is smooth. Since the door will be fitted to this end, it is important to get as good a seal as possible. With the drum seam side down (or bung down), draw a vertical line from top to bottom through the center of each end of the barrel. Then mark the layout for the fuel door opening. Cut the opening with a sabre saw and metal-cutting blade. Cut carefully to keep the face of the drum smooth. Drill mounting holes for the door. Before mounting the door, the legs should be attached.

Lay out the holes for the legs according to the manufacturer's instructions. Then drill the holes and bolt the legs on with stove bolts which should be included in the package. The washers and nuts should be on the outside (unless otherwise specified) so as not to interfere with ash removal. Be sure the legs are aligned.

The door can now be bolted to the front of the barrel with stove bolts. Don't tighten the bolts completely. The steel will expand with the first few fires. After a couple of hot fires, your drum will be seasoned and the bolts can be firmly tightened.

The smokepipe will be installed at the other end of the barrel. Scribe a circle to the size of the smokepipe. The circle should remove the bung. Cut the hole with a sabre saw and metal-cutting blade. Drill holes for the flange, then bolt it to the barrel. Buy however many lengths of pipe will be necessary. A

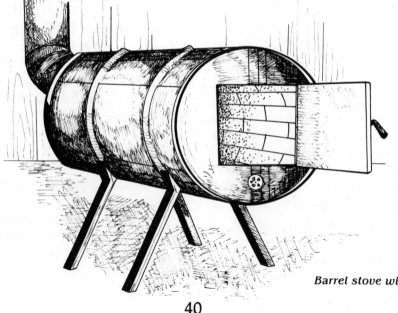

Barrel stove with firebrick lining

40

damper should be installed in the first section of the pipe. See page 45 for installation and safety requirements.

If the barrel has paint, burn it off. Let the barrel cool, then rub it with steel wool and apply black stove polish. Grates aren't necessary, in fact they will only increase the rate of burn which may mean the room will overheat. Two inches of ashes or sand or gravel should be placed in the bottom of the stove to protect the barrel.

Barrels will burn just about anything, but check them frequently. If the metal should burn through, remove the cast-iron parts and reassemble the kit on a new barrel.

OTHER CONSIDERATIONS

1. Check to be sure that the stove you decide to buy is available locally. You may learn that some stoves are back-ordered for three or four months, which in some locations may be the entire heating season.

2. If at all possible, visit a home where you can see the stove being used that you are thinking of buying. Other stove owners are a good source of information.

3. Repair parts may be a problem. Stove companies can disappear as fast as they can appear. Every month a new manufacturer appears with a new stove. In five years he may be gone and replacement parts may be impossible to find. Ask your dealer how long the company has been in business and whether it is likely to be around in ten years. Ashley, Washington Stove Works, Locke Stove Company, many of the foreign manufacturers, etc., have been in business for years and are likely to be there when you need them. Baffles and lids may have to be replaced. On the sheet-metal stoves, the inner liner will need replacing within ten years.

4. Think about the safety of the stove. With small children, cabinet models decrease the likelihood of burns. Small or non-existent ash lips, awkward loading doors, ex-cessively small doors, poor latches or cast aluminum doors and/or handles which transmit the heat so rapidly as to be unsafe are all features which may be hazardous in a stove. Lightweight stoves can be inadvertently knocked over and are much less durable.

5. Convenience should be a concern. Consider thermostats if you won't be around to adjust the draft, overnight burns if you don't want to rebuild the fire in the morning, heavy rugged construction for safety, airtights if you want to keep wood cutting (or buying) to a minimum, updraft stoves if you want less creosote, and sheet-metal stoves for "instant" heat. Top loaders may smoke as may stoves with fuel doors much larger than 8" x 8". Ash pans and ash lips decrease the mess of ash removal.

6. Aesthetics are important, particularly if the stove will be centrally located. Current stove sales would suggest that most Americans are buying circulators or Franklin-style stoves. Circulators are popular because they are safer with children. Domestic stoves with the "old-fashioned look" include the Franklins and the Defiant and can be burned with the doors opened or closed. Many people think this is the best of two worlds—the open fireplace and the efficient stove. The Defiant is expensive but airtight and of excellent quality; the Franklins are notoriously inefficient.

After cutting two extra cords per year for a "beautiful" but inefficient stove, your views on "beauty" may change. Some of the most efficient stoves are "ugly," but if an "ugly" stove saves you cutting an extra two cords for "beauty," you may wish to change to a more efficient stove. Franklins may mean twice the amount of wood as required for an airtight.

There are a number of combination stoves on the market for people who want both the romance of an open fire and the efficiencies of an airtight. In these stoves look for airtight doors and good draft control. The combis include: Franklins, Morsø, Defiant, Jøtul 4.

Number of Stoves

If you have the choice of whether to buy one large or two small stoves, one large one is better, theoretically. One large stove offers greater flexibility. Because of its larger firebox, it will take much larger chunks of wood. One stove also means only one set of stovepipes to be cleaned, and since the process of dismantling and cleaning is arduous, you will save yourself a lot of work.

However, in some house designs a single large stove isn't possible, particularly with one-story ranches where it is difficult to move the heat. In such cases, two stoves may be necessary.

Stanley cookstove

COOKSTOVES

Cookstoves haven't changed much in the past hundred years. Since people are less concerned about their gas and electric bills for cooking than about their heating bills, old cookstoves still can be found. New stoves of good quality will cost $600–$1400, old stoves $100–$600.

Cookstoves have small fireboxes and many have insulated sides to prevent excessive heat loss. The stoves are made of cast iron and will burn either wood or coal. If you intend to use wood, it will have to be cut into short splits, usually one foot long, to fit the firebox.

Cookstoves are being manufactured in the traditional stove designs, but there also are new, highly efficient stoves which are porcelain-coated to look like any modern appliance. Some come with ovens, reservoirs for hot water, and surface plates for boiling and frying.

Periodically check the stove to be sure that soot isn't collecting on the top of the oven, in the flue, or under the oven. This can substantially decrease the oven temperature. The ovens should always be used with an oven rack. And food, particularly bread, will have to be tended frequently to prevent it from burning.

In buying a cookstove, look for ones with large fireboxes, large surface plates, insulated walls, large ovens, and of quality cast-iron construction. Weight is again an indication of durability.

No book on wood stoves can be thorough enough. For that reason, a reliable dealer is good insurance. Every house is different; every stove is different; every installation is different. For the idiosyncrasies of your specific situation, someone who is nearby and knowledgeable is an asset.

In addition, the wood-stove market is growing rapidly. Even reputable dealers don't have the time to scrutinize every stove they sell. Therefore you want as much help and advice as possible plus the assurance that if you discover a part missing or a faulty baffle, you will be able to have it replaced. Some stoves have warranties for their parts which is a guarantee that the manufacturer stands by his product. Stores selling only or mainly wood stoves are likely to stand by the stoves they carry, and should be able to give you advice on installations.

Stove Location & Installation

The majority of destructive fires which occur from burning wood are a result of unsafe location and installation of the stove. Fireplaces and wood stoves aren't inherently dangerous but when installed without regard to safety, your house becomes a firetrap. Take extreme care to follow the clearance distances recommended by the National Fire Protection Agency and to double-check the safety of your chimney.

Location

Stoves can be located anywhere as long as there is a three-foot clearance on all sides for radiating heaters. But some locations make much better sense than others. Closets for either the stove or stovepipe are dangerous. The enclosed space provides poor circulation for the air, thus causing temperatures around the stove to rise and increasing the possibility of fire.

If you wish to take advantage of gravity, the lower the stove is in the house the better. A basement stove will warm the first floor, and if there are floor registers the warm air will travel between the floors. However, in an uninsulated basement, much of the heat may be lost through the walls, in which case the stove should be located on the first floor. If the stove is located near a stairwell or if the house is equipped with floor registers to allow the heat to rise, a first-floor stove can heat the upstairs. The stove also should be centrally located, in or near the living room, den, or wherever sedentary activities occur in the house. Kitchens or playrooms are poor locations because they generate their own heat. Ideally the stove should be in the center of the space it will heat, but situated so that it will not interfere with family traffic patterns.

A stove may be vented out a window or vertically through the house. If you intend to vent through ceilings and the roof, thereby keeping the chimney within the house, careful calculations must be made so that the chimney is between rafters, if possible, and passes near to but not through the roof ridge. Stovepipe which goes through the house will keep the stack warmer, produce a better draft, make the pipe easier to support, simpler to clean and repair, and keep the house warmer.

If you intend to vent a stove into an existing fireplace, your stove choice will be limited by the height of the fireplace opening. Usually fireplace openings range in height from twenty-seven to thirty-two inches, but they can be much smaller or much larger. In figuring whether a specific stove will fit, you must allow for a half-inch of insulation under the stove and a quarter-inch incline for every foot of stovepipe. If the stove vents out the top, you also must allow for the height of an elbow. Elbows will add six to eleven inches, depending on the diameter of your pipe. If, for example, your pipe is six inches in diameter, you may lose another eight inches for the elbow. If the stove vents both top and back, the crucial dimension on the stove specifications will be the height to the top of the back flue collar.

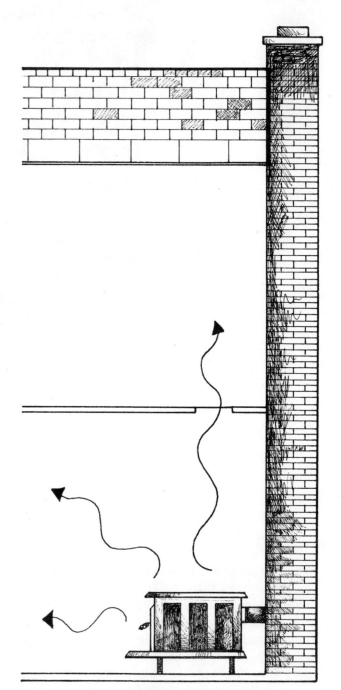

Position your stove for maximum heat circulation

INSTALLATION

There are a number of possible safe installations. For a house with a single flue for the furnace or no flue at all, there are no shortcuts. A factory-built insulated chimney will have to be used. However, you may have a fireplace which provides alternatives, although you will have to forego the option of a fireplace fire which may be too precious a pleasure. The third possibility is an existing but hidden flue, either free standing or in the chimney masonry. Go on the roof and look down the chimney(s) to discover the number of flues. Since it's much easier to build multiple flues into a single block of masonry, you may have a fireplace plus a second flue starting in the basement or first floor.

Check masonry chimneys for flue liners and for mortar deterioration. Some flues are best left unused if the damage of the ages is too extensive. On the other hand, you may have lessened your work load considerably.

Check Your Chimney

No matter whether you are planning to reactivate a long-unused fireplace, or venting a wood stove into an existing chimney, the chimney should be checked thoroughly before you proceed any further. You may find problems as simple as bird nests plugging the flue or as complicated as eroded mortar and loose bricks.

The first step should be to make certain that the fireplace was built for burning logs, and not for a gas-log hookup, or for coal or some other fuel. Those fireplaces are usually narrow and shallow, and may not be built to withstand the intensity of wood heat.

If you know the chimney was built for wood fires, make a methodical check of it. If the bricks are crumbly, loose, or missing, or there are cracks and fissures in the mortar,

the entire chimney may be in poor condition. Have it checked for safety by a mason. The chimney may have to be partially rebuilt or extensively repaired.

In older homes there may be inadequate clearances (should be two inches) between the chimney and the framing, or the fireplace may have been built on the floor joists rather than on a concrete foundation. Both cases create a fire hazard.

Go up on the roof to inspect the mortar more closely even if the chimney "looks" in good condition. Most of the masonry damage is likely to be above the roof line. The weather, particularly repeated water penetration and freezing, gradually erodes mortar.

Common sense will dictate the best way of getting up there. If possible, put the ladder against a gable rather than against the side of the roof where you might do damage to the shingles, drip edge or gutters. Place the ladder so that it makes about a four-to-one slope with both legs firmly planted. Have someone steady the ladder. If the chimney is near the peak, you should have no trouble maneuvering across the ridge. If the chimney exits through the center of one side, you'll need another ladder with a ridge hook.

Place ladders securely with about a four-to-one slope

Dark stains on the bricks mean that sooty water has been seeping through the mortar. Try to insert the blade of a pocket knife between the bricks and mortar. If it penetrates, or flakes or crumbles the mortar, the chimney is unsafe. Chimney fires can spread through these gaps. Small cracks, however, can be repointed. Dig out the deteriorating mortar with a cold chisel and replace it, being sure that you use a chimney mortar. You can use a dry-mix mortar to which you need only add water, or mix a mortar made of one part masonry cement (mortar cement already contains the correct amount of lime) and three parts sand.

Check also to be sure that the chimney flashing is present and in good repair. The flashing will be metal strips embedded in the masonry and extending four inches under the shingles. Without the flashing, water can seep into the house between the framing and the chimney.

While on the roof, check the chimney opening. You may have to remove a spark arrester, chimney cap or bonnet which will be secured with a nut and bolt or some screws. Some tops come off by twisting them counterclockwise. When the cap is off, check to be sure there is a flue for each heating appliance and that the flues are lined.

Flue Liners

Flue liners are a relatively recent safety precaution. If your house was built before the early part of the twentieth century, you may have an unlined chimney. Such thin walls of single brick construction with bricks sometimes laid edgewise will transmit the heat of a chimney fire to nearby combustibles. These flues should be lined by a mason. Lowering and mortaring sections of flue tile is no easy job, and poorly mortared joints make bumpy surfaces which can collect creosote and may affect the draft. If you have a choice, round flues are more efficient but more difficult to install.

Fireclay liners decrease the possibility of drafts between flues; they protect the masonry from creosote deterioration; and because they do not respond as quickly to sudden changes in temperature as masonry will, they help to contain chimney fires. If you don't wish to install flue liners, metal chimneys can be dropped down the flue. (See pp. 109-10).

Before leaving the roof, examine the inside of the chimney. If the chimney bends, drop a trouble light on the end of a long extension cord. Fallen bricks which may have lodged in the throat will probably cause smoking. Check the flue liners to be sure they are not cracked or broken and free of creosote build-up.

With a small pocket mirror look up the flue from the hearth opening. This may be difficult in fireplaces with narrow throats, or with smoke shelves and dampers restricting the view upwards. Tilt the mirror to such an angle that you can see light at the chimney top. If there is no light, birds or squirrels may have nested in the chimney and their bedding will have to be cleaned (not burned) out. If you are working from the fireplace hearth, you may be able to dislodge and remove the obstruction by using a broom or hoe. If you are working with a small flue opening this will have to be done from the roof with a weighted rope.

Again look carefully for soot and creosote deposits. Soot will be a black powdery substance, while dried creosote will be a black, brittle, tar-like residue. If it is more than a quarter-inch thick, the creosote should be cleaned out. Creosote will obstruct the draft and if the flue gases are sufficiently hot, the creosote will ignite. In addition creosote has a corrosive effect on mortar. If left unattended, water from both rain and snow will drip down the chimney causing the creosote, which is acidic, to erode the mortar and/or steel. Therefore, chimneys should be cleaned in the spring before the rains.

Chimney Sweeping

No matter whether you are using a fireplace, a wood stove, or a wood-burning furnace, sooner or later you must face the task of cleaning the chimney.

There are two approaches. One is to hire a chimney sweep. He will arrive with top hat and, more important, the right equipment and a knowledge of how to do the job. When he finishes, he will probably report on the condition of the chimney, warning you if it needs the services of a mason. He'll do the job well, will save you the danger of climbing up on your roof, and will make no mess.

But you want to do it yourself. And it needs cleaning, because you have seen a deposit of a quarter-inch or more inside the chimney, or it has been at least a year since last it was cleaned.

What do you need for the job? What will scrape away that buildup of soot or creosote?

First, let's forget some of the often-suggested methods. Let's not try last year's Christmas tree, or a bucket filled with concrete, or a bag with several pounds of sand in it. Any of these may damage the flue or somehow get stuck in the chimney. And let's leave that hoe for the garden; use of it in the flue may crack the mortar joints.

Let's spend the few dollars to get some of the equipment needed, recognizing that if we're heating with wood, we'll get our money's worth as we make this cleaning at least an annual event.

Sure, you can save money by using a burlap bag filled with straw, tire chains or sash weights. And if you try it, tie a half-inch rope to the bag, and let the bag down into the chimney as far as it will go, then drag it back up, making certain each time you do this that it is dragging against different sections of the flue. Do this until you are certain the walls have been well brushed.

But for best results, buy one of the wire brushes made especially for this purpose. They are made of strong stiff wire bristles and must be sized to fit your flue.

If you buy an extremely stiff brush, it should be exactly the size of your flue. Stiff brushes will take off more soot but they are harder to work with. No harm is done should you discover you've bought a brush slightly too large, since the ends can be trimmed with wire cutters. There also are brushes with more flexible bristles. If you buy one of these, get one slightly larger than the flue size. (Flue size can be determined by looking up the hearth, beyond the damper of the fireplace, or into the flue opening for a wood stove. You should be able to reach in far enough to measure the exact size with a measuring tape.) You may be offered a choice of a plastic or steel brush. Choose the latter.

The brushes can be used in two ways, either with a rope plus a weight of ten to fifteen pounds, or with a series of four-foot extension handles. Metal extension handles allow you to clean the chimney from the hearth. Otherwise you will have to clean the chimney from the roof.

Let's pick the right day for this job. It's warm, so the fire has not been burning in the stove or fireplace. And it's not mid-winter, when snow makes the roof the least desirable place to climb.

Remove the damper which in some cases is easier said than done. Dampers are usually attached to the damper support with two cotter keys. These may be taken out. Others may have to be rotated. Still others won't come loose. If not, you will have to work around the opened damper.

Next comes the trip to the top of the chimney — and make certain the route there is a safe one. If your chimney has a cap, arrive at chimney-side equipped to remove it. Next attach the weights to the brush and lower it on the rope from the top of the chimney. Pull the brush back and forth at least five or six times. The weights are unnecessary with two people, one on the roof and one near the hearth opening. Attach rope to both ends of the brush and take turns pulling the brush through the flue.

You also will need a method to prevent the

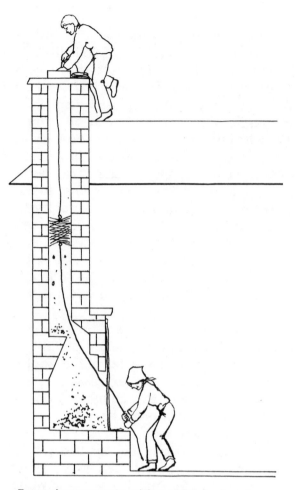

Removing creosote with a chimney brush

To complete the task of cleaning the fireplace, clean out the ash pit, located in the chimney foundation. The ash pit door may be either outside or inside the house near the base of the chimney. This pit will fill with ashes falling through the ash dump (a trap door in the center of the fireplace hearth). If water leaks into the pit it will mix with the ashes to form an almost concrete-like mixture. A bucket, trowel and work clothes are needed for this task.

When the system has been cleaned, check the safety of your chimney if you're in doubt. Light a small smoky fire (damp leaves will do) in the fireplace or stove. Block off the fireplace with a wet blanket. A second person stationed on the roof should then put a wet burlap bag or blanket over the chimney top. If there are cracks in the mortar, the smoke will be forced out of them. These cracks should be marked, the mortar chipped out, and the bricks repointed.

spread of dust inside the home while the chimney is being swept. (This is not a problem with a stove, as we will explain on page 115.) Close off the hearth opening by taping a tarp or several sheets of plastic across the front. Leave an opening in the tarp if you intend to clean the chimney from the hearth.

Find something else to do for about an hour after completing the brushing. This gives the dust time to settle. Then shovel the soot into the ash pit through the door, or shovel it into a bag, using a fireplace shovel or a dust pan. Use a vacuum cleaner to remove any deposits left on the hearth and smoke shelf and around the damper. It may pay to rent an industrial vacuum for the job, since the fine dust can get in the motor of your household vacuum and burn out the bearings.

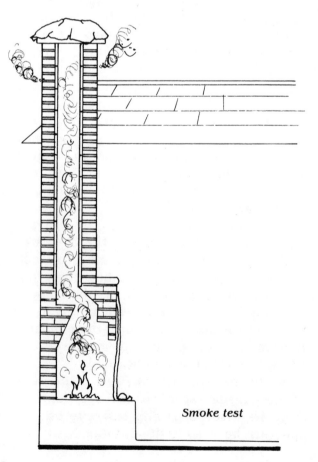

Smoke test

VENTING INTO AN EXISTING FLUE

Of the three options for installing a wood stove, venting into an existing but **unused** flue is the easiest and preferable. (You should never vent two heating appliances into the same flue. Be sure the flue actually **is** unused. The furnace should have its own flue.) When coal or gas stoves were taken out of old houses, round metal disks were inserted in the flue openings to cap the vent. Holes can be located by a little judicious tapping on the wall. If the wall has been sheetrocked, papered, or paneled, these will have to be removed.

Pull out the round metal disk. If the cap is stuck, start it with a pry bar. To check for the presence of flue liners, shine a flashlight inside the hole. Go up on the roof to check its condition and that of the chimney. Within and extending above the brickwork should be the fireclay liner of 5/8-inch or thicker. Check the masonry carefully for deterioration. If the chimney runs through an attic, scrutinize its condition there as well. If at all in doubt, consult the local fire department or a mason.

There also should be a metal or fireclay thimble leading into the flue. Repoint between the thimble and the masonry if necessary. Check the thimble diameter to determine what size stovepipe it will accept. Keep this potential limitation in mind when purchasing a stove.

The flue collar diameter on a stove should not be reduced. If the stove is designed for eight-inch pipe, you should not adapt down to a six-inch hole because you may be bothered with backpuffing. The reverse, however, is possible. If the stove takes six-inch stovepipe, you can buy an adapter which will allow you to vent into an eight-inch hole.

NFPA Clearances

Before proceeding further, give some thought to the positioning of the stove and the path the smokepipe will follow. The National Fire Protection Agency (NFPA) has strict recommendations but no way to enforce them since most stove installations are done by the homeowner. The regulations may seem stringent, even annoying, but they **should be followed.** The seemingly excessive clearances for radiant heaters are based on in-the-middle-of-the-night chance occurrences and on ignition temperatures of materials around the stove which with time will be lowered substantially.

Radiant energy is absorbed by the first thing it hits, be it you, the walls, or furniture. Most floors, walls, and ceilings contain combustibles, usually wood, which will be continually absorbing heat from the stove. Gradually the wood or wallpaper will dry and as it dries it will ignite more easily. What is not a fire hazard this year may be one next year. Continuous moderate heat can lower the ignition temperature of wood from 700°F. to 200°F. Therefore, comply with the recommended distances.

There should be a minimum of thirty-six inches between the radiant stove and all combustible materials in the walls and ceiling. Wood framing, plaster and lath walls, paneling, and sheetrock are all considered combustible. This distance can be decreased to a minimum of eighteen inches **only** if the walls are protected by a heat shield.

Circulators require less distance than radiant heaters because they have a protecting cabinet around the radiating heater; however they need ample clearance in front because they are usually loaded from the front. With

49

no heat shield, they require eighteen inches; with a heat shield only nine inches is required.

NFPA lists the following minimum clearance distances for free standing stoves installed without protection.

Type Heater	Above Top	From Front	From Back	From Sides	Floor
Radiant (includes parlor, box, Franklin, etc.)	36″	36″	36″	36″	18″ or 4″ with stoveboard extending 12″ on three sides, 18″ on ash door side
Circulating	18″*	36″*	18″	18″	4″ if stoveboard under stove
Cookstoves with lined fireboxes	30″		24″	24″ on firing side 18″ on opposite side	18″ from firebox
Cookstove with unlined firebox	30″		36″	36″ on firing side 18″ on opposite side	18″ from firebox
Stovepipe	18″	18″	18″	18″	

*Circulators are sometimes loaded from the top or front. Leave 36-inch clearance on loading door side.

Assembly

For constructing heat shields and installing your stove, you will need the following materials:

      1/4-inch asbestos millboard (4 foot × 4 foot sections sell for about $11.)
      28 gauge steel metal
      bricks, tiles, pebbles, or whatever you intend for decorative purposes
      scrap lumber for frame, if you plan to use bricks
      stovepipe (sized to the diameter of your flue collar size)
      damper (if applicable)
      elbows (if applicable)
      furnace cement
      sheet metal screws (three #6 screws for each piece of pipe including the elbows)
      electric drill with a metal bit
      sheet rock screws or 8d nails
      tin snips
      hammer
      saw or utility knife
      screwdriver
      porcelain electric fence spacers (4 for each 4 foot × 4 foot sheet of millboard)
      pliers

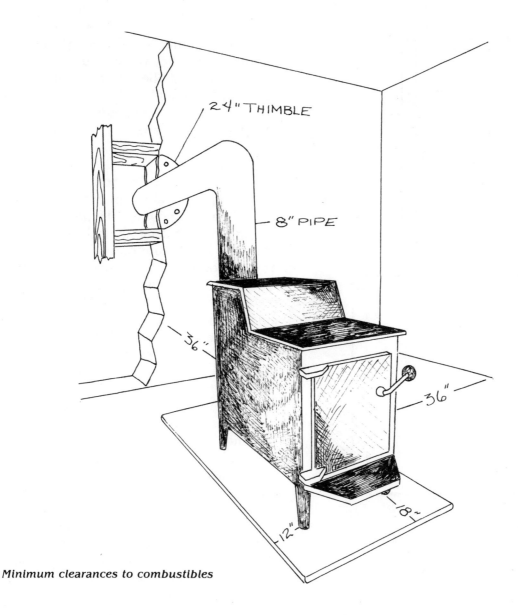

Minimum clearances to combustibles

Making a Heat Shield

The best heat shield is made of 28 gauge sheet metal over quarter-inch asbestos millboard.

Do not confuse asbestos millboard with asbestos cement board, which should not be used. Cement board is a hard, slate-like material made to protect boiler rooms in case of explosion. Millboard is softer, lighter, and can be cut easily with a utility knife or saw. Clamp the edges to be sawed between two pieces of plywood to prevent the millboard from breaking. Asbestos produces a dangerous dust when being cut, so wear a mask over your mouth and nose while cutting it.

Cut the millboard to the desired size—a minimum of thirty-six inches square. With tin snips cut the sheet metal to the size of the millboard plus two inches. Cut out one-inch squares from each of the four corners of the sheet metal. Pilot holes for the nails should be hammered through the sheet metal in each corner. The metal lips can be hammered to a 90° angle on four sides by laying the sheet on a 2 x 4 or the edge of a work bench. Next slip in the millboard and bend the lips of the sheet metal around the millboard with pliers.

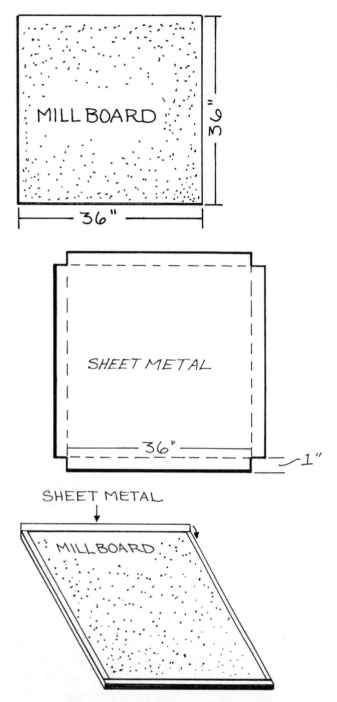

A one-inch air space **must** be left between the heat shield and the wall. Any non-combustible may be used as a spacer between the shield and wall. Some people use porcelain electric fence insulators. Be sure they are porcelain, not plastic.

When mounting the shield, place it one inch up from the floor to permit an air current to pass between the wall and the shield.

Remember that if nails are used in mounting the shield, they will conduct heat into the wall. Nails should be driven in only at the far edges of the shield.

Follow the same procedure for protecting the ceiling and mantle.

Floor Protection

Other pre-installation considerations include floor protection. Tile, linoleum, or carpeting only obscure the fact that beneath your feet is the subflooring and floor joists, both of wood and therefore combustible. The legs of the stove should be at least eighteen inches in height to allow sufficient air to circulate beneath the stove. That height can be reduced to a minimum of four inches if the stove rests on stoveboard (1/4-inch asbestos millboard covered with 28 gauge or thicker sheet metal). For fire protection the sheet metal isn't mandatory, but you will soon discover that millboard is flimsy. It will accumulate dirt, and can be scuffed, or damaged. Covered with sheet metal it is easily moved and cleaned.

Brick, Z-brick, slate, stone, iron, cement board and cement of less than eight inches thick do not protect the combustibles beneath them because they conduct heat. Although stoves installed on these materials seem "apparently" safe, the heat will gradually dry out the subflooring and floor joists. In addition heat travels through the legs of the stove, and should you have a chimney fire or severe backpuffing, the floor could be endangered. Combination stoves also give off intense heat when burned with the doors opened.

Regardless of what's on the floor and how great the clearance between the stove and floor, the floor should be protected. Sparks and embers can fall out of the stove, particularly when ashes are removed or the stove reloaded.

The stoveboard beneath the stove should extend eighteen inches beyond all sides of the stove where there is the possibility of glowing coals or embers dropping to the

52

floor, and twelve inches on all other sides. (These dimensions are the minimal safety code requirements.) Ash removal particularly in stoves which do not have an ash pan or an ash lip is dangerous. For this reason you may wish to extend the stoveboard beyond eighteen inches.

Stove stores invariably display their stoves on a brick or pebble hearth to increase the aesthetic appeal. If you wish to do the same, be sure the bricks, tile, pebbles, sand or whatever, is placed on top of the stoveboard.

A simple frame can be made from scrap lumber, sized to fit around the stoveboard. Then place the frame around the stoveboard and fill it with whatever you find pleasing. Your choice of material will be critical only if you vent into a fireplace hearth. If, for example, your stove measures twenty-eight inches to the top of the flue collar and you intend to vent through a fireplace which is thirty-one inches high, every inch is valuable. The millboard will add 1/4-inch and if you intend to set the stove on bricks of a two-inch thickness, the height to the stove flue collar will now be 30 1/4 inches. A two-foot section of smokepipe from the stove into the hearth will require a rise of 1/2-inch, leaving only 1/4-inch clearance.

Stovepipe

Stovepipe should be 24 gauge, heavy duty, black pipe designed for use **inside** the home. Galvanized pipe is a real danger should there be a chimney fire. This pipe is designed for oil or gas furnaces and is too thin for wood-burning appliances. Above all, it is **not** designed to be used on the outside of a building. The humidity combines with the ash and forms lye which will erode the metal very quickly. It also produces toxic fumes at high temperatures.

If you find used stovepipe, check for rust corrosion. Thin areas or pinholes are a danger in case of a chimney fire.

Black stovepipe usually comes in twenty-four-inch lengths of six- and eight-inch diameters.

To install single wall stovepipe the proper distance from combustibles, measure the diameter of the exhaust collar on your stove to determine the size of the pipe you will need. Single wall pipe must be three times its diameter away from combustibles, including the ceiling and the mantle. Thus stovepipe with a six-inch diameter will require clearance of eighteen inches on all sides. A heat shield of stoveboard spaced out one inch from the mantle, ceiling or wall will allow you to reduce this distance to nine inches. To go closer than nine inches or through a wall or ceiling, you should use stainless steel, factory-built, insulated pipe.

When venting into an existing flue, double check clearance distances. Having an unused

Minimum clearances with heat shields

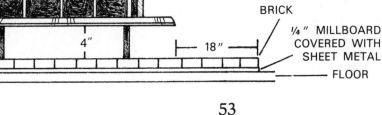

BRICK

¼" MILLBOARD
COVERED WITH
SHEET METAL

FLOOR

53

flue probably means yours is an older house. Partitions may have been added, walls moved, etc., so that an existing flue may no longer be a safe flue. If, for example, you have an interior fireplace with extra flues yet the distance from the opening to the now existing wall is less than nine inches, installation of a heat shield plus one-inch air space will not be possible. Instead of single-wall stovepipe you will have to choose pre-fab insulated chimney pipe. It is expensive but will permit clearances of no less than two inches on all sides.

In your mental calculations, remember that the pipe should be installed with as few elbows as possible (certainly no more than two; one is even better), and a vertical rise of at least a quarter-inch per foot of pipe. Anything in your smokepipe design which retards the flow of gases will allow for creosote accumulation.

Installing Stovepipe

Some stovepipe is pre-assembled, but if not, the pipe is easy to assemble. One edge has a groove, the other a flange. They will fit when pressed together. In estimating the amount of stovepipe you will need, remember that when the pipes are fit together, the total length will be one to three inches shorter per section. For twenty-four-inch pipe the useful length is 22 1/2 inches.

The European stove manufacturers use the metric system which means different sized exhaust collars. Metric pipe is available, but if you can't find it, you will have to buy an adapter. Reducing the flue size from that of the stove's flue collar diameter may cause backpuffing when the stove is reloaded, create a bad draft situation, or reduce combustion efficiency. Pipe diameters increased too drastically will slow the exhaust gases too much, and circular draft patterns may be established, causing downdrafts in the pipe. It is best to adapt to the next larger pipe size. Six-inch stovepipe is the most popular size for small stoves.

The sections of stovepipe should be

secured together with three #6 self-tapping sheet metal screws for each connection. If only two are used, a hinge effect is created; the third screw is important. Holes can be made by using a nail as a center punch.

Be sure that each section of pipe fits into the one below. Phrased differently: the crimped ends should face towards the stove. Since a wood fire produces creosote, a runny substance when sufficiently hot, the creosote will collect on the inside of the pipe and drip back towards the stove. If the pipes are reversed, the creosote will seep out between the pipes and either run down the outside of the pipe or drip onto the floor. With the crimped ends towards the stove, smoke will not leak out between the sections because draft is a suction phenomenon; rather, air will leak into the pipe.

For pipe running horizontally, keep the seams on the top of the pipe and be sure there are no screw holes on the down side through which creosote could leak.

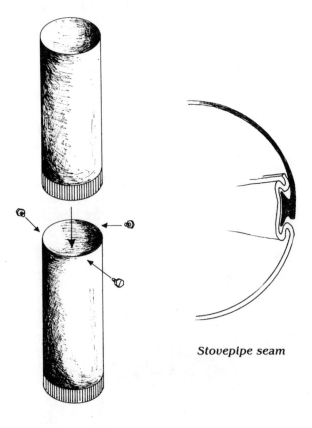

Stovepipe seam

Stovepipe assembly

Damper

Some stoves require a stovepipe damper (airtights usually do not) which should be installed in the first section of pipe about six inches from the collar. Don't install one unless it is required because it will only collect creosote.

Damper

The damper is a steel pin handle plus a disk (called a damper plate) that fits inside the pipe. Two holes must be made in the pipe to fit the damper. Drill the first hole, then insert the pin of the damper handle, and thread it through the disk. Turn the disk so that it is in a closed position, and press on the opposite side of the pipe with the damper-handle point, making a dimple to show where to drill or punch the second hole. After drilling it, run the handle through the first hole, then through the damper plate, and out the second hole. When the handle is horizontal, the damper is open; when the handle is vertical the damper is closed.

Elbows

Non-adjustable elbows are locked into a 90° turn. For angles between 0° and 90° an adjustable elbow can be purchased. Nonadjustable elbows are corrugated and preferable; adjustable elbows tend to leak creosote.

How Much Pipe?

The length of stovepipe should be as short as possible. If you must have a lengthy horizontal run, the pipes should not only be secured with sheet metal screws, but at two-foot intervals the pipes should be reinforced with strap iron supports (used for hanging copper pipes) or be wired to the ceiling. This may seem overcautious but in the event of a chimney fire, the fire suddenly will demand vast quantities of oxygen. This will cause inordinate stress on the pipes which may vibrate, then fly apart.

The length of the stovepipe involves several tradeoffs. The longer the pipe, the more heat moves into the room, and not up the chimney. But with this comes more creosote, as well as greater danger in the event of a chimney fire. The National Fire Protection Association recommends the shortest, most direct exit between stove and chimney. The horizontal run of the stovepipe should never exceed 75 percent of the height of the chimney, from the flue inlet to the top of the chimney.

The pipe should have a slope from the stove up to the chimney of at least a quarter-inch per foot. Nearly horizontal pipe will slow down the gases, allowing greater heat transfer but also cooling the stack temperature and increasing creosote deposits.

Perhaps you've seen photographs of old meeting halls or schools in which the stovepipe ran the length of the room. They got away with this because the stoves weren't airtight, burned hotter, and so produced much less creosote.

Creosote problems in horizontal pipe can sometimes be cured by encasing the stovepipe in a second piece of pipe with a diameter one inch larger. The air space is then filled with fiberglass insulation. This will lessen heat loss through the pipe.

For the least creosote buildup, keep the stovepipe close to vertical. With adequate draft, smoke may be able to negotiate a slightly downhill run or 90° curves, but in both cases you may have increased creosote.

Trial Assembly

Assemble the stovepipe and elbow(s). Be sure the stove is resting on stoveboard and bricks or whatever you intend for floor protection. Begin from the chimney and work back to the stove. The section of pipe which fits into the thimble should be flush with the inner face of the flue. If the pipe extends any further, it will obstruct the draft.

Pipe passing through a thimble and a brick wall requires eight inches of brickwork on all sides of the pipe. Combustibles or framing beyond this twenty-two-inch square (for six-inch pipe) of brickwork must be protected. Line the combustibles with 22 to 28 gauge sheet metal.

On long, vertical runs of stovepipe, check clearance distances. Unless combustible walls are protected, there must be at least eighteen inches of clearance. If the chimney connector must pass through a combustible partition wall or will be too close to combustibles, read the section on "Venting Into the Fireplace Above the Damper" (pp. 59-60) for ways to solve clearance problems.

A length of smokepipe may have to be trimmed so the pipe will fit onto the exhaust collar snugly. Make a pencil mark around the uncrimped end. Then cut the pipe with a hacksaw or sabre saw.

For permanent assembly, connect the pipes with the sheet metal screws and caulk the joints between the pipes and between the pipe and the stove with furnace cement. Before using the cement, be sure the surface is clean. Then dampen the surface and apply the cement. It will dry in twenty-four hours and provide an airtight bond. With lateral runs, only the lower portion of the pipe needs to be caulked. Try to leave as smooth a surface as possible so as not to obstruct the draft. Periodically the furnace cement will need to be reapplied. Remove what has cracked, again dampen the surface and add another layer of cement.

Check around the stove collar and the seams of the pipe where you may need to re-caulk. You also may have unwanted space between the smokepipe and the fireclay or metal thimble. This space can be filled with asbestos rope which your stove dealer will have. Stuff the rope in between the thimble and the smokepipe with a screwdriver so that you have as airtight a seal as possible. When you wish to remove the pipe for cleaning, replacement, etc., the rope can be dislodged and used again.

FIREPLACE CONNECTIONS

An existing fireplace can be adapted for a wood stove hook-up. Some stove units such as Better 'n Ben's (C & D Distributors) are sold with a fireplace cover and need no stovepipe. They can be installed rapidly and have the advantage of taking very little space.

For those making their own units, there are two possible fireplace installations which don't involve any damage to the masonry. A third installation, venting into the fireplace flue above the damper, entails cutting through the flue tile and is more complicated. In the two simpler procedures, stovepipe is vented into the fireplace hearth either at the fireplace opening or at the damper.

Closing off the fireplace opening necessitates stoveboard to seal off the fireplace and a length of stovepipe to run from the stove to an opening in the stoveboard. Fireplaces blocked off in this way may collect messy creosote deposits on the fireplace hearth, but this problem can be eased if several inches of sand are laid on the hearth before the entrance is blocked off.

Stovepipe installed directly into the fireplace and up to the flue requires an extra elbow and one or two extra sections of pipe, but will keep the fireplace cleaner and is easier and cheaper to fabricate. There will, however, be more pipe to disassemble for cleaning (which should be done frequently if you use the stove with any regularity). In addition, one or two elbows are required. No more than two 90° turns should ever be used. Angles of 45° are better in that sharp curves can adversely affect the draft pattern and are natural repositories for creosote.

To vent the stove into the fireplace flue, use one of the following methods.

Blocking off the Fireplace

For a fireplace cover you will need a piece of sheet metal or ¼-inch stoveboard in which a hole the size of the stovepipe has been cut. (Just millboard is sufficient but the addition of sheet metal will reflect heat back into the room as well as making the millboard much stronger.)

The hole can be cut with a sabre saw and a metal-cutting blade. To gauge the height of the stovepipe opening, decide whether you will be top- or back-venting the stove. If the flue gases will exit from the top of the stove, it's best to use an adjustable elbow with as gradual an angle as possible. Measure to the top of the elbow to find out the height at which the pipe will be entering the fireplace. If the stove is back-vented, measure to the top of the flue exhaust collar.

Add a quarter-inch for the stoveboard under the stove and a quarter-inch for every foot of pipe. (This measurement can be greater than a quarter-inch per foot, but no less.)

The fireplace cover material should be six inches wider than the fireplace opening and three inches higher to allow large enough margins on three sides to bolt into the brick. Mark on the cover where the bolts will attach to the masonry. Pre-drill these holes. Drill into the masonry between the bricks, then insert masonry anchors into the holes to prevent ripping up the bricks. Run a bead of non-flammable caulking around the edge to insure that the cover will be airtight, then screw through the stoveboard so that the screws will be imbedded in the anchor. Two screws on each side should be sufficient.

If you prefer not to deface the fireplace

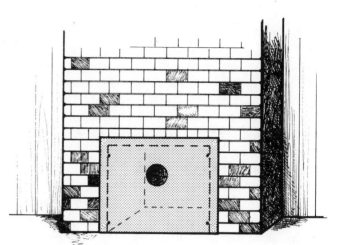

Closing the fireplace opening with stoveboard

The stove in place. A layer of sand will help catch dripping creosote.

jambs, a simple bolt system can be devised. Four carriage bolts, two on each side, can be run through the metal covering and held against the brick lip with a nut and large washer. The only difficulty with this system is that if you have a small stovepipe hole and a large fireplace opening, it may be difficult to tighten the bolts. The tightening will have to be done by reaching through the stovepipe hole and holding the nuts in place while turning the bolt from outside.

57

A sheet of asbestos with metal covering can be inset into the fireplace and lag screwed to the brick jambs. Cut the asbestos to fit the size of the opening. The metal covering should extend three inches on three of the sides, with a three-inch square cut from two corners. Temporarily clamp the metal to the asbestos, using a scrap piece of lumber under each clamp to protect the asbestos. Drill holes on each side. Bolt the two together, metal side up. Bend the lips 90° away from the asbestos. Push the unit into the fireplace opening until it fits tightly. The metal will be on the outside. Four screws, two to a side, should be ample to hold the sheet metal. Then caulk around the edges with furnace cement.

Before closing the fireplace opening, be sure the damper is opened or removed, and the ash pit is closed. Place a layer of sand over the inner hearth to catch any creosote drippings.

Up the Flue

The second type of fireplace installation involves running the stovepipe up to but not into the chimney flue. To do this, take the measurements of the opening just below the damper. Add six inches to these dimensions. From a piece of black sheet metal, 18 gauge, cut out squares of three inches from the corners so that a three-inch flange will be possible on all sides. Bend the flanges just less than 90°. Cut an opening for the stovepipe. The metal then should be treated with heat-resistant, flat black paint. With the damper opened, insert the sheet-metal unit into the chimney, being sure that it fits tightly and that the flanges face the fireplace hearth. The flanges should hold the unit in place. Caulk around the edges of the pipe and flanges with furnace cement to insure an airtight seal.

A unit of this sort is made-to-order by some hardware and welding suppliers. Their units are usually built with a small section of pipe slightly larger than your stovepipe which is welded to the sheet metal. This section of stovepipe has holes for sheet-metal screws which will secure the pipe to the unit. No caulking should be necessary. In installing stovepipe, keep in mind that at least two or three times a year (or more frequently, if you have a creosote problem), the pipes should be dismantled and thoroughly cleaned. Hence stovepipe installations shouldn't be impossibly difficult to take apart.

Up the flue installation

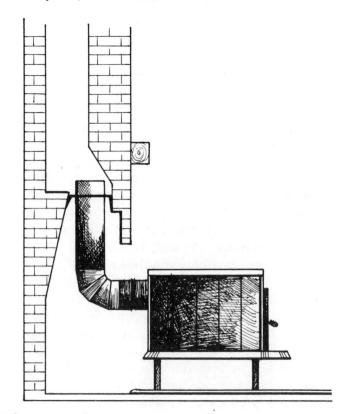

Flimsier installations can be fabricated, the stovepipe even flattened to fit partially through the damper. This should give it some stability. Fill the remaining air space with fiber glass.

Venting Into the Fireplace Above the Damper

You may wish to vent the stove into the fireplace above the damper. This will allow you to use the fireplace in late spring and early fall as long as you cap the hole for the wood stove connector pipe. Then during the colder parts of winter the wood stove can be used if the flue is blocked off just below the connector pipe entrance. Such an arrangement gives you some flexibility, but does not allow you to use both systems concurrently.

To vent above the fireplace opening also allows greater choice in the height of the stove you buy and may produce a better draft than venting directly into the fireplace hearth. The additional smokepipe will increase heat transfer, but the work involved will be greater. You may wish a skilled mason to undertake the job since foreseen and unforeseen complications can occur when going through a wall into masonry, particularly into an exterior chimney.

Determine where the studs are. There may be one dead-center over the fireplace. Six-inch stovepipe will need a hole of twenty-two inches. In regular frame construction, studs are sixteen inches on center. Therefore a stud will have to be removed and 2 × 4 framing added.

Installing factory-built insulated pipe is easier. The pipe requires a two-inch clearance, meaning the hole through the wall will have to be four inches larger than the outside diameter of the pipe.

The perimeters of the opening will be determined by the type of connection you intend. Also consider stovepipe clearances to the ceiling. Again the eighteen inches (for six-inch uninsulated pipe) can be reduced to

Above the damper installation

nine inches if protection is provided, or to two inches if insulated pipe is used.

Outline the hole on the wall. Paneling can be cut with a circular saw set to the proper depth. Cut through sheetrock with a utility knife. Plaster can be removed with a masonry chisel and hammer, the lath cut with a hammer and wood chisel.

Single-Wall Pipe with Fireclay Thimble

For single-walled six-inch pipe, cut a twenty-two-inch hole. Ideally one edge of your hole will butt to an existing stud. The stud which must be removed can be cut with a sabre saw. You may wish to extend your hole to the next stud to make the framing in easier (a hole of about thirty inches).

Insulated Pipe

Most likely no studs will have to be removed if insulated pipe is used. Factory-built pipe of a six-inch diameter has an outer diameter of eight inches, and requires a four-inch air space, meaning a twelve-inch opening. Try to center the hole between the studs.

59

Cutting through the Masonry

If there is insulation, it should be removed and the masonry exposed. The hole through the masonry should be the size of the outer dimension of the fireclay thimble, or insulated pipe. With a masonry bit, drill holes at mortar joints between the bricks until one is loosened. Pull out the brick. Continue the process until all the center bricks are removed. Break the bricks around the outer perimeter with a cold chisel. Bricks will be much easier to handle than concrete block because they are easier to crack and have more frequent mortar joints.

Between the bricks and liners there usually will be an air space which allows the tiles to expand. Flue liners are fragile. Avoid cracking them in the process of making your hole. You can use an electric drill with a masonry bit to make a line of holes sufficiently long to accept the blade of a sabre or reciprocating saw. With the saw, cut out the circle to the outer dimension of your pipe. Since fireclay will rapidly destroy both the bit and the blade, using a star chisel and hammer to work your way around is a better idea. They also are less likely to crack the liners.

Assembly

Fireclay Thimble

Slip the fireclay thimble into the hole to be sure it will fit. It should be flush with the inner face of the flue liner. If it extends into the flue, it will block the draft. Be sure the thimble is long enough to reach far enough into the room so that the lip will rest against the inner wall surface.

Check the inside diameter of the thimble to be sure it is large enough to accept the diameter of your stovepipe.

Frame in the hole you've made in the wall. Toenail the crosspieces to the studs and end nail them into what remains of the framing member. Between the crosspieces, add an additional member to square off the opening at the proper distance.

The thimble now should be put in place and attached securely. It should enter the chimney horizontally. Cement the thimble to the adjoining masonry using refractory mortar and spread to make a smooth joint. The special mortar is needed to withstand the constant changes in temperature. It can be made of one part Portland cement, one part hydrated lime, and six parts of clean sand, measured by volume.

The bricks of the chimney can be left exposed, in which case the exposed side of the 2 x 4 framing should be lined with twenty-two to twenty-eight gauge sheet metal. A layer of new bricks or firebricks can be mortared to fill the hole. They will provide a more finished appearance. Although less pleasing aesthetically, the space also can be filled with stoveboard nailed to the 2 x 4's. Leave a small gap between the thimble and the covering material in case any settling occurs.

Assemble the stovepipe. The stovepipe connector should slide into the thimble and be easily removable for cleaning and repairs. It shouldn't project **into** the flue liner. Be sure the crimped end faces the room. Then assemble the rest of the pipe. A section of pipe may have to be cut-to-fit which can be done with metal cutting shears.

Be sure the connector rests tightly enough in the thimble so that it won't be dislodged should there be a sudden puff from the firebox. You may wish to fill this space with asbestos rope which can be wedged into the space with a screwdriver.

Insulated Pipe

Insulated pipe will need two inches of air space left on all sides. Cover the gap with a trim collar which can be nailed to the 2 x 4 crosspieces which should be added between the studs. Never place insulated pipe in direct contact with combustibles.

If you use insulated pipe, remember that you can't change to smokepipe until you are more than eighteen inches from combustibles.

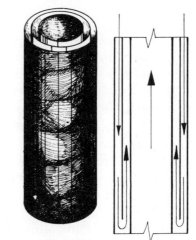

Triple walled pipe

Disadvantages

Chimney flues are made to accommodate large volumes of air. They are usually 8 × 8 (64 square inches) or 8 × 12 (96 square inches), while the stovepipe may be only six inches (twenty-eight square inches). The flue gases may move too slowly through the chimney, then cool, condense, and produce creosote, or downdrafts can occur. Installations vented into the fireplace may reveal any of these difficulties.

FACTORY-BUILT INSULATED CHIMNEYS

There are different kinds of factory-built pipe, all based on the principle that multiple-walled pipe will insulate the rising smoke and gases sufficiently to reduce clearance distances to two inches. The insulated outer surface will not be cool—just less hot. The greatest installation mistake and the greatest cause of fires is using single-wall pipe through a wall and up along a building. Factory-built pipe is **mandatory** whenever your installation goes through walls, ceilings, windows or the roof. The pipe should be listed as "All fuel" or "Class A" and be UL approved (Underwriters Laboratory) to insure that the brand has been tested and approved. Do not use UL pipe listed as "vent" because it is neither insulated nor ventilated for wood or charcoal fires.

Triple-wall pipe is three pipes of graduated sizes which nest within one another. They may be air insulated or air ventilated. In air ventilated pipes cold air travels down between the outer two surfaces and rises between the next two—hot air rises—while smoke and gases exit through the innermost. Air-ventilated pipe creates creosote.

Triple-wall pipe also may be air-insulated, which produces less creosote. The least creosote is produced by double-wall, factory-built, insulated pipe. This insulated pipe has a stainless steel outer casing, one inch of insulation (fiber glass and agglomerates of silica particles), and a stainless steel liner.

For temporary installations only, you can make your own insulated pipe. Buy two sets of pipes with a one-inch difference in their diameters. Wrap the outside of the inner pipe with asbestos paper to prevent the fiber glass from melting. Add the second pipe with the crimped end facing the same direction, and stuff fiber glass into the intervening space. The process is tedious and time-consuming but even double pipes without insulation are better than single-wall pipe. In a couple of years, however, the inner pipe will rust out and the process will have to be repeated. Factory-built pipe is expensive ($12 per lineal foot) but is sturdy and should last ten to twenty years.

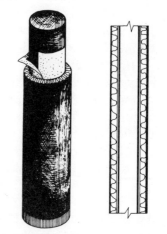

Home-made insulated pipe deteriorates quickly and should be considered a temporary measure only

Factory-built pipe comes in eighteen- or thirty-inch lengths with an inside pipe diameter of six, seven, eight, ten, twelve, and fourteen inches. "UP" is written on each section. The lengths of some brands fit together with a ring which slips down to lock the sections together. If the rings don't slip easily they can be tapped into place. Other pipe is threaded and locks together with a ⅛ turn to twist-lock the connection. Follow the manufacturer's instructions.

If you are handy with tools, installing a prefab chimney should take no more than a day. Don't begin until you have purchased your stove. Flue diameters differ; radiant and circulating stoves have different safety clearances. Then check your local building codes for special regulations.

There are three kinds of installations. The pipe can exit 1) out a window, 2) through an exterior wall, or 3) through the ceiling, attic, and then roof. The last gives the best wood-burning efficiencies because there is no more than one elbow and most of the pipe remains within the house. The first two entail at least one, most likely two elbows, and a long run of pipe outdoors. Both these conditions increase creosote formation.

In calculating the amount of pipe you will need, remember that the minute you are within eighteen inches (if your run of pipe will begin with six-inch uninsulated pipe) of combustibles, uninsulated, single-walled smokepipe cannot be used unless protection is provided. Under no circumstances should uninsulated pipe be used outdoors.

Don't mix brands of insulated stovepipe. Each one is assembled a little differently. To be sure you don't run out of pipe, buy an extra section or two. You can always return what's left over. Remember the chimney must be three feet above the roof—and two feet higher—than anything within ten feet.

Insulated Stovepipe and Fittings

The following fittings are available for insulated chimney installations:

a) An **insulated tee** starts the chimney out-doors when it will run up the outside of the house. It is a cleanout entrance.

b) **Elbows** in 15°, 30°, 45°, or 90° are available for fixed offsets or can be used in pairs for greater angles. Offsets greater than 30° are not recommended.

c) The **ceiling support package** is for joist-supported chimneys. The support and trim plate are nailed onto the framed opening. A bucket section fits inside and supports the first length of chimney thereafter.

d) The **wall support kit** is intended for use with an insulated tee which will start the chimney from an outside wall.

e) The **roof support package** contains a length of pipe with plates and brackets to be mounted on the roof. It is designed to support twenty feet of chimney and is intended

Installation through a window

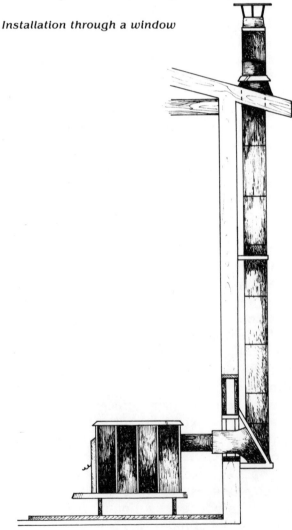

for open cathedral chimneys. Over this, special flashing and a storm collar are dropped.

f) Various **chimney tops** are available to keep out animals, arrest sparks, and provide rain protection.

g) **Wall bands** are used along an exterior house wall to insure stability and provide the required two-inch clearance. They should be used every eight feet.

h) **Trim collars** provide a finished appearance whenever the chimney passes through a wall or ceiling.

i) **Wall spacers** maintain clearance distances wherever insulated pipe passes through a combustible wall.

Installation

For insulated chimney installation you will need:

plumb bob	pliers
hand saw	screwdriver
sabre saw	utility knife
electric drill with bits	pry bar
ladders	hammer
2 x 4's	tape measure
common nails	square
roofing nails	level
roofing cement	

insulated pipe, supports, cap and accessories depending on your installation

Out the Window

This is the easiest of the installations for the do-it-yourselfer because there is no cutting through walls, roofs, or floors. (You may have to cut through the roof overhang if the roof or gutters project more than four inches into the path of the pipe. If less, 15° elbows may be used to clear the roof.)

Measure the amount of pipe needed, remembering that a radiating stove must be thirty-six inches away from combustibles unless you have a protective shield of stove-

board. Since one elbow will be needed outside the window, back vent from the stove if possible to decrease the number of elbows.

The first section of pipe from the stove can be single-wall pipe if you are still eighteen inches away from combustibles (for six-inch pipe). You may even want to top vent to keep more of the pipe within the house, but this means a second elbow.

Experiment with the pipe to be sure you understand how it fits together. Getting the smokepipe to fit inside the insulated pipe may be difficult. If pressure doesn't work, crimp the edges with a pair of pliers. Hardware or stove stores will crimp pipe, but for this connection it may reduce the diameter too much.

Remove one frame from a double-hung window. Take its dimensions and cut a piece of plywood to fill the space. A sandwich of window thickness, the plywood spaced apart with blocks and the intervening space filled with fiber glass, will give a better insulated opening. Both pieces of plywood will need stovepipe holes. These should be cut to the outside diameter of the insulated pipe. (Six-inch pipe will have an eight-inch outer diameter, etc.) To this number add four inches. Cut out either a square or circle with a sabre saw. The holes should be cut so they line up when the two pieces of plywood are in place.

The pipe is installed following the directions for venting through an exterior wall.

Through An Exterior Wall

Decide approximately where the stove will be located. The first hole should be made through the wall from the inside. To establish the height of the hole, decide whether the stove will be top- or back-vented. If the stove will be back-vented, measure from the floor to the center of the stove exhaust collar. Be sure to include the height added by the stoveboard, bricks, tile or whatever you intend to use for floor protection. Top-venting a stove means a run of horizontal pipe plus an elbow. Temporarily assemble the pipe including the elbow. Measure the distance from the floor to the center of the elbow. Mark this height on the wall. It will be the center of your hole.

Rap on the exterior wall with your knuckle to locate the studs. A rough approximation can be had by measuring eighteen inches in from an exterior corner, then every sixteen inches. Studs are usually sixteen inches on center. A stud finder may help, or look for a vertical row of nails in the Sheetrock. If you are near a light switch, there may be electric wires going to an overhead light. To prevent accidental contact, turn off the current. Re-route the wires later, if necessary.

Mark the approximate location of your hole being sure it will be at least eighteen inches down from the ceiling (unless you plan to put stoveboard on the ceiling). Draw a square or circle to the outside diameter of your pipe plus four inches. Drill enough holes in succession to get the blade of a key-hole or sabre saw into the hole. Saw around the outside. You may hit a stud unexpectedly. Readjust the location of the hole. Then continue. You want the hole to be between the studs.

Six-inch insulated pipe (with an outer diameter of eight inches), plus two inches of air space, requires an opening of twelve inches. A trim collar will be needed to cover the opening for a finished appearance around the stack. The collar has an outside diameter of fourteen inches. Since the opening between the studs is usually fourteen and a half inches, you may want to nail a piece of 2×4 to the stud for a better nailing surface.

After the hole on the inside has been made, drill four holes from the inside through the exterior wall at the corners of your opening. Use an $\frac{1}{8}$-inch drill bit or larger.

From the outside, draw a line to connect the four holes. Increase the size of any one of them so that the blade of a sabre saw will fit. Cut out the hole. Nail a wall spacer into place. The recessed portion of the spacer should project into the partition. It has been

sized to maintain the proper clearance from combustibles.

Next assemble the wall support package. It consists of a plate, two angle iron braces and hardware. The braces are fastened to the wall above or below the plate. The support has a load capacity of forty feet of vertical chimney.

Before lag screwing the support tightly to the wall, connect the insulated tee to the plate of the wall support. Check the alignment. Place a level on the tee to be sure it is horizontal. From the inside, slide the piece of horizontal insulated pipe through the hole and connect it to the tee; the connection will

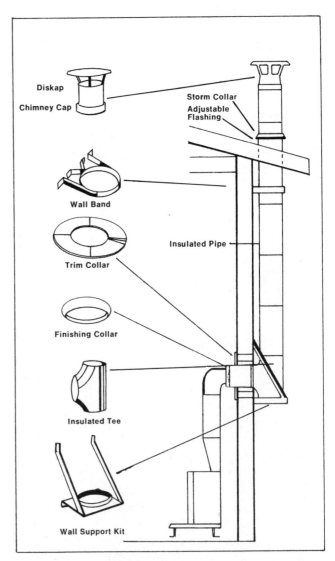

Installation through an exterior wall

be made somewhere within the wall. This will take two people, one to hold the tee firmly while the second person pushes from the inside until the two sections of pipe lock.

Slip on the trim collar with the finished side toward you and nail it to the wall. The rest of the interior run of pipe can be assembled. The stove may have to be moved slightly in order to make all the connections snug. Be sure all stovepipe screws are tight.

Tighten all screws on the exterior wall when you are sure the tee is level. Place the tee cap over the bottom opening from beneath the support. This cap can be removed for cleaning and inspection.

There should be an eighth of an inch clearance between the wall spacer and the pipe. Caulk this with furnace cement.

Assembly from this point is simple. Add the pipe section by section. Tap the rings into locking position or twist the pipe until it locks firmly. At eight-foot intervals slip a wall band matched to the chimney diameter over the pipe. Tighten the screw clamp to secure it to the pipe. Then screw the wall band into the exterior wall to assure stability and the two-inch safety clearance.

Stop the pipe below the overhang. An overhang which projects less than four inches from the center of the pipe can be handled with two 15° elbows to go around the roof. A plumb bob from the roof edge should align with the edge of the pipe (for six-inch pipe). Add the elbows. Wall band brackets mounted on blocks of wood will provide extra stability for the pipe as it goes around the fascia. Then continue the rest of the vertical length of pipe.

Cut through roof overhang if it projects too far. Mark where the pipe will meet the soffit. The location of the hole can be found with a plumb bob. Add two inches on each side for clearance. If the hole means cutting through a rafter, add a 15° elbow to adjust the location of the hole. Make holes from underneath with a drill. Cut through the soffit. Drill pilot holes from the soffit hole through the roof. Cut the roof opening from above. Remove the shingles within the pilot holes

with a pry bar and a utility knife. A sabre or circular saw can be used to cut the hole.

A firestop spacer should be nailed to the soffit to provide proper clearance, and the pipe passed through the soffit, then locked into the lower section of pipe. The above-the-roof installation is covered on page 67.

Through Ceilings and Roof

For a pre-fab installation which will keep most of the pipe within the house, you will need a ceiling support package for every ceil-

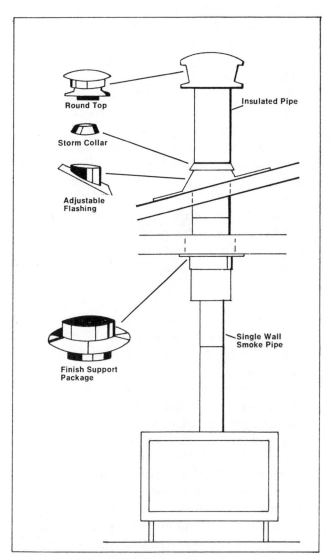

Round Top

Storm Collar

Adjustable Flashing

Finish Support Package

Insulated Pipe

Single Wall Smoke Pipe

Through the ceiling

ing you pass through as well as a roof support package and sufficient factory-built pipe for the vertical run—plus an extra three feet (at least) for the chimney height above the roof. You also will need a chimney cap and possibly guy wires or roof braces for further support.

The length of pipe depends on the location of the stove and where the pipe will pass through the roof. Best location is as close to the ridge as possible, particularly on steeply pitched roofs. Since pipe should extend three feet above the roof and be two feet above anything within ten feet, snowy and windy climates will be troublesome when the pipe exits close to the eave on a steeply pitched roof. Snow sliding down the roof can push against the pipe causing the flashing to tear and the tar seal to break. Severe windy weather can snap the guy wires, and in the middle of winter, climbing on roofs is no joy. I've seen one installation plagued by this problem. In desperation the owners ran the pipe up the roof to the ridge.

It may seem more work and expense to bring the pipe out near the ridge, but the chimney will cause fewer problems and have better support.

Choose what room you want for the stove. Ideally it should be near the center of the room, but this may be impossible because of the second floor layout. Pipe passing through a hall, bathroom or closet is inconvenient and dangerous; nor do you want it going through the center of a bedroom. The pipe should pass vertically through the house and through the second floor where it won't interfere with traffic patterns.

The attic is also a consideration. The roof hole should be between the rafters and as near as possible to the ridge. In an unfinished attic it should be easy to locate a likely exit.

To determine the best location you will have to juggle the various options for the stove (remember to calculate for minimum clearance distances from the stove to the walls) and for the chimney opening on each floor. Once the best location has been determined, return to the attic. You will be cutting

a hole in the roof slightly more than four inches wider than the outside diameter of the insulated pipe.

There are two methods to use to figure out the size of that hole that must be slightly larger because of the slant of the roof. One is to figure it out mathematically. Here's an example:

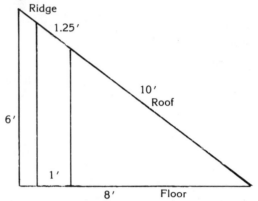

In this example the hole through the roof should measure 15″ (or 1.25 feet) if the hole through the attic floor is 12″.

The simple mathematics:

$$8:10 :: 12:X$$
$$8X = 120$$
$$X = 15$$

Want to avoid that figuring? Simply draw the hole size on the floor of the attic, then, using a plumb bob, mark the corners of that hole size on the ceiling above you.

Flooring is easily pulled up. Remove a board or two to find out where the joists are. Otherwise drill a few pilot holes, first in the center of the square, then towards the perimeter to insure that a joist isn't running directly through the intended hole.

Adjust the floor and roof opening positions so that structural members won't have to be cut. The pipes can absorb some slant (three to four inches in an eight-foot run) without adversely affecting the draft.

Measure from the top of the attic opening to the attic floor for the length of stovepipe needed. The same will have to be done for the floors below in order to compute your stovepipe order. Buy an extra length of pipe in case your calculations are off. It can always be returned.

Since you now know where the pipe will pass through the attic floor, drill a hole in one corner, sufficiently large for the blade of a sabre saw. Once the square has been cut out, drill four pilot holes from the attic through the ceiling below so that they line up. Connect the holes from the floor below and cut the opening with a sabre saw or utility knife. If the ceiling is plaster and lath, you may need a hammer and chisel.

The opening will have to be framed in to provide support for the pipe. This is best done from above. Follow the manufacturer's instructions. You may have to widen the opening in order to have sufficient room in which to operate. Toenail 2 x 4 supports. Cut the supports just a hair too long. Drill pilot holes if necessary to prevent the supports from moving out of square. Use 8d nails. Check with the level before driving home the nails. In an unfinished attic you may be able to end-nail the supports. If the existing framing is almost right, shim out to the necessary distance.

Nail the ceiling support package in place with 8d nails. The package is intended for joist support and is different from the wall firestop spacer. The ceiling support will provide the two-inch clearance and will allow the pipe to be suspended below. Beginning at the stove, start adding lengths of pipe, keeping the crimped end down for single-wall pipe, and locking the insulated pipes into place. The section which connects with the insulated pipe may need to be crimped to allow the pipe to slip inside the insulated one. Be sure the joint is tight. The pipe which will go through the ceiling will have to be dropped in from above, through the support. This job takes two people.

The pipe through the ceiling should have a two-inch space on either side of the pipe. On the ceiling a trim collar is nailed into place.

Pipe passing through an uninsulated attic may need to be wrapped in fiber glass to maintain sufficiently high stack temperatures. Use batts of the six-inch fiber glass insulation.

The Roof

This still leaves cutting a hole in the roof. Drill four pilot holes through the roof from the attic side which align with the four corners of the square you have drawn. This prevents accidentally cutting a rafter. Make one of the holes large enough for the blade of a sabre saw. (Use a coarse-toothed blade.) The rest is best done from the roof.

To get to the roof put a ladder against a gable and make certain both legs are firmly planted. Pipe coming through near the ridge will be easy to reach; pipe exiting near the

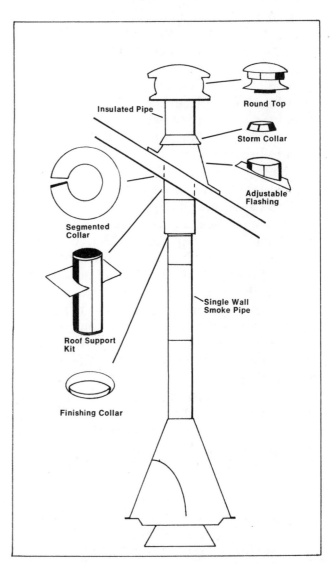

Through the roof

eave will be easiest to reach with two people on two ladders; pipe coming through partway down a steeply pitched roof will call for another ladder and a ridge hook.

There may be other considerations. Slate roofs are extremely slippery and downright dangerous in the snow. Don't do roof work in adverse weather.

Once you are secure on the roof, begin removing the slate or shingles. You'll need a pry bar for removing the nails in slate roofs; asphalt shingles can be cut with a utility knife. Remove the roofing material within the pilot holes. To cut the sheathing you will need either the keyhole saw or the sabre saw. The hole shape can be elliptical, circular or square as long as you leave at least a two-inch air space on all sides of the pipe.

Slide the next section of pipe down through the hole and into place. A second person should be below in the attic ready to put the pipe in place. Lock the two sections together. In the space below the flashing and above the trim plate, stuff fiber glass insulation to prevent drafts.

The roof flashing in the roof support package will direct runoff water and snow, but it must be weathertight. Spread around roofing tar where the flashing will make contact with the roof. Then slip the flashing over the chimney. It will adjust to the pitch of most roofs. If possible, slip the flashing under the row of shingles on the roof-ridge or high side. Nail the flashing to the roof with roofing nails. Tar the heads of any nails and around the edges of the flashing. If you don't, water will in time work itself into the hole around the nailhead.

The storm collar is a skirt which fits over the pipe and rests just above the flashing. It will cover the opening between the chimney and the flashing. Tighten the screw clasp on the collar. Dab roofing tar between the chimney and storm collar but not between the flashing and the chimney. The ventilation will keep the pipe from overheating. Assemble the last sections of pipe, stopping when you reach a height of three feet and are two feet above anything within ten feet.

A chimney cap should be added to the last section of pipe to keep out animals, rain and snow. Water is very corrosive when it mixes with creosote.

Some of the caps rotate to keep the flue opening always out of the wind. They are helpful if you have consistent cross currents or general wind turbulence. Others are revolving ventilators which pull out the gases. Unless you anticipate a draft problem, a diskap or round top cap should be sufficient.

If you are using metalbestos, do not tighten the screw on the chimney topper. It will not loosen once tightened and you will be unable to get the cap off for cleaning.

Chimney caps demand maintenance. They provide a cool surface where acidic exhaust gases can condense. The creosote may then drip down the outside of the chimney, seep into the mortar, digest the flashing, and stain the roof. Be sure the cap is cleaned every year. The rotating type should be oiled at least annually.

Once the chimney cap is in place, tighten the trim plate in the attic. Before attaching the guy wires or roof braces, check to see that the chimney is level. Chimneys which extend six feet or more above the roof will need bracing. Adjustable roof braces (adjustable from five feet to eight feet) are available. They fit around the pipe and screw into the roof. You may wish to make adjustments before tightening the bolts.

To hide the "above the roof" chimney, fake factory-made masonry units are available. They slip over the pipe and are purely decorative.

Before firing up the stove, go back through your installation, joint by joint. Remember that once you start a fire in the stove, the pipes will begin to heat and last-minute repairs will be close to impossible. Joints which leak smoke and lengths of pipe not firmly attached may be difficult to fix. For this reason check everything before the first fire, and make the first fire small.

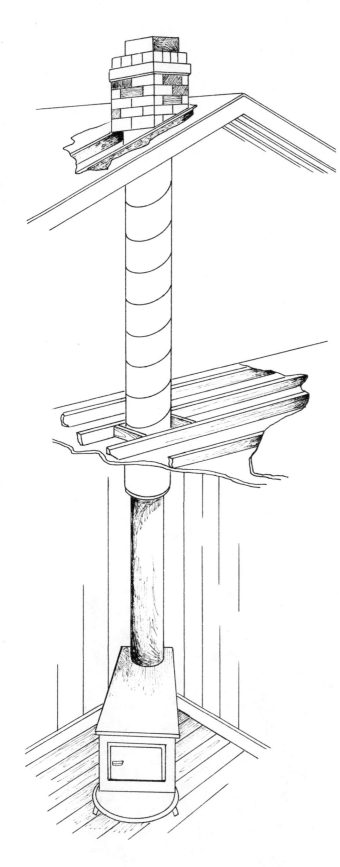

A two-story installation using a factory-built chimney.

Remember, do not:

1) reduce the size of the smokepipe or flue to less than that of the pipe boot on your stove,

2) run single-wall smokepipe through windows, roofs, ceilings, walls, etc.

3) set combustibles (furniture, firewood, etc.) next to the stove,

4) install pipe in a closet or alcove.

Factory-Built or Masonry Chimney?

Usually masonry chimneys are less per foot for materials—$7 for cement block and $12 per lineal foot for factory-built pipe—but more expensive to build since you'll probably have to hire a mason. Anyone handy with tools can install a factory-built chimney.

Although factory-built chimneys are expensive, for one-story installations they are cheaper. For a two-story installation, a lined cinder block chimney is cheaper and almost indestructable. Factory-built pipe will last ten to twenty years.

Interior masonry chimneys also provide a large heat sink which will radiate heat long after the fire has died out. Stack temperatures in masonry chimneys are lower because the factory-built pipe is so well insulated; therefore, creosote may be more of a problem with masonry. If the chimney is on an outside wall, the heat storage capacity of the masonry is lost and stack temperatures may be quite low.

Pre-fab chimneys are extremely flexible, allowing greater choice in pipe diameter (six to sixteen inches) and location, and are easy to install.

There is little difference in draft between the two types, but pre-fab pipe can usually be installed with fewer elbows than masonry installations.

The natural downdraft of a masonry chimney should be utilized in summer. The cool air in the chimney can be used as an air conditioner in summer, but the stove will have to be disconnected and the damper left open. This downdraft will help dry out the masonry.

Round or Square Tiles?

If you have the option of building with round or square flue tiles, the round tiles are better though harder to work with. Flue gases move in spirals as they rise. The sharp corners of the rectangular flues slow down the gases and therefore the flue size must be larger than for the round flues, for equal efficiency.

Getting Your Wood Supply

Now that your wood stove is installed, the problem that defeats many woodburners begins. Would that there were wood! In Vermont there are fifty-two acres per person. And there are 150 national forests in forty-four of the states. The wood is there, enough to heat one-third of America, but getting it still can be a frustrating preoccupation.

As the demand increases, so will the supply. At present there is little "method" in the business of raising, harvesting, and delivering wood. Many people who burn wood rely on the few extra acres they have, cutting indiscriminately, and hauling out whatever they can pile into a pickup truck. But as other sources of fuel diminish, there will be pressure to standardize, regulate, manage, and automate wood-harvesting procedures. At our present level of technology, most of the wood is harvested by the woodburner himself or by local outdoorsmen who enjoy an extra income from doing the physical work they love. Like every other facet of the wood industry, much remains to be learned by the scientists, foresters, and manufacturers; with more knowledge, methods will change.

For the homesteader with a heating requirement of seven to ten cords per year (the average requirement if you are heating entirely with wood), a seven to ten acre woodlot, if properly managed, will take care of fuel needs forever. As a general rule one acre of wooded land will yield one cord of wood year after year. But just because the wood is available doesn't mean it is good fuel wood (a cord of white pine, for example, is equal to 96 gallons of oil while a cord of hickory is equal to 178 gallons). Nor is there any guarantee that the wood will be there year after year. Woodlots require careful management for a sustained yield.

And even if you have the land, you may not be willing to sacrifice the time and energy necessary to harvest ten cords. It's hard work. Someone in top physical shape, but not harvesting wood for an occupation, may only cut, buck, split, and stack a run a day. If the wood is cut to twelve inch lengths (with four runs per cord) ten cords may be a month of work. With only weekends available, you may spend most of your free time getting in the wood. And wood is heavy. A cord of green wood weighs two tons.

Professional woodcutters can produce four cords a day; you may never be in their physical shape, but with a little patience, you should produce a cord a day.

It is also worth remembering that the tools used in harvesting wood are extremely dangerous and even if you can use them professionally, the forest is unpredictable. Loose footing, wind, a bad saw cut, and kickback on the chain saw are all the makings of a lethal situation.

MARKING TREES

Forests if left untended will gradually move to peak growth. A lot left to reforest itself will begin with 4000-6000 stems per acre; of these only 100 will survive. Softwoods will be replaced by hardwoods, and smaller trees by larger ones, but the process of natural selection takes 150-200 years. By managing a woodlot, the natural process will take less than 100 years. The remaining stand of trees will be larger and of better quality. For wood to become an alternate fuel, serious consideration must be given to speeding the growth of the forest.

Before felling the first tree, examine your woodlot carefully. Take along a tree identification book if you don't know the different species.

First to be removed are the dead, diseased, and damaged trees. Damaged trees will be unsound, rotten, crooked, forked, or short trees with bushy crowns. Diseased trees will have swollen stems, seams, breaks in the bark, or poorly healed branch stubs. Don't bother with an obviously punky or rotten tree. It's a waste of time, won't offer much heat, and will probably fall over in the next windstorm.

Trees that have been damaged by other trees or logging equipment should be removed. They are taking water and nutrients from the soil and shading trees which might be good sawlogs.

As you walk over your land, decide which species of tree are most predominant. Hardwoods, found mainly in the eastern United States, are deciduous (broadleaved trees which lose their leaves every year). Softwoods, found in abundance in the western United States, are conifers (with spiny needlelike leaves that stay green all year). The desired species for lumber include the hardwoods: sugar maple, yellow birch, white ash, red maple, red oak, black cherry, basswood, and the softwoods: white pine, soft pine, red spruce, and Douglas fir.

Improving your land is a long-term project, best done gradually. Tree maintenance should begin when the trees are four to ten inches in diameter at breast height (dbh). At this diameter they are in intense competition with each other and will respond rapidly to thinning. If the trees in your stand are between ten to twelve inches (dbh), they are of sawlog size. Consult your state or county forester before you go further.

How Much Wood?

Can you figure out how much wood you will need to heat your home, if you haven't used a wood stove before?

The University of Wisconsin Extension Service in its publication, **"Wood for Home Heating,"** suggests this method.

"The easiest way to figure how much fuel wood you will need for a heating season is to convert your present fuel consumption to wood equivalents.

"Below are figures to help convert your present fuel to wood equivalents. A standard cord of wood is a stack $4' \times 4' \times 8'$; it includes 80 cubic feet of solid wood. The heavier (better) hardwoods weigh, per standard cord, between 3,000 to 4,000 pounds when air-dry, so you can use an average of 3,500 pounds per cord for your estimate.

"1 gallon of #2 fuel oil = 22.2 pounds of wood

"1 therm (100 cubic feet) of natural gas = 14 pounds of wood

"1 gallon of propane gas = 14.6 pounds of wood

"1 kilowatt-hour of electricity = 0.59 pounds of wood

"1 pound of coal = 1.56 pounds of wood.

"Using #2 fuel oil as an example, if you burn 1,000 gallons of fuel oil, then 1,000 × 22.2 = 22,200 pounds of wood. Dividing 22,200 by 3,500 means you would need 6⅓ standard cords of wood."

Gauge your firewood needs for the coming year before doing any cutting, and approximate the number of acres on which you will have to cut by figuring on one cord per acre. You will want to take your firewood from the land you can reach the easiest.

Crop Trees

Before deciding which trees to cut, you will want to identify the crop trees, those you wish to save for timber. They will be healthy, well-formed and straight, and are too valuable to cut for firewood. These trees have relatively small branches, with few or no branches on the lower ten to sixteen feet of the trunk. They are free of wounds and seams.

Begin in one corner of your woodlot, and walk twenty feet (or eight steps) along the boundary, then mark the nearest crop tree by tying a ribbon to it, or blazing it with spray paint.

If there is none within twenty feet, extend your horizon by five to seven feet and pick the best of the lot. Then go another twenty feet along the boundary and pick and mark a second crop tree. Continue this process until you have reached the furthest boundary. Turn at right angles into the lot, walk twenty feet, mark a crop tree, then turn another right angle and return on a line parallel to your first line, marking trees at twenty-foot intervals. There should be about 100 crop trees per acre.

Co-dominant and Intermediate Trees

The next marking is based on the age of the forest. A very young stand demands less space between trees than a mature stand because the crowns of the trees are smaller. Since the crown or leaf area of a tree is its means of gathering sunlight for photosynthesis and hence growth, the distance between the crowns is important.

Trees must be left between crop trees, but the number will depend on the maturity of the forest.

Ideally you want a co-dominant tree in reserve between dominant (or crop) trees so that should anything happen to a crop tree before it is harvested, another healthy tree will be ready to take over. And you will want intermediate trees which given time can become dominant crop trees. Remove co-dominant trees (those of approximately the same age and of a desirable species) if they are so close to the dominant tree that they interfere with or touch its crown. They are direct competitors and will lose in nature's competition. These can be harvested for firewood.

Tree	Diameter at Breast Height	Distance Between Crowns
Saplings	0"–6"	3-5 feet
Pole	7"–10"	6-12 feet
Saw Timber	11"–24"+	13-25 feet

Supressed Trees

The remaining are understory trees which may have little life. Their branches probably have died back, and in their struggle for sunlight they have become bent and crooked. They may be pencil thin and of little or no use as firewood. Leave them alone. They are no threat to the other trees and aren't worth the effort for firewood.

TREES FOR FIREWOOD

Your firewood will come from removing the co-dominants and intermediate trees which are crowding each other or the crop trees, and the "wolf" trees. **Wolf trees** are the granddaddys with large spreading branches —old holdovers from the past which are probably defective and take more than their share of space, though they may have sentimental value. They should be removed to allow sunlight, moisture, and soil nutrients to reach the remaining trees for faster growth and better timber production. If these wolf trees are still sound, they can be used for firewood.

Although you may be used to seeing half-acre city lots with one tree, remember forest trees can be given too much space too fast. When the wind break of other trees is removed, the remaining trees are suddenly more vulnerable to wind. In summer the trees in a heavily thinned stand have little protection from the sun and can be killed by sun scald.

A still further danger with intense thinning is insect blight. If you leave only one species of tree it may be attacked by insects (witness the decimation of the American elm) and your whole crop is gone. For these reasons it is best to thin the land over a three-year period, taking only enough trees to be two years ahead of your wood-burning needs.

The best tree size for the beginning wood harvester to tackle is twelve to fourteen inches (dbh). It will yield a half-cord of wood. Fourteen trees of this size will yield seven cords. They are of a manageable size, easy to fell, not too heavy to heft, and of a good diameter to split.

County foresters can be of immeasureable help. They will walk your land at no charge, marking trees that should be removed. In addition there are government programs on a cost-sharing basis, with the government paying 50-75 percent of the cost to encourage the landowner to manage his investment. Your county forester will know about them.

Government Programs

The Forestry Incentive Program (FIP) will share the costs of timber stand improvement and tree planting with the private landowner who owns less than 500 acres. A second federal cost-sharing program is the Agricultural Conservation Program (ACP) which offers cost-sharing assistance to improve forest stands. They will help in planting trees and shrubs for conservation and timber production as well as for windbreaks, wildlife shelter, and erosion control.

Such programs recognize that because much of the land in America is owned in small parcels and therefore by people probably not willing or able to make long-term investments, the government, in order to meet the increasing demand for wood, must share the expense. When you are interested in improving and managing your woodlot, investigate these programs.

Sawlogs

The current interest in wood heat has foresters worried. They are concerned about high value timber production and managed use of forest lands. They foresee weekend mayhem in the forests with thousands of families revving up their chain saws and ravishing what has taken hundreds of years to produce. They worry about environmental impact, the wanton destruction of our resources, and the devaluing of our lands as we make the forests more accessible for fuel wood harvesting. Their worries are legitimate.

Theoretically firewood production can dovetail beautifully with the interests of lumbermen, but only if the landowner realizes some simple economic facts.

The following table gives the price per cord for various woods sold as sawlogs.

Wood	Price/Cord
Yellow birch	$45-$200
Hard maple	$45-$200
Red maple	$33-$115
Basswood	$33-$115
Black cherry	$45-$150
Oak	$50-$150
Ash	$50-$200
White birch	$33-$90
Butternut	$33-$125
Elm	$33-$90
Beech	$60
White pine	$90
Hemlock	$0-$80
Spruce/fir	$60-$90

Another important fact: trees increase in value.

Age of Tree (Years)	Diameter in Inches (dbh)	Board Feet*
40	12	110
55	16	260
70	21	525

Economically it makes no sense to burn your investment, unless that is the most economical use for it.

The woodlot owner should also want the greatest return for his labor.

© St. Louis Post Dispatch

*A board foot is a unit one foot square and one inch thick.

75

Clearly the species which are top firewood are not top sawlogs. Why, for example, burn black cherry if you have hophornbeam? Most woodlot owners have as clear a choice. The value of the wood for timber should guide what is removed for firewood. White ash and yellow birch should be kept for timber. Beech and red maple are better cut for firewood. Of the birches, yellow birch is a much better fuel wood than either grey or white birch. (Be sure to split the birches or the wood will rot.) White oak is better than red. Hophornbeam and elm (if it can be burned round) should be thinned out.

BTU's Per Cord	
Apple Black birch Hickory Hophornbeam Locust White oak Black beech	26,800,000 BTU's/cord
White ash Beech Yellow birch Sugar maple Red oak	23,400,000 BTU's/cord
Black ash White birch Grey birch Norway pine Pitch pine Black cherry Elm Soft maple Tamarack	19,900,000 BTU's/cord
Aspen Basswood Butternut Hemlock White pine White cedar Balsam fir Spruce	14,500,000 BTU's/cord

Wood Characteristics

One season devoted to gnawing your way through an American elm, and oil at any price is a bargain. So there are other considerations besides BTU and sawlog value. Consider availability, splitability, tendency to spark, coaling qualities, smoke, ease of starting and fragrance.

The table on the next page gives the characteristics of various dried woods.

In general, trees whose fibers intertwine (white oak) or grow in a spiral pattern (elm) are very hard to split; fibers which grow vertically (in ash, for example) make the wood easy to split.

Softwoods (or conifers) such as hemlock, larch, spruce, and cedar, and hardwoods such as hickory, butternut, and sumac have moisture pockets. As these woods are heated, the trapped gases and water vapor are released and a popping sound is heard. When the pockets explode, sparks and burning embers may go up the chimney. Should an ember lodge, it could ignite unburned creosote. Drying will reduce sparking.

White birch gives off soot. Aspen (popple) is easy to split but it burns quickly and smokes. Hickory and elm usually are infested with beetles; other woods have carpenter ants. Elm and excessively knotty woods are difficult to split. To say that you should avoid softwoods and burn only hardwoods is too simplistic. Softwoods produce a quicker, hotter fire, leaving very few coals and producing more creosote.

Fruitwoods (apple, avocado, cherry, citrus, mulberry, peach, pear, persimmon, and plum) are hardwoods. They are available in most of the United States. Besides being excellent firewood, they produce an appealing fragrance and unusually colorful flames.

For an all-purpose firewood, white ash is good. It is fairly easy to split, won't spark, and is the best of the woods to burn green.

					Does it	
	Relative			Does it	pop or	
	amount	Easy to	Easy to	have heavy	throw	General rating
Hardwood Trees	of heat	burn	split	smoke?	sparks?	and remarks
Ash, red oak, white oak, beech, birch, hickory, hard maple (sugar, rock, black), dogwood	High	Yes	Yes	No	No	Excellent.
Soft maple, cherry (red) walnut	Medium	Yes	Yes	No	No	Good.
Elm, sycamore gum	Medium	Medium	No	Medium	No	Fair—contains too much water when green.
Aspen, basswood, cottonwood, yellow poplar	Low	Yes	Yes	Medium	No	Fair—but good for kindling.
Softwood Trees						
Southern yellow pine, Douglas-fir	High	Yes	Yes	Yes	No	Good but smoky.
Cypress, redwood	Medium	Medium	Yes	Medium	No	Fair.
White cedar, eastern red cedar .	Medium	Yes	Yes	Medium	Yes	Good–Excellent for kindling.
Eastern white pine, Balsam fir, hemlock, red pine	Low	Medium	Yes	Medium	No	Fair–Good kindling.
Tamarack, larch	Medium	Yes	Yes	Medium	Yes	Fair.
Spruce	Low	Yes	Yes	Medium	Yes	Poor—but good for kindling.

Ratings for Firewood*

* Adapted from: "Firewood for your Fireplace." U.S. Forest Service, U.S.D.A. Leaflet No. 559.

HARVESTING

Wood should be allowed to dry at least six to nine months before it is burned; to be burned in December it should be cut the previous spring. Wood seasoned one to two years is even better, but you'll have to plan ahead to do this. If trees are felled in winter, then bucked and split, they will benefit from the warmth of the spring breezes (March-May). Drying conditions are best then. Pulling out the logs when the ground is covered with snow and/or ice will aid greatly in skidding, and it's usually easier to split wood, particularly elm, when it is frozen. (Be careful — the wedge may bounce at first because of the ice.) And a crisp winter day is bug-free!

Girdling

If you run out of time during the winter, you can girdle the trees which will kill them. Then in summer or fall they can be felled and split.

Girdling a tree cuts the outer layer through which the nutrients flow from the soil to the leaves. This can be done with a chain saw or an axe. Cut a circle approximately two inches deep around the tree. Most trees will slowly dry after being girdled; the birches will tend to rot. Don't leave girdled trees more than a year before you fell, buck, and split them.

For late winter wood, trees can be felled in the summer with their leaves on. Let the trees lie on the forest floor a week or so before limbing and bucking. The leaves will continue to draw moisture from the limbs and trunk, and hasten the drying process. Once the leaves have completely withered, the tree can be cut up.

Girdling a season ahead will help dry most trees while still standing

How to Cut

Felling trees is dangerous business and the tools are only part of it. You can never calculate sufficiently for the unexpected, and the unexpected can lead to further unexpecteds — cutting aspens, for example, is like taking a three-year-old to a poetry reading — you have no assurance of the outcome.

Glance furtively at an aspen and it drops a limb; calculate carefully where by all rights it should fall and at the crucial moment a tiny gust of wind will jam the saw. Begin with the wedge to free the saw and the aspen will rock the other way, making your efforts futile. Then without warning it will begin clattering around in the tree tops, turn on the stump, drop branches everywhere and get hung up in the crotch of another tree. But at least you now have your saw back. You can cut the aspen through at the stump and it can still hang. You can cut the spruce holding it only to increase the problem and the danger. You may attempt dangerous aerial cutting to divide the load. You can have both lunch and dinner and still be trying to fell the same tree. And if you haven't been bopped a couple of times on the head with the debris, your saw is dull, and your nerves and temper shot. Even when you exercise the best practices, the unforeseen is always possible. So learn how to fell trees with an experienced companion. You may even wish to hire someone to do the felling. And above all — never work alone.

EQUIPMENT

Before cutting your first tree, you should have the following equipment:

a) A **hard hat** is a must if you intend to cut standing timber. "Widow makers" (dead

branches) are likely to fall while you are in the process of cutting.

b) **Safety goggles** will protect your eyes from twigs, sawdust, and debris. They can steam up unless vented both top and bottom. They will limit your peripheral vision and are likely to become covered with sawdust. If you already wear glasses, it is possible to buy lenses of safety glass. Or you may be more comfortable wearing a hard hat with an eye shield.

c) **Ear plugs** or ear protectors are a must unless you have a low-noise saw. Human hearing is damaged at 90 decibels; many saws operate at 105-110 decibels. With time your hearing will become seriously impaired if some kind of protection is not worn. Sonic ear plugs will protect the ear from high frequency noises but permit the passage of normal low frequency sounds such as conversation. They cost about $6. There also are ear protectors which look like ear muffs and can be worn under safety helmets ($10.95).

d) **Safety chaps** are made from heavy army duck covered with multiple layers of ballistic nylon cloth and weigh approximately four pounds. They fasten twice around each leg and at the waist. Slacks also are available. They lack cuffs and have nylon or fiberglass pads sewn into the knees. Safety pants will protect your thighs should the saw slip as can happen when you are limbing a tree.

e) If your **clothing** is too loose it will catch on branches, twigs or the saw; if too tight your mobility will be impaired.

f) **Boots** should have non-skid soles for traction with sturdy leather uppers and steel-capped toes to protect your feet should the saw slip or a log roll over.

g) **Bow saws** are not essential unless you prefer a relatively silent forest. The Swedish bow saws now available have a tubular steel frame, are short (18-20 inches are best), lightweight, and if kept sharp are a pleasure to use. Replacement blades are so cheap that it's as practical to buy a new blade as to sharpen the old.

When beginning a cut, let the saw's weight do most of the work. Then bear down only on the "push" stroke. A rocking action with the blade will increase the cutting speed. An experienced cutter can produce a standard cord in a day's time, but it's lots of exercise.

h) **Wedges** are essential regardless of whether you fell with an axe, bow saw or chain saw. You will probably want two or three wedges. They should be of plastic, wood, or magnesium so that the teeth of the saw won't be ruined if they nick the wedge. Wood (which are hard to find) or magnesium wedges are better than plastic. You will probably want two or three of different sizes, with one of them fairly thick.

i) The **peavey** is a curved metal hook on the end of a pole. The end of the hook is pointed so that with the hook embedded in the bark of the tree, a log can be rolled. Peaveys are very useful should you want to roll a tree off a stump or off another tree. They save both time and fingers.

j) **Splitting mauls** are blunt-tipped axes, or sledges with a sharpened edge. Splitting wood with a maul is much easier than with an axe. Axes cut the wood while mauls, because of the shape of the head, force the wood apart. The head of a maul is about twice the weight of an axe (6-10 pounds) which means the head hits the log with much greater force. Wedges and a sledge can do the work of a maul but the wedge can fly out of the log if not squarely hit.

It is easy to split the handle of a maul because of the weight of the head. Be careful not to overshoot a cut.

Axes

An axe is essential if only for minor emergencies. Or it may be used for felling, limbing, driving wedges, and cutting underbrush. Even if you plan to do all your cutting with a chain saw, take along an axe.

A good axe will cost about $12 to $15. There are double-bitted (two blades) axes but for use with a chain saw a single-bitted axe should be sufficient. The heavier the axe the more you can take advantage of the natural momentum. In addition you are less likely to think of it as an overgrown hatchet and swing it in the air to cut twigs. It also will stick into the wood better and bounce less, which in winter is a real danger. A 2½-3½ pound axe is average—a 3½-4 pound one if you can handle the weight. The handle should be crotch high or about 26-30 inches.

Axes, like other tools used in the woods, are easily lost. The handles of axes, sledges, mauls, and any other tools should be painted a bright color, preferably orange, so that they aren't lost in the ground cover. Don't buy them already painted because you won't be able to examine the grain. Check the grain carefully. It should run the length of the handle, and the wood be free of knots.

The head of an axe should be protected when not in use. A #5 bean can, with both the top and bottom lids removed and the can flattened, can be used to protect the blade. Bend the end over with a pair of pliers.

Most axes come with a fawn's foot handle. To check the alignment (or "hang") of an axe, set the axe on a flat surface with the cutting edge down and the blade vertical. The axe should rest on the center of the cutting edge or towards the heel of the handle. Also check how the head has been secured. Wood or steel wedges are preferred. Some axes come with a plastic wedge which is very difficult to remove. The steel head will last, but you will replace the handle many times.

Over the course of a year the width of the wood in the eye will vary. In summer the wood will shrink and the handle will become loose. If the axe is stored indoors, the same thing will occur in winter. Always check the head before you use an axe. Heads may fly. If the head is loose, it should be soaked overnight in water to make the wood expand. Before putting it in water, be sure that the end of the handle is flush with the edge of the head. This can be done by holding the axe, head down, and gently tapping the handle with a hammer or mallet. Axes are best left with the head resting on a dirt floor. This provides sufficient moisture to keep the head tight.

Axes can be used for driving felling wedges or pounding stakes, but never for pounding in steel wedges. This may crack the eye of the axe. For limbing, axes are best sharp; for splitting wood they are best slightly blunt. Axes nick easily. Never try to split wood on the ground, for the axe head could easily hit a stone and dull the blade, or worse, it could glance off and hit you.

Hanging an Axe

It's very easy to overshoot a cut and split an axe handle. Minor scrapings of the handle can be lessened. Wrap the first three or four inches of the handle with steel or copper wire. Tighten the wire with pliers; then wind the wire with electric tape. This won't prevent the handle from cracking when the handle rather than the head makes speedy contact with a log.

To replace the handle, remove the old one. Saw off the old handle near the head. Drive out the remaining wood in the eye with a hammer and a scrap piece of hardwood. It may be necessary to drill holes in the head to loosen it. The new handle may come with its own wedges. If not, cut a one-inch wedge from the heel of the old handle. Rip saw the handle to fit the eye of the axe. Next rest the heel of the handle on the floor and lightly tap the head on with a hammer. Then with the axe head down, tap the heel of the handle until the axe head is securely in place. If the axe handle is too wide for the eye, you may have to shape it with a rasp. Once the head is flush, the wedge should be driven in as far as it will go, running the long axis. If there are two steel wedges, they should be driven in at 90° and evenly spaced. Shavings around the head or the wedge can be removed with a rasp.

Sharpening an axe

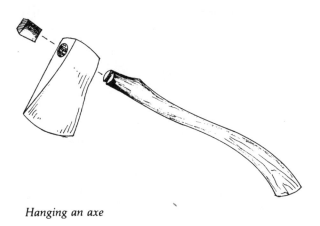

Hanging an axe

With time you will begin changing the relationship of the cheeks to the edge. It is important in the sharpening process not to alter the original angles.

Chain Saws

Chain saws are available in many different sizes including the mini-saws, lightweights, medium-duty, and production saws as well as the electric chain saws, and are priced anywhere from $79 to $300 or more. Your decision will depend on how much you are willing to pay and how much wood you plan to cut. If you are intending to cut no more than a half-cord a year, then you should consider the mini-saws, a bow saw or the electric saws. Of these, the bow saw is cheapest, and the electric saw is half the price of a small gasoline saw. Electric saws are light and easy to start, and produce no fumes. If you want to

Sharpening an Axe

A blunt axe is better for splitting wood, but you will want a sharp one if you are going to fell and/or limb a tree. An oval sharpening stone, which is fine grained on one side and coarse grained on the other, works best for sharpening an axe. Add a coating of light oil to the surface of the stone to prevent the accumulation of grit. Use a rotary motion with the stone, taking off no more of the metal than necessary. Don't worry about getting rid of all the nicks; they aren't crucial.

cut wood in your garage in the winter, they allow you to keep warm while accumulating a wood pile.

Chain saws come in various bar lengths. A bar somewhere between sixteen and twenty inches is sufficient for most jobs. A twenty-inch bar will cut almost anything you find, but as the bar becomes longer, the price and weight of the saw increase. A fifteen- to sixteen-inch bar is probably best if you aren't going to be cutting regularly. However, if you will be cutting more than a cord a year, you want a saw that will run all day and is capable of handling big cuts. You should buy a saw which can carry a bar one size larger than you will be using. This provides extra margin. If the bar isn't long enough, you can replace it with a longer one. On the other hand, you should keep weight in mind. Fatigue is the largest cause of accidents in the woods, and heavy chain saws only become heavier as the day wears on and you wear out.

Stihl, Homelite, and McCullough are the trade names of three of the better saws, but you may be limited by what your dealer has available. Be sure that for any saw you buy, you can get repair parts and service. Your local dealer also will be able to show you how to sharpen the chain which should be done at least twice daily, when you are cutting all day.

There are many new devices to make saws easier and safer to handle such as automatic oilers to give you one less thing to think about; a "chain brake" to protect you should the chain kick back at you; throttle safety catch to insure that the chain doesn't move unless you are ready, etc.

Sharpening the Chain

It is very easy to dull a chain and a dull chain is dangerous. If you hit a rock, saw into the ground or through a muddy piece of wood you will have to sharpen the chain. Otherwise watch what's chewed away by the chain. It should be small wood chips but if the saw starts producing sawdust, the chain needs sharpening. Tighten the chain tension so the chain can just be pulled around the bar.

Using a pen or the file, mark the tooth on the chain where you are beginning to file. It is best to begin somewhere between the middle and tip because the chain won't wiggle as much. Wear gloves so as not to get cut. The file should be round and the correct size for your chain. A depth gauge and a guide bar to hold the file will assure the correct angle.

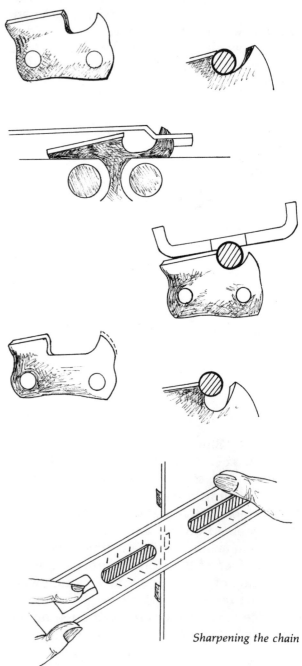

Sharpening the chain

82

Place the guide and file on the tooth to be sharpened. Keep the guide level. Line up the guide lines so that they are parallel to the chain in order to hold the correct angle. The cutting is all done on the "away" stroke. File until the tooth is sharp. Move the chain, and sharpen tooth by tooth so that the sharpening is always done in the same place on the bar.

Do all the teeth on one side first and use the same number of strokes per tooth. To finish off, remove the file from the guide and file down and towards the outside edge of each tooth to clean out the gullet. Avoid touching the cutting edge.

Periodically you should have the chain sharpened professionally, particularly if you don't think you have the proper angle. Watch out for the drag teeth or depth gauges. At some point they will have to be filed down or the chain will ride on these teeth.

Chain tension will need adjusting. When the chain begins to loosen, the tensioning bolt should be tightened. It requires a wrench and screwdriver. If the chain has loosened too much, your dealer can remove a link in the chain.

Read the operator's manual carefully; all saws work somewhat differently.

Safety Rules

The following safety precautions should be observed.

1) Hold the chain saw firmly with both hands when the engine is running.

2) Be sure you have the right fuel mixture. The standard mixture is two gallons of gasoline to six ounces of oil. Oil can be bought in a six-pack of six-ounce cans.

3) When the engine isn't running, carry the saw with the guide bar pointed behind you and the muffler away from your body.

4) Place the plastic or wood guard over the chain when the saw isn't in use.

5) Turn off the engine when carrying the saw around.

6) Start the engine with the saw on the ground. Do not start the saw on your leg or knee.

7) Do not smoke near the fuel can or chain saw. Be sure to replace the fuel cap, and leave the fuel can twenty-five feet away from where you will be working.

8) Check the sharpness of the chain and the tension on the guide bar. If they need adjusting, do so. The chain should be sharpened at least twice a day.

9) Keep the saw free from dirt, fuel, and sawdust buildup.

10) A two-gallon metal gas can will be necessary. File, depth gauge, and guide bar are needed to keep the chain sharp; a wrench and screwdriver are needed to adjust the tension on the chain. An extra chain is not worth taking every time you go out into the woods, but if you are working from a base camp you should have a spare one handy. Chains will break periodically.

11) Always take a companion along.

Sawbuck

Trouble Shooting Chart

The following chart lists the more common troubles with their probable causes and remedies.

Trouble	Probable Cause	Remedy	Trouble	Probable Cause	Remedy
Engine fails to start	(Fuel Troubles) *Empty fuel tank	Fill fuel tank with correct fuel mixture	Engine lacks power	Wrong fuel mixture	Check in owner's manual or see your dealer
	Engine flooded	Follow procedures in Operating Instructions		Main fuel adjustment needle set too rich	Readjust main fuel adjustment needle according to owner's manual
	Water or dirt in fuel. Dirty fuel tank filter	Drain fuel tank. Remove and clean or replace fuel tank filter		Spark arrester and exhaust ports clogged or dirty	Clean spark arrester and exhaust ports
	Main fuel adjustment needle closed or set too lean	Correct adjustment needle setting as described in Operating Instructions		Dirty air filter element	Remove and clean filter element
				Poor compression or piston and cylinder scored	Take your chain saw to your dealer for overhaul
	(No Spark)* Spark wire grounding on engine	Tape bare part of wire. Tape wire to hold away from engine	Engine starves on acceleration or idles too fast	Idle fuel adjustment needle set too lean	Readjust idle fuel adjustment needle according to owner's manual
	*Ignition switch in "STOP" position	Move ignition switch to "ON" position		Idle speed adjustment screw set too high	Readjust idle speed adjustment screw
	Dirty or defective spark plug	Clean or replace spark plug. Adjust spark plug gap		Loose spark arrester; missing or damaged gasket	Tighten spark arrester attaching screws; install new gasket
	Breaker point gap too wide, points not opening, or points burned or pitted	Adjust breaker point gap, or take chain saw to your dealer		Worn or damaged crankshaft seals, air leaking into engine	Take your chain saw to your dealer for overhaul
	*Bad coil	Have your dealer replace it	Chain oiler fails to deliver oil to bar and chain	Oiler tank empty	Fill tank with correct grade of clean oil
	*Bad condenser	Have your dealer replace it			
	Connections loose or wire grounding on engine	Tape connections tight. Tape bare parts of wires		Wrong weight oil Oil congealed from cold	Use lighter weight oil
				Dirt in oil plugging valve system	Have your dealer clean the oiler system
Engine hard to start	All above causes. Those preceded by an asterisk (*) will prevent any starting at all			Oiler not working: leaking seals or valve assembly	Have your dealer overhaul the oiler system

FELLING

Before leaving for the woods, be sure the chain on your saw is sharp. A dull tool is unpredictable and vastly more tiring.

Don't cut trees on a windy or snowy day. The wind will wreak havoc with all your calculations; snow will obscure your vision and make your footing hazardous. Be careful of rotten trees. They are hard to predict, if not impossible, because without a central core, there can be no hinge to control the direction in which the tree will fall. These trees provide homes for squirrels, rabbits, and other animals, aren't damaging to other trees, and a good wind will topple them. Unless there's a reason to do otherwise, let nature takes its course.

The trees to be removed should be marked. Examine the crown of the tree carefully to find out which way the tree leans (most will lean). A large branch may be enough to determine which way the tree will fall. If there's no more than a 5 percent lean in one direction, you will be able to fell the tree in any direction you wish.

Examine the limbs. Dead limbs directly above your head are potential widow(er) makers. Dead limbs in nearby trees which your tree may hit are also dangerous.

Cut away the brush around the work area. This includes whips and branches of neighboring trees which might interfere with your activity. Calculate where the tree will fall and your "escape" route which should be diagonally back and away from the stump at a 45° angle from the line of fall. Cut branches and whips which will obstruct your retreat. Trees can kill.

The more felling you do, the more accurate you will become. A tree surrounded by others can easily get "hung up," and if it drops into the crotch of another, your firewood may be there for years. You want the tree to fall far away from the trunks of nearby trees and out of reach of any large limbs where the tree might get caught.

Three cuts are made in the tree; the first is the **undercut,** a horizontal cut entering the tree on the side facing the direction in which you want the tree to fall. Be sure the undercut is parallel to the ground. If you make the undercut with the tip of the saw, the cut will probably be angled. This you want to avoid because the tree might break off prematurely and pivot to one side. The cut should be made with the teeth closest to the motor. The second cut is the **face** or **notch cut** which is a diagonal cut made to release a wedge-shaped piece of wood about ¼-⅓ of the diameter of the tree. It should begin a few inches above the undercut on the same side of the tree. When the wedge has been removed the tree has been severely weakened. Before the back cut has been completed, the tree should tip.

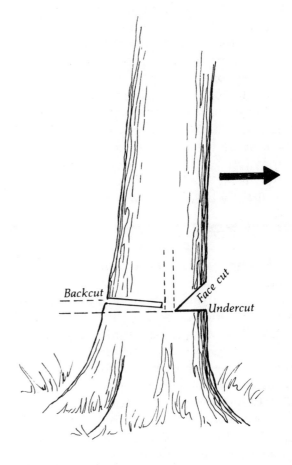

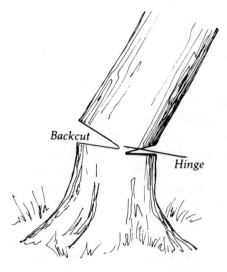

Backcut

Hinge

If the backcut is made too low, the tree may fall over backwards. Therefore, particularly when you are learning, make the backcut too high. If you overshoot by too much, you can always make a lower second backcut.

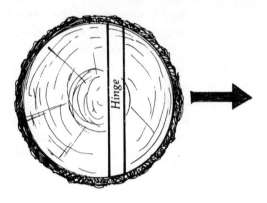

Hinge

The **back** or **felling cut** is made about two to three inches higher than the horizontal cut and angled slightly towards the undercut. For large trees, the felling cut should be even higher. You want to leave a hinge of uncut wood, so stop two or three inches from the undercut. Before the tree falls remove your saw. Never cut all the way through because the hinge controls the direction of the fall.

Should the tree top begin to move, stop, turn off the motor, and place the chain saw to one side out of your and the tree's way. If all is going according to plan and the tree is quite small, you may be able to further guide the direction of fall by pushing on the trunk. If it is a medium- or large-sized tree, move away quickly. Should the hinge snap, the tree may jump straight back off the stump. If the tree is in the process of falling, don't stand directly behind or even near it.

Holding a Side

Trees may not lean precisely in the direction that you want them to fall. Power lines, buildings, or most likely the crotch of another tree may be directly on target. To avoid these undesirables you want the tree to alter its course slightly. Both the undercut and the face cut should be made the same but the backcut will vary so that the hinge is shaped like a piece of pie with the pie crust on the side where you want the tree to fall. The hinge should extend across the entire diameter of the tree. Do not cut through even a portion of the hinge.

Pointers

1) Always work with someone else around.

2) Keep the guard or dogs tight against the tree or log. Dogs are the large teeth which help steady the saw during the cut.

3) Brace your body against the engine handle so that if the saw pinches you will be pushed rather than struck.

4) Always stop the chain before wedging. If you wedge with the chain moving, you may break the chain, or cause the saw to kick back or the engine to stall.

5) Watch the actions of other persons (and dogs) to be sure they are out of range.

6) A grease pencil may be helpful if you aren't used to felling trees. On smooth-barked trees, mark the three cuts on the tree.

7) Take a rest whenever you feel the least bit tired. Chain saws are heavy. If you begin relaxing on the job, you may lose your balance or control of the saw. Fatigue is a by-product of working with a chain saw. The vibration, noise, and exhaust smoke, as well as the physical exhaustion and mental concentration, all contribute to fatigue.

To be sure that you don't inadvertently extend the backcut to the undercut, begin the hinge on the side which is to be narrower. Then work around the tree, stopping the backcut within an inch or two of the undercut on the far side. Since these cuts take more skill, only practice will tell you how much to leave on trees of various sizes.

Once all the cuts are made the tree still may refuse to move. Remove the saw and drive a wedge (or wedges) into the backcut. The wedge may gentle persuade the tree to fall in the proper direction.

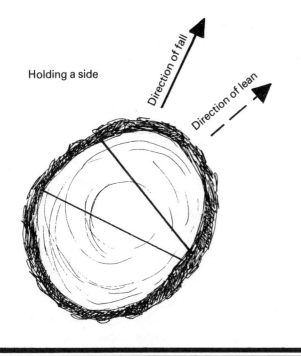

Holding a side

Direction of fall

Direction of lean

Wedges

Even if you don't use wedges to fell a tree, you will need them sooner or later to free your chain saw. Every wood cutter has gotten a saw stuck, and sooner or later will learn to fell with wedges.

Here's how to use them in felling a tree: After the backcut is large enough to accept the bar of the chain saw, stop the motor, leave the bar in the cut, and drive a magnesium, wood, or plastic wedge squarely into the cut behind the bar and pointed in the direction the tree will fall. Tap it in with an axe head or sledge. Since the wedge may come in contact with the saw teeth, never use a steel wedge. It may damage or dull the saw teeth.

8) "Kick back" is a common occurrence with a saw. The chain catches near the nose, the chain jumps out of the cut and forces the saw backwards towards the operator. If you are not alert, you can get hurt easily. The more powerful the saw, the greater the chances of serious injury.

9) Check the chain tension frequently. The chain should move easily by hand and lift only slightly at the middle of the bar.

10) Always clear the work space. Thick, brushy ground cover is hazardous.

11) Don't let either your axe or chain saw make contact with the ground. It will dull the cutting edges.

12) Avoid using the chain saw above shoulder height or in awkward positions. Don't operate the saw in a tree or on a ladder unless you have the proper training.

13) Don't run the engine slowly at the start of or during the cut. The saw should cut only at high speeds (or at full throttle). Let it do the work. Never operate a saw unless the chain stops when the engine idles.

Restart the engine. Periodically drive the wedge (or wedges if it is a large tree) in further but not so far as to obstruct the chain. As soon as the tree tips or when the backcut is of proper depth, turn off the motor, slide the saw out, and hammer the wedges in further. Wedges, particularly for the beginner, are cheap insurance. It is easy to miscalculate how a tree is weighted, some trees have no obvious lean, and who can calculate the vagaries of the wind? The tree that tips backwards, even slightly, has trapped your saw and the procedure thereafter is frustrating, dangerous, and time-consuming. In addition, since the saw often binds when the backcut is almost finished, the tree could fall at any moment, and if there are two of you (as there should be), the escape routes will never look big enough, wide enough, fast enough, or safe enough.

Recovering Your Saw With Your Life

If your saw gets stuck, disconnect the saw's power unit from the bar. Try pounding in a wedge, if the bar is in deep enough. Or with a second saw, start a second backcut above your saw. If an axe is your only tool, extend the undercut until the tree begins to teeter. You should have time to get the bar out before the tree falls.

Other dangerous situations occur when you plan to fell a tree which already leans heavily in one direction. The pressure on the hinge will be so intense that before the backcut is sufficiently deep, the wood may split along the grain rather than at the hinge. If you are cutting firewood, this doesn't much matter; however, it can split with a spring which neither you nor the chain saw wants to be in the way of.

It is best to avoid this situation by making your cuts so as to reduce the strength of the hinge. After the face cut has been made, extend the undercut a few inches around the circumference. Then make the backcut. This will weaken the force along the grain, and the tree will fall on the remaining hinge. This also can be accomplished by making a

Tree may split along the grain

deeper undercut though keeping the same sized face cut, but you risk pinching the saw.

Trees can be persuaded to defy gravity, but unless there is **very** good reason, you may only be asking for trouble. If the tree has a substantial lean in the wrong direction, leave it alone—if you are determined, wedges are the key. Make a shallower undercut and face cut; the backcut should be only slightly above the undercut and the rest must be done by driving in two or three wedges.

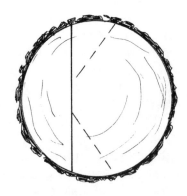

Extend the undercut to weaken force along the grain

88

Hung Up?

It is bound to happen—regardless of precautions. When a tree gets hung up after it has just begun to tilt, part of the hinge will still be intact. Finish cutting through the stump. This may dislodge the tree enough so that it rolls over on the stump, the base falls to the ground, and the rest of the tree follows. Though this may not happen, be prepared for it. Trees can quickly jump to the side or uphill of the stump—be ready to move.

If the tree remains immobile and you have a peavey, you may be able to roll the trunk or pry it off the stump. Lacking a peavey, a good stout sapling wedged under the trunk can be used as a pry bar and two people may be able to free the tree.

The next method to try involves cutting through the trunk. Since the saw will pinch on the top side, start your cut there, going in a few inches, but avoiding getting the saw pinched. Then make the rest of the cut from the underside. The base will land with quite a thud, so be mindful of your saw and your feet. You may do this a number of times to no avail. A come-along or winch may be of assistance, or the wind may have to do the rest. It is possible to fell the tree causing the problem, but you will be working with two incalculables and no assurance the problem won't escalate.

LIMBING

Difficulties in the air may be matched by those on the ground, and now that the tree is down and all the nervous anxiety has been dispelled, careless enthusiasm should not take over. Trees sometimes pin their own branches or other trees to the ground. Because they didn't break under the weight, it's a sure sign they are young and supple. Cut a sapling caught under pressure and it will

snap back sharply, with no warning and with lightning-like speed. Don't fool around with them.

To release saplings you may be able to move the tree with a peavey, or work up the trunk, limbing and bucking. By then you may have sufficiently lightened the load to move the trunk with a peavey.

Limbs also are prone to snapping quickly if they are caught. Position yourself so you won't get hit. Realize that when you cut branches caught under the trunk, not only may the the branch snap, but the tree may roll. Calculate where it might move and be ready to get out of the way.

If there are no complications, begin limbing. Start at the butt end and work towards the crown. Stand on the side of the trunk opposite from the branch to be trimmed. Clear away any limbs or saplings that might interfere with the safety of your work. Gauge each cut carefully by checking where the pressure is. Freely hanging branches should be one-third undercut, then top cut; branches under pressure from the ground should be top cut, then undercut.

HAULING

You may wish to limb, then haul the trees home to reduce the number of times you have to move the wood. Slide or pull smaller logs out with a toboggan, horse, tractor and winch, or come-along.

BUCKING

If you intend to cut firewood lengths (buck) in the woods, remove the limbs, leaving several caught under the tree to elevate and support the tree to make bucking easier. Use a marking stick to mark off firewood lengths with a grease pencil. A marking stick has ticks at intervals just under firebox size (twelve, sixteen inches or whatever intervals you require for your stove). It will be easiest to mark from the stump to the crown. Clear out your work space. Then start at the crown. With the tree suspended in the air, the first cut should be made underneath. Go only one-third of the way through. If you cut too far the saw will bind. Then make the top cut.

When the trunk is resting on the ground, you can make a series of cuts on one side, then roll the log over to finish the cuts. If you try to go all the way through you will dull the chain on dirt and stones. Or roll one of the short lengths under the trunk to keep the log off the ground.

Bucking at Home

Bucking firewood to length is a good way to begin using a chain saw since conditions are more controlled. Logs can be cut to length on a sawbuck, but the struggle of lifting all but poles is more than the pay back for having the tree just below waist level. Usually a log is rolled crosswise to another and gradually fed by one person to a second person using the chain saw. This keeps the wood tilted somewhat off the ground. Both people also have a small respite between either cutting or hefting.

If you are bucking alone, this system can be used, or the log can be raised on two smaller logs. Pay attention to when the blade will bind. With the portion to be cut cantilevered, make an undercut one-third of the way through, then the top cut. If the cut is made between two supports, make the top cut first, then the undercut.

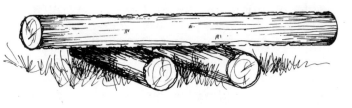

Be sure the wood is free of mud. Mud will dull the chain very quickly. Wood bought by the pulpwood truckload will present this problem and though you get the wood cheap, you may spend a great deal of time filing. A stiff wire brush to clean the bark where you will be cutting may be helpful.

Sawbucks

Sawbucks can be made in a few minutes with 2 x 4's or preferably 2 x 8's either nailed or bolted together.

Bucksaw

Bucksaws are called that because they were used to saw wood on a sawbuck. The blade fits into a wooden H-shaped frame. To adjust the tension, twist the turnbuckle.

Cutting Cribs

Cutting cribs are easy to fabricate. Pound four stakes into the ground and at more frequent intervals depending on the size of firewood you want. Pile the logs between the stakes and saw through the entire set of logs at one time.

SPLITTING

Whether in the woods or near your storage shed, you should buck the wood to length and split it immediately to prevent decay and to accelerate drying. Trees left on the forest floor will soon begin rotting from the moisture of the earth.

Wood can be left round if under six inches in diameter, but wood larger than that should be split. Splitting breaks the water barrier—the bark—and reduces the sizes to be burned. With greater surface area, more rapid drying can occur.

For most people splitting is the real pleasure of getting in the firewood. Feeling pale, undernourished and trapped in the land of "no sun," you can depart with the maul in the middle of winter, split a run and feel there is no better vacation than that of watching a horrendous log reduced to kindling.

You will need a **chopping block** or tree stump which has been cut off near the ground. It shouldn't be more than 1½ feet off the ground. The log to be split is then balanced on top. Do not split on the ground.

The ground gives with every stroke, lessening the effectiveness of your work, and is sure to dull an axe instantly if you hit it.

Examine the log carefully. A log may have **checks** or cracks where it has begun to dry. These will be radial lines from the center to the outer bark. Aim for the checks. The log has already begun the cut for you. In the interest of your own safety, don't stand rigid. Flex the knees so that when wielding an axe the blade comes as close to a 90° angle to the wood as possible. This way you are less likely to get hurt should the axe or maul bounce off the wood.

Many logs have knots where the branches were originally. This means that the grain of the wood will be going in another direction. To cut across the grain is tough, so make your first cut as far away from the knot as possible or between knots. Large logs usually resist that "big blow" down the middle, but they can slowly be reduced by splitting around the outside and leaving a hexagonal shape which may need still more around-the-periphery work, or if the core is small enough you may be able to split it in half. This is the only way to split elm.

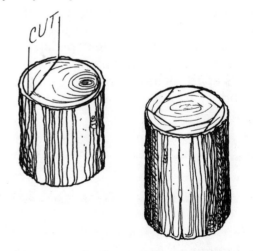

Don't be shy about cutting wood down to fairly small splits. There is never enough kindling. You may wish to leave this process until winter.

Splitting is easier when the wood is green and frozen. Some woods can be split only when frozen; elm is the most notable example.

Logs too large for the maul will call for a **sledge** and **wedges.** The wedge should be driven with the sledge. Don't use an axe or you may crack the eye of the axe. Drive the wedge in at the center. With logs of larger diameter you may need two wedges. Place them equidistant from the center. A third wedge may be needed should either of the two be driven in all the way before the log splits.

If you are splitting long logs down the outside, space the wedges. Even with smaller chunks, a wedge can easily be lost before the log splits. Drive a second, even a third wedge, being careful not to place them so that they go through one or more knots.

When the wood is bucked, avoid leaving forked logs. They will be hard to get into a small stove, and are difficult to split. You may have to saw down the crotch, then split the legs apart, or stand the piece on the two legs and try to wedge down the center.

Wood splits best when the lengths are straight grained, free of knots and green. Although split wood will not burn as long as unsplit, it burns better and will dry twice as fast.

The easiest to split are the conifers: pine, cedar, redwood, fir and Western larch; the worst to split are elm, sycamore, dogwood, red gum and black gum. It is essential to split both birch and alder or they will rot.

Power Splitters

For those who don't like splitting or have ten cords to split and not much time before the snow flies, renting or buying a power splitter may be very practical. Hydraulic splitters are relatively new (1959). Home-made varieties can be rigged up by anyone with a tractor.

The hydraulic splitter has a wedge and ram. The log is placed against the wedge and is split or diced. Some hydraulic splitters have a star-shaped wedge which will reduce one large piece to five small ones.

There is a substantial difference between $500 and $800 splitters, enough to make the additional expense worth it. Hydraulic splitters should have at least 10 tons' ram pressure, accommodate logs of 22 inches in length, and work on a 15-second cycle time. Most people who are used to splitting wood find that they can split wood faster than the hydraulic splitters, but for elm and other "hard to split" wood, they will save time.

Screw Type Splitters

Companies also make a less expensive screw type splitter which fits onto the axle of the car. They are a greater gas consumer per cord than any hydraulic splitter on the market. Hydraulic splitters are powered by small engines and generally use only a quart of gasoline per cord. Vehicle-driven screw log splitters use around four times that amount —at least a gallon per cord.

To split wood with a screw type splitter, the log is pressed into the turning screw with the butt of the log against the ground and fed into the screw at a slight angle. The screw will then pull the log onto the widening screw and split it open. There is no possibility for the log to spin on the threads if it is firmly against the ground.

Some log splitters necessitate removing the rear wheel of a car, pickup, four-wheel-drive or tractor. Others bolt directly onto the wheel. Both types mean the car has to be

Hydraulic splitter

jacked up every time you do any splitting.

Mechanical log splitters may be the only way to encourage the use of wood as a fuel. If a $200 investment produces a cord a day, then the 65¢ for gasoline is worthwhile. However if you are cutting firewood for a fireplace (15 percent efficient at best), then you are just increasing the drain on non-renewable resources. "Energy input" must be calculated against "energy output." Not only is energy expended in manufacturing splitters, but they take gasoline and oil to operate.

Screw type splitter mounts on rear hub of car

WOOD STORAGE

Once the wood has been split, it must be stacked to dry or season. It is best to locate your pile nearby, but if it can be placed on a hilltop or knoll where there are more air currents, the wood will dry faster. Drying occurs more rapidly **along** the grain. Therefore don't stack the wood for drying until it is split.

Wood piled against the house can be a fire hazard or lead to an insect invasion of your home. The exterior house walls also will cut down on air circulation. Avoid damp places or depressions where water will collect after a rainfall. The pile should be free-standing with maximum exposure to air and sunlight.

If you have a concrete patio, pile the wood there. Otherwise lay down two stringers (poles of 2-3 inches in diameter) running the length of the pile. Anything can be improvised for support (stones, boards, metal pipes) as long as it will raise the woodpile four inches off the ground to allow for air circulation beneath the wood to prevent decay. Place the stringers a foot or so apart so that the splits will straddle both supports. Leave plenty of space between the rows.

The stringers can be of any length you want, but if you are curious about the number of cords you've cut, they should be eight feet long. At either end, stakes should be driven in to prevent the pile from collapsing. Cut them so that, when driven in, they are four feet high. Begin stacking the splits between the stakes. It is a real annoyance to have the pile tip over in the middle of winter. As an added precaution, pile the last two splits of every other row cross-wise and tilt them slightly towards the pile. Lay the logs of the top row barkside up. The bark will shed the rain and snow.

A **standard cord** is a pile 8 × 4 × 4 feet; a **face cord** or **run** is a pile eight feet × firebox length × four feet. For a face cord of twelve-inch lengths, you will need four runs to equal a standard cord. If the wood has been cut to sixteen-inch lengths, three runs will equal a cord.

Stacking wood on stringers speeds curing

GREEN WOOD

Green wood can be as much as 65 percent water. Much of this moisture evaporates very quickly. In three months of reasonable weather (evaporation depends on temperature and humidity), the seasoning is half complete and the fuel value is 90 percent of what it will be when thoroughly dry. After six to nine months, the wood is reasonably dry; in two years the wood is as dry as it will get.

There is an appreciable difference in BTU rating for woods burned green or air-dried. Completely dry hardwood has about 7850 BTU's per pound whereas green wood when burned loses over one-eighth (1200 BTU's per pound) in evaporating the moisture.

It requires no work to let the wood sit for at least a year. In the process you are increasing the heat value, the wood will be lighter, ignite better, and produce less smoke and fewer sparks. But we're not always forethoughtful enough to harvest in time.

Approximate Weights and Heat Values for Different Woods				
	Weight/cord		Available heat Million BTU	
	Green	Air dry	Green	Air dry
Ash	3840	3440	16.5	20.0
Aspen	3440	2160	10.3	12.5
Beech, American	4320	3760	17.3	21.8
Birch, yellow	4560	3680	17.3	21.3
Elm, American	4320	2900	14.3	17.2
Hickory, shagbark	5040	424C	20.7	24.6
Maple, red	4000	3200	15.0	18.6
Maple, sugar	4480	3680	18.4	21.3
Oak, red	5120	3680	17.9	21.3
Oak, white	5040	3920	19.2	22.7
Pine, eastern white	2880	2080	12.1	13.3

Hastening Drying

Wood will dry faster if it is split. Much depends on the humidity. In some areas in May and June wood will dry rapidly; it will reabsorb water in July and August, dry out again in September, reabsorb water in October. Potentially wood can increase its moisture content if not properly stored.

Drying can be hastened if the pile is stacked criss-cross for three months, then stacked in the normal parallel fashion. If you lack space to do this, stack the wood normally, with one month's supply stacked criss-cross.

It is absolutely necessary to season the following woods: black ash, birch, American elm, hickory, butternut, the maples, oaks, black walnut, honey locust, pine, sycamore. Drying is not as essential for: ash, beech, box fir, shagbark hickory, pine (lodgepole, red), larch, locust (black), spruce (red, white). In an emergency white ash is not difficult to burn green.

More Permanent Structures

Even more permanent structures can be built for drying wood.

1) A **solar drier** will produce air-dried wood in three months and the high temperatures will eliminate beetle or insect problems.

Protect the stack from rain or snow by covering the pile with four-mil, clear polyethylene. This works best for fall and winter protection. (The intensity of the summer sun will deteriorate the plastic which may mean re-roofing the pile sometime during the summer.)

If plastic is used, don't wall in the pile. If you do, as the temperature beneath the plastic rises, the water vapor which escapes from the wood will only condense on the surface of the plastic, then later be absorbed by the wood. Use plastic only over the top or make a tent-like structure which will provide ventilation. Wood without bark will dry faster, but stripping it is impractical. Strip elm of bark to prevent the further spread of Dutch elm disease. The bark should be burned or the beetle will continue its nefarious activities once the weather warms.

2) A **woodshed** will promote better drying. If the shed is attached to the house you will have easy access to the wood. That is much easier than endlessly climbing stairs from the cellar. Wood should be seasoned outdoors for one year, then for one year in a protected shed for best results.

3) If you can store wood inside, it will dry even more in an **insulated basement.** Outside air drying reduces the moisture in wood by 14-25 percent; a woodshed will reduce it another 10-15 percent; while indoors adds still another 5-15 percent. For the benefit of dried wood you may have to contend with dirt and insects.

4) There are other **alternatives.** Houses designed for wood heat can be built with an exterior woodshed attached to the house with a trap door between it and the house. Each week wood can be piled next to the door, then reached from inside. This keeps the mess outside, and eliminates the constant march in and out with loads of wood, open doors, and sawdust and dirt tracked through the house.

It is also possible to bring in a week's supply of wood, then store it in the basement for further drying before it is put on the fire. If you vent the wood stove with a pipe up to the damper, the unused fireplace can be used for storage.

There are various wood storage bins on the market. Or you can fabricate your own. A laundry tub next to the stove allows you to bring in snow-covered logs. The water will drip into the tub, then be evaporated.

Recognizing Dry Wood

Green wood is easy to identify. Just split a piece. The core will look wet and shiny; dry wood looks dull and the saw marks are less pronounced. Green wood is almost twice as heavy as seasoned wood and will make a dull thud when two green sticks are hit together. It is hard to handle, hard to light, and burns slowly. Much of its energy is lost in heating, then evaporating, the excess moisture. As wood dries, the moisture evaporates naturally and the wood begins to shrink. (Wood even when air dry is still 20-25 percent moisture.) Since wood shrinks unevenly, cracking and checking of the wood occurs. Dried wood can be recognized by the weathered ends and by the cracks which will radiate like spokes out from the heartwood.

Green wood can be used to dampen an excessively hot fire or used at night to help hold the fire over. It tends to smoke more than dry wood and therefore increases creosote deposits and soot. If you must burn green wood, use it during the day when the fire is the hottest.

To be much more scientific about the process, you can weigh a split just after it has been cut; then weigh it again in nine months and figure the weight loss. Oven-drying also will give you an indication of moisture loss. Weigh the wood, then leave it in the oven at a low setting. After a few hours you should know how much by weight the wood has lost.

Can Wood Be Stored Too Long?

Few of us have the luxury of worrying about this problem but wood does have a storage life even when stored in a dry, well-ventilated place. Decay markedly reduces the wood's heat value. Dead trees are likely to be moist and punky inside because the bark has prevented water loss. Therefore split wood will last longer than round wood, but it too will rot if stored too long. Birch will rot quickly; hickory, beech and hard maple are susceptible to rot and fungi; cedar, oak, black locust and black walnut are more durable.

SCROUNGING WOOD

If you don't own your own woodlot, there are places where you can pick up wood very inexpensively. For $3 a cord you can take out "cull" (weed or unwanted) trees in some state forests. Other state land programs charge $1-$2 a run. The National Forests (there are 150 national forests, some near metropolitan areas) have a "Dead and Down" program. They issue free permits or there may be a $1 nominal charge. The program sets a ten-cord limit per person and is aimed at providing firewood for the personal use of the woodcutter. Such programs save the Forest Service from marking the trees and supervising the removal procedure, while cleaning the forests of unmarketable timber.

Orchardists always prune their trees in winter, and there is nothing better to burn than apple. Electric and telephone companies can be found along the roadside cutting trees away from the wires. Severe windstorms and hurricanes are a windfall for the woodburner. Landscapers have extra wood. Town dumps are sources for usable firewood. Municipalities, particularly those now trying to keep up with the devastation of the Dutch elm beetle, have extra wood which usually is hauled to landfill areas. Tree-cutting services and neighbors are other sources of wood.

Crews at highway projects and construction sites are often prohibited from burning refuse. Their waste wood must be buried or hauled to the dump. Sometimes it is possible to clear out the trees before the bulldozers move in. Sawmills sometimes give away slabs or edgings; some deliver; some sell them for $6-$18 a cord. Lumberyards have kindling for a nominal fee.

You may be able to go into land after it has been lumbered. Loggers use only one-third of what they cut. They leave the butt and the tree top, and both are valuable for fuel. There may be woodworking factories in your area which always have leftover scraps. Many farmers have woodlots and for a minimal stumpage fee will give you permission to cut on their land. Wood product mills, dowel factories, old wood pallets, bowling pins, hockey stick plants, etc. are all good sources.

The wood you scrounge will vary tremendously in quality. Leftovers from sawmills, lumberyards, and woodworking factories usually are softwood which has a high resin content and should be used for kindling. Don't plan to stoke a fire solely with these scraps. And do not use painted or varnished wood as fuel.

BUYING WOOD

Wood can be purchased by the cord and generally to your specifications. Even if you've gotten in the wood for the winter, you may deplete your supply before the end of the heating season and have to order an extra cord.

The delivery of wood is not yet a regulated business. Whether you are actually "taken" or not, you probably will think so. One delivery won't appear as large as the next, will be piled differently if at all, and may have assumed another name by the time it arrives. Wood is sold by the truck load, by weight, in cords (standard, long, stovewood, short, face, and running cord), ricks, runs, or units. All this is as confusing to the woodburner as to many dealers. Others simply take advantage of the fact that most homeowners don't know the difference between wood species or understand wood measurements.

Wood usually is sold in divisions of a **standard cord** which is a neatly stacked pile eight feet long × four feet wide × four feet high covering 128 cubic feet. Since wood can't be stacked without air space, only 60-110 cubic feet of the 128 may be solid wood. (Usually it runs between 80-90 cubic feet with more solid wood content in roundwood than split.)

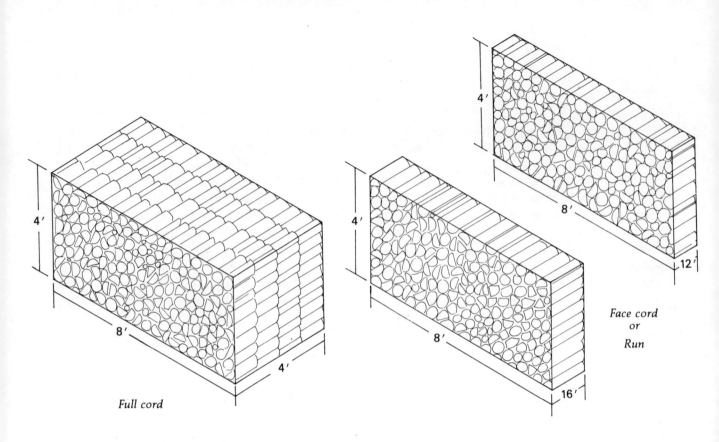

Full cord

*Face cord
or
Run*

Few people have four-foot fireplaces and many lack the equipment to reduce four-foot lengths to stove dimension. Therefore wood sold in face cords, or lengths corresponding to either fireplace dimension (twenty-four inches) or stove dimension (twelve or sixteen inches), is more common. When you buy a **face cord** you are buying a pile eight feet × four feet × whatever length dimension you specify. A **rick** usually refers to sixteen-inch lengths.

A **run** is also a face cord, and varies in size depending on the wood length. For example, wood cut to twenty-four-inch lengths means there are two runs in a cord; cut to sixteen-inch lengths, three runs to the cord; cut to twelve-inch lengths, four runs to the cord. To further complicate matters, there is a **unit** which is 1/24 of a standard cord or a pile two feet × sixteen inches × two feet — the amount of wood which will fit into a station wagon or car trunk.

You may have difficulty judging whether you have what you paid for. If you pay to have the wood stacked in a eight × four × four pile there's no problem, but if it is stacked in nooks and crannies, it's hard to check your purchase. For each neatly stacked pile, multiply the height by the length of the pile by the stick length (all in feet) and divide by 128. This will give you the percentage of a cord you have bought. Even that is only a rough estimate because of the endless variables.

Wood Prices

Prices for cord wood reflect the amount of wood, the kind, and the work involved. For example, a standard cord will be cheaper than three sixteen-inch runs, a run cheaper than eight units. Cheapest is four-foot green wood by the cord, unpiled, selling in New England for about $40. (This price can be reduced if you truck it yourself.) An uncut cord means the homeowner will need a chain saw or bow saw, axe, maul, wedges, and a strong back. A green cord should measure two-four inches higher than a seasoned cord. (Wood shrinks more in girth than length.)

Buying green wood by the cord in the off-season (late spring to early summer) is the most economical; in January prices go way up. Wood cutters sell little wood in late spring. You will have more choice and prices can be as much as 30 percent lower. Unsplit wood of stove length sells for $55-$65 per cord. Prices are sure to continue rising. If this is your first season burning wood, pay for air-dried wood (not green wood or you will have bad creosote problems) and, if you can, save money on the trucking ($12) and splitting ($12) by doing it yourself. At the same time order green wood for next year. It will be cheaper and the wood is easier to split green. Order hardwood or mixed wood. Some softwood will come in handy for kindling. It ignites easily and burns rapidly. If you unknowingly get a whole cord of softwood you've been taken. (A cord of hickory is the equivalent of 24,600,000 BTU's, while a cord of white pine has 12,022,000 BTU's, or half as much heat value.)

Even among the hardwoods there is a difference in BTU value. You can expect to pay $10-$15 more for hickory or ash than for maple or elm. Aspen (or popple) is a hardwood but with no more available heat per cord than white pine. It's worth shopping around. You will find wood dealers in the classified ad section of your newspaper. Ask what kind of wood they can deliver as well as the price. Then check the BTU value. For the same price, you may be able to get more heat.

See p. 76 for BTU ratings, for various wood species.

Wood by the Truckload

If you don't pay to have the wood stacked, there will be a large disorderly mound in the middle of your yard. To know whether you got what you paid for, check the vehicle in which the wood was delivered. The bed of most pickups is four feet wide, nineteen inches deep and eight feet long — space enough for a sixteen-inch face cord. If the pickup has a 6-foot body, it won't be able to hold a sixteen-inch run.

Be wary of buying by the truckload unless you have some idea of how much the truck can hold.

In some places wood can now be bought by the pulpwood truckload. You will be buying tree-length logs the diameter and length of those which are delivered to lumber mills. Truckloads of this size advertise that when the wood is bucked and split it will equal eight to ten cords; in some cases four to seven cords is a more realistic estimate. Such truckloads are still much cheaper; a cord can cost as little as $20 — which is a bargain if you like the exercise.

The logs may be exceedingly muddy unless they have been cut and hauled in the winter. Brush off the dirt before bucking. It will quickly dull a good saw.

Wood by Weight

Wood also is sold by weight which is a much fairer measure if you can be sure the wood is well-seasoned. Don't buy water — it's cheaper from the faucet. An average cord will lose 1000 pounds as it seasons. Check the wood carefully to be sure it is dry.

There is a considerable difference in weight between woods; a standard cord of air-dried hardwood weighs 4000 pounds while a standard cord of softwood will weigh half that. In heat value per pound there is no difference between soft and hard wood, but the heavier the wood, the less space it takes and the fewer times you'll have to load the stove.

Beware

There is nothing in the law regulating wood quality. Wood can come sound or rotten, dry or green, with or without bark. Until you know the reliability of your wood dealer, don't pay for a load until it has been delivered, inspected, and stacked. There are a number of sleights of hand to watch for.

1) Measure the log lengths. They may be a little less in length to make it easier to load the stove, but if they are uniformly two-three inches too short, you're not getting what you paid for.

2) Logs can be piled in numerous ways to increase height. A rock or tree stump will do this. Wood piled criss-cross will stack much more loosely than logs piled with the grain in one direction. Knots and branch stubs can be used to the advantage of the seller.

3) Rotten or decaying logs can be piled on the bottom. By the time you reach them, they will be reduced to pulp. Or the pile can be stacked with more than ample ventilation. Mice and squirrels should be able to make their ways through the pile, but anything larger and you're buying too much air.

4) Avoid loads which are only softwood or hardwoods of low heat value.

To insure against these misfortunes, check with others more knowledgeable about local wood dealers.

You're Running Out of Wood

Most of us get part way through the heating season before admitting the obvious: we're running out of wood and it's still the dead of winter. There are interim measures which can be taken.

1) Dilute! When you begin to realize that the pile is diminishing much too fast, the dry wood can be mixed with freshly cut green wood. This is a less than ideal solution. Creosote formations will increase and must be monitored carefully. Never burn only green wood. (You won't be able to anyway because green wood will resist igniting.) Less than half the fire should be of green wood, and mixed with dry wood only when the fire is well under way.

2) Choose the woods which burn best when green such as: yellow birch, black birch, sumac, white ash, American beech, box fir, hickory, pine, black locust, white spruce, pine, spruce, cedar. Ash is preferred.

3) The logs can be split into smaller pieces to air-dry more quickly. They can be added to the back or side of the fire, allowed to dry gradually from the heat, then moved onto the blaze. This process may take overnight. When you open the stove in the morning, the logs can be used to rekindle the fire. By then they should be seasoned enough to burn.

If the furnace is used, wood can be dried next to it, or under the wood stove while it is in operation. The latter is a risky process since the heat from the stove may ignite the splits. If you dry wood this way, never leave the wood drying overnight or when you aren't at home.

4) You can strike out into the woods. Kindling will be easy to find. Evergreens always have dead lower branches which because they are above the snow won't be wet. If they are brittle and snap, then the wood is dry enough to burn. You may find hardwood branches, but usually they grow much higher off the ground.

Dead trees should be available. If you can push them over with your own weight, they're too rotten to be of use. Others will have to be felled to see whether they're any good. Birch won't be worth felling. Dead wood will be more difficult to split, but will burn well.

Tips

1) Don't pile firewood near the smoke outlet or under the stove unless you will be tending the fire constantly.

2) If your wood is decayed or buggy, bring it in just before burning it.

3) Bark has heat value. Except for elm, there is no reason to peel it off unless you want to accelerate the drying process.

SELLING FIREWOOD

I have yet to meet anyone who has produced more than subsistence wages from selling firewood. Most of the wood sold is being harvested by the part-time logger who has invested in a tractor, a pickup, a chain saw, and maybe a hydraulic splitter or tractor attachment. Chain saws are difficult and dangerous. High insurance premiums must be paid. In addition there are gas, oil, and maintenance costs, and the depreciation of the pickup.

Unlike other fuels, wood is heavy and bulky. Roundtrip drives of twenty to fifty miles for wood are common since wood is harvested in rural areas and taken to urban centers. For this a 3/4 ton pickup is minimum. As the truck gets larger the per-cord expenses become less, but this means that wood if it is to be a competitive fuel will have to be moved in larger quantities. Wood collectives, with their largest outlay going for transportation, may be the only way for effective, efficient, and economic harvesting of firewood.

Wood Substitutes

There are wood substitutes, usually near the check-out counters in the supermarkets. Synthetic logs are made from wood waste (sawdust, shavings, etc.) with paraffin as a binder. They come in neat, easy-to-carry packages, but at $350 a ton, they are expensive and a questionable product. The paraffin logs burn with a colorful flame for about three hours, but produce no coals. Most of the heat goes up the chimney. Should you have a fireplace chimney fire, the logs can be a hazard because they are almost impossible to remove.

There are advantages to wood substitutes. Certainly they are cleaner, easy to handle, burn with low ash content and are consistently much drier than firewood. But they are more costly and can be dangerous.

Newspaper logs can substitute for wood logs and are easily made. Soak the newspapers in water or a solution of laundry detergent and roll them on dowels into cylinders. Bind the sheets tightly together with string. The hole left after you remove the dowel will help combustion; the detergent will keep the sheets together. Dry the newspapers, then burn. If the papers aren't bound tightly, they will peel off, produce a smoky fire, and leave a mess of ashes.

Flame Color

For special occasions you may wish to add color to the fire flame. Driftwood will produce a blue or lavender flame; apple after it has aged will produce multiple colors; sodium chloride (table salt) and calcium chloride will produce yellow colors.

Ten causes of stove troubles and their cures

No.	Fault	Examination	Correction
1.	Broken clay tiles.	Can be found by light and mirror reflecting condition of walls.	All breaks should be patched with cement.
2.	Clay lining fails to come below opening of smoke pipe.	Found by observation through flue opening into chimney.	Clay tiling should be extended below flue opening.
3.	Partial projection of smoke pipe into flue area.	Found by measurement after pipe is withdrawn or by sight from chimney opening, using light on a cord.	Projection must be eliminated.
4.	Loose seated pipe in flue opening.	Air leaks can be determined by smoke test or examination of chimney while fire burns below location.	Leaks should be eliminated by cementing all pipe openings.
5.	Smoke pipe enters chimney in declining position.	This is observed by measurement.	Correct the pipe to permit smoke to enter in an ascending pipe.
6.	Second flue opening below that for smoke pipe.	This is found by observation from within basement.	Change to allow only one opening in each chimney.
7.	Accumulation of soot narrows cross sectional area of pipe.	Examine pipe from cleanout opening.	Remove soot.
8.	Hand damper in a full closed position.	If handle does not give true position of plate remove section of pipe to ascertain position.	Allow sufficient opening of plate for needed escape of gases.
9.	Clean-out opening on pipe leaks air.	Flames visible when furnace is under fire.	Tighten or cement to eliminate leak.
10.	Clean-out pan not tightly seated in base of chimney.	This air leak can be determined by watching action of small fire built in bottom of chimney shaft.	Cement to eliminate all leaks.

Operating the Stove

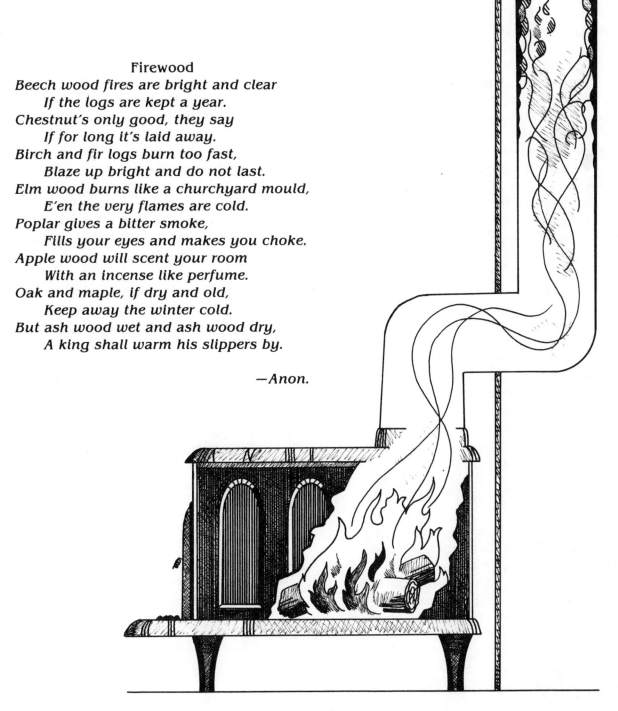

Firewood

Beech wood fires are bright and clear
*   If the logs are kept a year.*
Chestnut's only good, they say
*   If for long it's laid away.*
Birch and fir logs burn too fast,
*   Blaze up bright and do not last.*
Elm wood burns like a churchyard mould,
*   E'en the very flames are cold.*
Poplar gives a bitter smoke,
*   Fills your eyes and makes you choke.*
Apple wood will scent your room
*   With an incense like perfume.*
Oak and maple, if dry and old,
*   Keep away the winter cold.*
But ash wood wet and ash wood dry,
*   A king shall warm his slippers by.*

—Anon.

Most of us have had experience building campfires. And even if we have the badges to prove our success, we soon discover that building a fire in a wood stove is quite a different skill. Kindling is readily available for summer campfires so getting the fire going is usually no problem; for winter wood stove fires kindling is precious. You can't afford to start the fire with mounds of tinder. In outdoor fires the wood can be stacked in spacious tepee or log cabin arrangements. This permits easy circulation of air through the firewood. Wood stoves (cookstoves are even worse) have relatively small fireboxes. Many of them are long rectangles so that big pieces of wood have to be laid parallel to each other. This makes air circulation more difficult. Even if campfires provide more smoke than flame, there is always a "clean-air" retreat somewhere. Mid-winter wood fires require proper use of the damper; the only retreat from a house full of smoke may be sub-zero outdoor temperatures.

Campfires, if made in a pit or surrounded by a ring of stones, are relatively safe. When you're ready to break camp, they can be doused with a bucket of sand or water. Wood stove fires aren't that easy. Although the firebox should be able to withstand the intensity of the fire, accidents do happen. Some accidents will require the fire department and can seriously endanger your house and family.

Give your wood stove fire the utmost respect by learning how to operate the stove safely, skillfully, and efficiently.

A new stove of cast iron must be cured which means the fires should be small for the first week. The fires may smoke or smell peculiar at first. It's only the oils in the paint burning off.

For stoves with no ash pit, insulate the bottom of the firebox with two inches of sand.

Be sure the drafts are all wide open or you will fill the house with smoke when you light the fire. A sheet at a time, crumple up newspapers into a ball the size of a grapefruit. This will assure plenty of air circulation. Magazines and colored advertising flyers do not burn well.

Provide three inches or so of newspaper over the entire bottom of the stove. Cover the newspaper with kindling (split sticks are better than round), laid either tepee or log cabin fashion if there's room. Place the sticks close enough to one another so that the flame can move easily from one stick to another. If the kindling is packed too tightly, the fire will suffocate, smoke, and then die out.

Cedar, shredded bark, birch bark, grapevine bark, or shavings can be used for tinder. For kindling, softwoods cut into sticks 3/4 inch in diameter work best. Dead twigs of spruce, balsam, pine and sumac, or pine cones, corn cobs, dried citrus peels, lath, or scrap pieces from lumberyards also work well.

Graduate the size of the logs so that on top of the kindling you have a log slightly larger than the kindling. Light the newspaper and immediately close the firebox door. Resist the temptation to watch the fire ignite. By leaving the door open you will only interfere with the draft pattern. You should hear the fire catching and as it draws in more oxygen through the draft, it should burn more intensely. There even may be crackling sounds in the stovepipe as the gases pass through, heating the pipe.

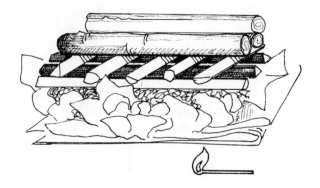

If your fire has failed, leave the logs in the firebox but move them to one side. Some may have charred. Add more newspaper and kindling. Check to be sure that you haven't packed the kindling too tightly. Fires need a free flow of oxygen to burn. If you have difficulty at this point getting the fire going, **never** regardless of your level of frustration, use any kind of liquid lighter fluid. Flammable liquids may flame up, even vaporize, then ignite, and blow up the stove. They are made for outdoor use only.

Once you know the kindling is burning well, add another log to the fire. To promote better drafts, leave a narrow air space between the logs. Heat will be reflected between the adjacent surfaces of the two logs which will keep the logs burning and temperatures in the firebox high. Stoves differ in the amount of wood they can hold and the rate at which they burn. For a while it will be trial and error. Usually you can tell just from the sound whether the fire is burning rapidly or has burned down, or out.

Softwoods (or lightweight woods) burn faster than hardwoods or fruit woods (heavy woods) because of the pitch and resin which they contain. Fires can be started with softwoods, but once they are under way, you should move to the hardwoods. Since softwoods tend to produce a lot of smoke, be sure the draft is wide open to keep the smoke moving.

When the first logs have burned to coals, open the door and add more logs. On stoves such as the Scandinavian front-to-back burners, the coals should be raked to the front of the stove before new logs are added. Once you know the new wood is burning well, the fire can be dampened (but not all the way for you will just produce creosote). In the first half-hour of each burn most of the gases which cause creosote are given off. To insure they ignite, keep the draft wide open so there will be plenty of oxygen. Then dampen the fire by partially closing the draft to prevent a fire hotter than necessary.

Laying the fire in a Tempwood stove is slightly different because the draft inlets are on the top of the stove. The larger logs should be placed in the stove first. Then add kindling in criss-crossed fashion, finally the crumpled newspaper, being certain that most of it is located under the draft tubes. Light the fire; at once replace the lid but leave the draft inlets open. After ten to fifteen minutes the fire should be going well and you can begin adjusting the draft controls.

When there is only charcoal in the stove very little draft is necessary because no creosote compounds are being formed. Let the coals burn down before you add more wood because to continue accumulating coals may cause the stove to overheat and warp. Be sure the damper is wide open before adding more wood. This is particularly important for top loaders which can be smoky. Then add the wood and leave the draft open for ten to twenty minutes depending on how good a coal bed you have and how much wood you added. A large log, for example, will be more difficult to burn. Therefore you want a brisk fire. Repeat this process with every new load of wood.

Tending the Stove

Tending a wood stove is complicated but generally the decisions you make will be based on what you want and what you are willing to cope with. For the most complete combustion (i.e. the burning of the gases) you need a hot (1100 °F.) fire, but this means frequent loadings of smaller pieces and plenty of oxygen. Unfortunately running a stove this way means much of the heat will go up the chimney, reducing the heat transfer value of the stove. For that loss, however, you will have a cleaner chimney.

If you wait until the fire has died way down, then fill the chamber to capacity, you have lowered the firebox temperature. The new wood must heat up and the moisture be driven off — a process which allows gases to escape unburned. This reduces the overall efficiency of your stove. However, heat will still radiate through the walls since it was absorbed earlier when the fire was hotter. To fill a stove at one loading slows down the fire, but moderates heat transfer.

Cookstoves

To fire up a cookstove, the drafts (on the left and front of the stove) and the damper should be opened. Leave all the lids on. Once the fire is under way, the side draft can be closed. If the damper is closed, air will circulate to warm the oven. Don't peek at the fire by lifting the lids. This will decrease the draft and bring smoke and ashes into the room.

CREOSOTE PREVENTION

A major concern should be creosote prevention. To warm the stovepipe and the chimney, let the fire burn hot after you reload the stove. This may be enough to melt creosote deposits which will begin forming as soon as the stack temperature falls below 250 °F. If the creosote is warm it will run back down the pipe towards the stove and be burned.

Creosote formation can be reduced by leaving the air inlet moderately open until most of the wood has been reduced to charcoal. Control the stove's heat output by the amount of fuel, **not** by the damper. Smaller pieces of wood added more frequently and burned with the draft wide open will moderate room temperatures and produce better stove efficiencies. This is particularly true in fall and spring when stoves fully loaded tend to overheat.

None of us has the patience to feed a stove small sticks every five minutes; on the other hand feeding the fire the largest unsplit log the stove will take should be avoided. Large logs drastically reduce firebox temperatures because there is inadequate air to permit complete combustion. The gases and tars escape, creosote is formed.

Stack Temperatures

Knowing your stack temperatures may be a good indication of what is happening in your installation. If you can keep your hand on single-wall, uninsulated stovepipe, little heat is going out the chimney; therefore creosote is being deposited on the pipe. For a further check, drill a hole in the smokepipe and insert a thermometer stem near the outlet collar. Stack temperatures below 300 °F. may mean soot and creosote deposits are accumulating. Adjust your installation and/or fire size so that the stovepipe heat registers between 300°-400°F. Temperatures above 400°F. usually mean you are wasting heat.

Such a method for monitoring creosote is only approximate. Soot can gather on the thermometer stem and lower the reading, or your stack may need high temperatures. To retain temperatures above 250°F. the entire distance in a stack two-and-a-half stories high, the exhaust gases may have to enter at temperatures greater than 400°F. The same will be true with an exterior masonry chimney in which the gases cool very rapidly.

The first year check your chimney frequently to learn where and how much creosote is forming. When you know how your system is working, you should be able to keep the exhaust temperatures in the correct range with the thermometer.

Holding a Fire

If you want your fire to burn overnight, one large chunk will outlast by two or three times the same volume of smaller wood. For nighttime, find the longest piece that will fit. Black locust, ironwood (hophornbeam), hickory, white oak, rock elm or apple give the best coals and the longest-lasting burn. Be sure the log is placed on a good bed of coals, then shut down the draft. Since running such low fires is undesirable, they should not be encouraged except when absolutely necessary.

The following morning, run a hot fire of kindling for ten to fifteen minutes to burn off the creosote which formed the previous night.

An Untended Fire

Whenever you leave the house, leave the stovepipe damper opened, but close the air inlet damper. The worst fear in leaving a stove going is that the wood will burn uncontrollably, or that a spark from the fire will escape through the draft inlet. Both these possibilities can be guarded against by closing the air inlet dampers.

If you have an old stove or a stove which isn't airtight, check before leaving to be sure

that the fire has died way down. Since these stoves have their own hidden air intakes, they are more dangerous. Even thermostatically-controlled stoves can become infernos.

Also check that you have left nothing combustible within three feet of the stove. It's easy to overlook clothes drying, kindling, newspapers, or logs left to dry under the firebox. All these things can catch fire from the intense heat radiation. Check also for flammables left on top of the stove (mittens, etc.).

When you return open the dampers. Stoke the fire and let it burn actively for a while. Damping down a stove permits creosote build-up. By letting the fire get hot again, some of this creosote will burn off before it becomes a problem.

An Untended Cookstove

Before leaving the house with a cookstove going, be sure all drafts are left opened a hair so that the fire won't burn out of control, but neither will the house fill with smoke.

ASHES

After a few fires, the ashes will begin to accumulate, if your fires aren't burning the wood completely. Stoves vary in the amount of ash they produce. In some stoves much of the ash is carried out the flue with the smoke. In others the ashes accumulate rapidly and have to be removed daily. With an efficient stove, you will have a bushel of ashes for every cord of wood burned.

Stoves with grates usually have ash pans. Let the pan fill until the ashes reach just under the bottom of the grate. While the fire is burning, embers and coals will fall through the grate and add their heat to the intensity of the fire. There is nothing wrong with letting the ashes accumulate, but don't let them fill to overflowing because they then will interfere with the draft.

Other stoves don't have grates. The fire is built on the ashes which serve as insulation for the bottom of the stove. In cast-iron stoves, the bottom should be covered with at least two inches of ashes (or two inches of sand if you have a new stove).

Reserve ashes can be used to bank the fire at night. Just cover the burning logs. This will retain glowing coals overnight and make the fire easier to rekindle.

Ash Removal

Exercise extreme caution when removing ashes. They still may contain burning embers even though you think the fire is out. Shovel the ashes into a non-combustible heavy metal container using fireplace tools. Don't use iron or aluminum vessels because the metals are affected by the alkalis. Some stoves are equipped with a woodstove hoe and ash bucket to make the process safer. Above all do not shovel the residue into a paper bag.

Ashes contain all the material that made up the wood minus only the water and carbohydrates which have gone up the flue. Gardens will benefit from the mineral-rich ashes. Potassium is good for encouraging strong stems, and phosphorus stimulates root growth. Ashes are also good for sweetening soils, and can be sprinkled over the crowns of root crops (onions, carrots, beets, etc.) to discourage the root maggot. They will prevent slugs and snails from attacking vegetables because these creatures don't like to crawl over the ashes.

If the ashes are for garden use, store them in a dry place. Don't put them on a winter compost pile for the water will leach out all the nutrients. Fifty to sixty pounds will be needed for 500 square feet, when scattering them on your garden.

Ashes—More Ashes

Ashes are caustic and can be used as a degreaser—ask any Scout caught streamside with all the pots and pans. They are also helpful in melting snow and for traction on icy roads.

Traditionally they have been used to deodorize outhouses.

CHARCOAL

Charcoal has twice the heat potential of wood and can be used alone or in a mixture with wood. It requires less attention than wood and is easy to control. Many people favor charcoal for cooking.

Be sure your stove can burn coal before you try to. Some coals (cannel) may burn too hot, particularly for the Franklin-type stoves. Overfiring is a problem with any wood-burning device but because the BTU rating for coal is much higher, it must be watched more carefully.

Charcoal can be ignited with crumpled newspapers, then kindling. Add the coal only a little at a time. When the charcoal is burning well, add more coal but **only** in small quantities. Charcoal can be deadly when burned indoors because it produces an odorless carbon monoxide. When burning it, be sure the damper is wide open and the coal is burned on a basket or grate for good air circulation.

Anthracite coal, which is from hardwoods, sells for about $70 a ton. Although it is difficult to ignite, it gives the hottest, longest burn without producing soot or smoke. Bituminous or soft coal burns more quickly, producing soot, smoke and sometimes a sulphurous odor; cannel coal ignites quickly and crackles like wood.

You will need less charcoal than wood for the same amount of heat. In addition charcoal is good to hold the fire overnight or if you plan to be away all day.

DRAFT

The draft depends on the type of wood, the draw of the chimney (i.e. chimney height and diameter), the size of the logs, the way the fire is built, the type of installation, and the house air currents. Infrequent draft problems are to be expected. Usually they are caused by a change in wind direction. The house will fill with smoke quickly and need to be ventilated. Open a window until the fire catches. If problems occur only at the beginning, nothing necessarily is wrong with your installation. It may only be a matter of establishing the proper draft. When, however, trouble getting the fire to catch is a prolonged and regular occurrence even in calm weather, something is amiss.

Stoves Vented Into a Fireplace Flue

Fires may be difficult to get under way in homes with exterior chimneys because of existing downdrafts. In an open fireplace this can be cured by holding a lighted newspaper up the flue, but if you have blocked off the fireplace, this is impossible. Use more newspaper and kindling than normal in laying the fire, and place a ball of newspaper on top. Ignite this first. The extra heat should turn the draft around.

Installations which have two flue sizes may or may not work depending on how radical is their difference in diameter. Stovepipe is commonly six inches in diameter. When fireplace flues into which stovepipe vents are too large, the gases will move more slowly and tend to condense more readily. The problem is even worse in an exterior masonry chimney. The gases, even if hot, will be cooled rapidly, particularly in sub-zero weather. Back-puffing may occur because, without the rapid rise of hot air in the chimney, there is little suction into the fire.

A **reducing collar** can be attached to the chimney top which helps to pull out the gases. The cone will taper the opening to a smaller size, thereby increasing the draft.

More complicated solutions include dropping six-inch pipe (or pipe the diameter of your stovepipe collar) down the chimney to provide a smaller, continuous flue. These pipes will be much more difficult to check for rust or pinholes and more difficult to replace. Therefore you may wish a sheet metal shop to make the sections from heavier gauge

SAFETY TIPS

Wood stove safety cannot be stressed enough. Wood stoves demand constant vigilance. They are perfectly safe but **only** if properly installed and properly cared for.

1) Check areas where creosote can accumulate. Chimneys should be cleaned or carefully inspected at least twice a year and stovepipes more frequently. If the damper in the stovepipe moves with any difficulty, or the fire needs more draft than usual or smokes more than usual, creosote probably is collecting. A "thud" instead of a "ping" heard when you tap the pipes indicates creosote residue. With stoves which vent out the back, it is easy to remove the baffle (if your stove has one) and shine a flashlight down the pipe. In stoves which have elbows, the elbows can be removed and both the vertical and horizontal sections of pipe examined by flashlight.

2) Check for rusted or corroded pipes. Because the pipes are under continued, intense heat, they are at some point bound to rust out and should be replaced. Thin gauge pipe can corrode through in a year.

3) Avoid burning trash in your wood stove. Not only do the plastics give off ex-

stainless steel. The extra cost for stronger pipe will be worth it. Check carefully to be sure you will be able to get through the damper opening. The damper may be difficult or impossible to remove. One or two elbows or pipe bent to an oval shape can be used to pass through the opening.

Measure the amount of stovepipe needed. Buy an extra section. You can always return it. Assemble the pipe, using three sheet metal screws per joint. Be sure you know in advance how you will pass through the damper, whether it be with one section of flattened pipe or an elbow.

Two people are needed for this installation because the unit will be lowered through the chimney from the roof. The stovepipe should enter living space through an existing chimney connector in the chimney above the damper or pass through the damper opening. One person should be ready to pull the pipe through the damper area or the wall (if you intend to vent into the chimney above the damper). A second person is on the roof to lower the pipe. If the pipe will be exiting through a hole above the fireplace, a certain amount of finagling may have to go on to get an adjustable elbow through the chimney connector.

Fill the space between the pipe and the chimney flue with mica pellets (pellets without styrofoam or they will melt). Stuff the flue opening around the damper with fiberglass insulation.

The Operator

Drafts are of course affected by the way the stove is operated. The more the stove is run with the damper closed, the less oxygen reaches the fire, the poorer the combustion, the lower the firebox temperature, the greater the creosote. Many stoves, the Scandinavian ones especially, operate more efficiently if the draft is never totally closed unless you won't be there to watch for sparks, backpuffing, or other dangers.

Other causes of smoke include using wet wood. Always use dry wood, but if green wood has to be used, mix it with dry wood, and add it only when you have a hot fire.

Installation Adjustments

If you have a long section of horizontal stovepipe and/or one or two elbows, you may have draft problems. Try shortening the horizontal run and/or eliminating any non-essen-

---

Safety Tips (cont.)
tremely corrosive acids but such fires can easily burn out of control.

4) "Chimney Sweep," "Red Devil," etc. advertise that they will keep the flue free of creosote and soot, but they will **not** clean the flue if the creosote has already been deposited.

5) Exercise extreme caution when removing ashes. They still may contain burning embers even though you think the fire has died out. Immediately dispose of the ashes outdoors. Be careful when reloading the stove. Glowing coals can slip out easily.

6) Double-check the size of a log before

adding it to the fire. You may discover once having set it on the coals that the log is too large and must be removed. Taking this log out of the stove and outdoors is a dangerous procedure. Keep a pair of work gloves nearby, for should this occur you must be able to remove the log quickly. Gloves or a pot holder also are handy when the handles of the fire doors get extremely hot.

7) One of the principal sources of fires is heat radiation. Be sure your clearances are adequate (a minimum of three feet). Keep this in mind before you get sloppy about piling wood, newspapers, or other combustibles too near the stove. Even plastics will burn.

tial elbows. When venting into a fireplace or into the fireplace above the damper, be sure the pipe doesn't stick too far into the flue. Draft problems can also be caused by chimney height. Or if you are venting into a masonry chimney, you may need to check for drafts between the flues. Or your installation may need a chimney cap.

HEAT EXCHANGERS

Once you have mastered the problems of maintaining a good fire by becoming artful in the use of the dampers, you will, no doubt, read with increasing interest advertisements which boast greater heat recovery. There are both active and passive systems to increase heat output.

Passive Heat Exchangers
Other things being equal, the greater the surface area of a stove, the more radiating energy it will give off. Complicated embossed designs or ribs with textured patterns increase the radiating surface area and improve heat transfer of stoves. Baffles increase heat transfer by increasing the length of time that gases and smoke are forced to remain in the stove. Even back venting, rather than top venting, slows the passage of gases.

Many of the Scandinavian stove models have arches, heat chambers, and ovens to increase heat output. Double-barrel stove designs such as that of the SEVCA and Hinckley Shaker stoves also provide greater heat transfer.

Heat transfer can be further increased (15-20 percent) by lengthening the amount of stovepipe which is exposed to the space you wish to heat. This is easily accomplished in installations with horizontal runs. Move the stove closer to the center of the room and add an extra section of pipe.

If your pipe exits vertically, a doughnut can be added between the first and second sections of pipe above the stove. Buy four non-adjustable elbows (to prevent creosote drips) and two tees. Add an elbow to either side of each tee; then attach the elbows together. Use three #6 self-tapping screws for each connection. Be sure the doughnut is sufficiently (18 inches) below combustibles in the ceiling unless protection is provided.

---

8) Be sure that your chimney is high enough. Burning material can come out the chimney and ignite the roof.

9) Flammable liquids should **never** be stored in the same room as a wood stove nor should they be used for starting a fire.

10) Always burn hardwoods which are well-seasoned. Wood should dry six to nine months, preferably two years before it is used. If you burn softwoods, exercise extreme care. They can send sparks through a partially closed draft.

11) Avoid using painted or varnished wood as fuel.

12) Be sure that only one person at a time is responsible for a wood stove. Too many responsible adults can cause overzealous feeding of a fire which creates a potential hazard.

13) Teach children to respect the stove. They've been known to knock over the stove accidentally.

14) Avoid stoking the fire until the wood has burned down to coals. Overheating a sheet metal stove can cause warping.

15) Never leave a fire untended unless it has died down and the draft inlet is closed.

16) If the furnace cement cracks, replace it. Sparks and smoke can escape through these openings.

Both these methods mean more pipe which NFPA does not recommend. In addition, for better heat transfer you may be paying too high a price—more pipe means the gases will have further to go. The further the gases travel, the more time they have to give up their heat, but the cooler they get and the more creosote they deposit. If your pipe already is long or if you vent into an exterior chimney, the likelihood of cooling the gases too much is more than possible. Doughnuts or lengthened pipe should be considered only for interior chimneys which prove during a heating season that they don't produce excessive amounts of creosote. They preferably should not be used on airtights.

Metal fins can be made to fit around the existing pipe. They act as mini-radiators, giving the heat a reflective surface to bounce off. You can make your own by bending a piece of metal with a pair of pliers, or by taking a thin piece of sheet metal, cutting strips which you can bend in any direction, then

Slip-on heat fins from Belanger Co.

folding over the edges so that the fin will stay hooked around the pipe.

Active Heat Exchangers
The simplest active system is a fan—for horizontal pipe it is the only system. Place the fan behind the stove, positioned so that it blows along the pipe. Once you have a good fire going, turn on the fan.

There are commercial heat extractors which fit into a vertical run of stovepipe. They force the gases to break up in order to flow around a series of horizontal tubes before being reunited and entering the smokepipe. Through the tubes, air is blown by an electric motor which extracts heat from the gases. The blower is thermostatically controlled.

Heat extractors may themselves collect creosote or cause creosote to collect elsewhere in your installation. They are best on small stoves which burn hot. Low draft or airtight stoves which are dampened way down burn so slowly that the outer surface of the tubes will accumulate creosote. Even the least bit of creosote or soot on the tubes will work as an insulator. Less and less heat is transferred until ultimately you are paying to run the motor. Be sure you buy a model with some kind of rake to clean the pipes.

Heat exchangers will improve the air circulation and heat efficiency of the stove, but if the flue gas temperature falls below 250°F. (which it is now likely to do since you are extracting even more heat), creosote will form rapidly. Clean the tubes frequently.

Safety Tips (cont.)
17) Be sure that upholstered furniture or rugs aren't within three feet of the stove.

18) Watch the damper. It can close accidentally.

19) Keep a fire extinguisher and several pounds of salt or baking soda within easy reach in case of fire. Fire extinguishers should be rated for wood and paper fires.

Avoid the soda-acid types because a sudden application of water can warp or crack stoves.

20) Never run stovepipe through a ceiling or wall without using an approved ventilated metal thimble to protect against the conduction of heat into the wood, wall or roof material.

If your chimney does not have a good draft, you may have to extend the chimney and/or install a **draft-inducing fan** in which case you may be better off without a heat exchanger. Also to be calculated is the electrical energy consumed and the noise of the blower fan which will go off and on at irregular intervals depending on the temperature of the fire.

Never add these devices to an especially long run of pipe. Nor should they be added to either horizontal pipe or to a short run with one or two elbows.

CHIMNEY FIRES

With the increase in the use of wood stoves and wood furnaces, chimney fires are increasing. In 1976, 40,000 chimney fires were reported; countless others went unreported. Modern wood-burning equipment which burns the wood more efficiently and more completely increases the likelihood of fire because of the way the stoves are operated.

The usual procedure for operating air-tights overnight is to pack the stove with as much fuel as possible and dampen down the fire. At some point the fire cools to the point where combustion is incomplete and the partially burned gases enter the chimney which has cooled to some extent. If it has cooled enough, the unburned gases and water condense to form an acid solution. The condensate will be a liquid brown or tar-like substance looking like varnish, with an acrid odor and very fluid. It contains a considerable amount of water and will drip back down the chimney. Gradually the water will evaporate, leaving the solid residues of acetic and pyroligneous acids. This substance will be thick, sticky and very much like tar.

With age the residue is transformed by the heat in the chimney to a hard, porous, shiny material or to a flaky dust. The form the creosote takes will depend on the temperature at which it condenses. Regardless of its form,

creosote may ignite at any time—some day when you have a roaring fire.

Even if the stove is operated properly, there will always be some creosote formation.

The ideal heating appliance should leave no residue in the pipes or chimney and emit nothing visible from the stack except heat ripples. But wood stoves aren't the "ideal" heating appliance because wood isn't the ideal fuel. All wood possesses some moisture, and moisture means creosote.

In addition to creosote, soot deposits will be found. The soot is a soft, black powdery substance which originates as small carbon particles in the flames, and can be brushed off.

The minor annoyance of creosote is that as it forms it begins to restrict the draft, increase the possibility of smoky fires, and decrease heat transfer through the pipes or masonry. A layer of creosote three millimeters thick is a better insulator than asbestos and can cause a 10-15 percent drop in efficiency. Therefore to clean the chimney regularly increases immeasurably the efficiency of your unit.

The greater concern, however, is the flammability of creosote. A simple experiment can be conducted by dropping a piece of creosote into a stove or fireplace. (If you haven't produced any of your own, a chimney sweep will have plenty.) Creosote doesn't burn like wood which gradually catches fire. The ignition temperature of creosote is relatively high, and therefore it will catch only with an excessively hot fire. As it heats, the substance expands, filling with air. Then expanding and smoking excessively, it suddenly, with a "whoosh," catches fire.

You'll have no trouble detecting a chimney fire—it will sound like a train roaring through your living room. Thereafter the pipes will begin to vibrate violently as more air is sucked into the stove to feed the fire. If the pipes are well secured and the chimney is lined and in good repair, your house should survive, though flames shooting up the chimney will provide a spectacular scare. If the chimney is in poor repair, there is a good possibility that the fire will burn out the lining, destroy the chimney and move through the house.

A creosote fire can become so intense (stack temperatures may rise to 2000°F.–3000°F.) that the heat will dislodge the mortar between the bricks. Pieces of mortar may fall into the flue, only to be caught in the tremendous up-draft of the fire and shoot out of the chimney onto the roof. This will endanger your roof, unless you have a spark arrester. In the meantime soot and creosote are likely to slide down the walls of the flue and drop into the fireplace. The heat will cause masonry and metal parts to expand and crack, thus allowing the flames to pass out of the flue to the combustibles of the house.

An unlined chimney increases the hazard. The acidity of creosote will corrode many materials including steel and mortar but not flue liners and stainless steel. Mortar deterioration from creosote build-up will allow the fire easy passage to combustibles. Two appliances hooked to the same flue create a dangerous situation, since, should a chimney fire occur, you are less able to cut off all oxygen to the fire.

The minute you think you have a chimney fire, call the fire department. Close the dampers on the stove. If the stove is airtight, this will help. Should the stove fire continue to burn, throw baking soda or rock salt (in quantity) on it. The chemical will travel up the chimney and often extinguish the flame. If you have time, move the furniture away from the stove for further safety and to give the firemen more room. Above all, **never** try to put out the fire with water. It will crack the cast iron and vastly increase the danger. It also will crack the flue liners which when heated so much are very brittle.

For a fire in an open fireplace, throw rock salt or baking soda on the flames and block off the opening with a metal cover, wet rug, or wet blanket (this may be dangerous, so you'll have to use your own judgment as to whether blocking the opening can be done safely).

Checking Your Stack For Creosote

When you have a fire going, go outside and watch what comes out the stack. Dense smoke means a smoldering fire and creosote accumulation.

Rap the smokepipe. If it makes a dull thud instead of a ping, it is gathering creosote.

Frequent checks of your pipes can't be stressed enough. For vertical pipe, take off the elbow or the first section of pipe and shine a flashlight up; in a fireplace, open the damper and examine the brick and flue tile; for installations vented out a wall or window, the tee cap on factory-built insulated pipe can be removed and either a flashlight or mirror used to check the build-up. Look for black deposits.

Check elbows and tee connectors often. Creosote is most likely to collect wherever the gases are slowed down the most.

Creosote can develop anywhere in the system. If you have no creosote in the first section of pipe, you may in the second, etc. So examine the whole installation.

Cleaning Your Flue

If you know your chimney is developing creosote deposits, the stack should be cleaned **immediately.** Professional sweeps are better prepared for mid-winter stove cleaning than the average homeowner, although you can duplicate their service if you have the right equipment. Cleaning a chimney from the roof in winter is dangerous; snow on the roof makes the footing precarious and wet slate roofs are lethal. Professional sweeps will do their work from inside with wire brushes and four-foot metal extension handles. It may be worth it for a group of woodburners to share the expense of purchasing chimney-sweeping equipment. You'll save the $35 or more which a sweep will charge each time he cleans your chimney.

Factory-built insulated pipe should be cleaned in place. Disconnect the pipe from the stove. Tape a garbage bag around the pipe opening to catch the creosote, but leave a sufficient opening in which to maneuver the brush.

The brush should be made of strong stiff wire bristles and be sized for the diameter of your pipe. Push the brush up the pipe by adding extension handles until the brush hits the chimney cap. The brush should go up and down the pipe at least four or five times to clear the pipe of creosote. If you can't tell

where the brush is in the pipe, have a second person go to the attic. He should be able to hear the brush moving in the stack.

Installations which are vented through a wall or window will have to be cleaned from outdoors. Remove the drip cleanout at the base of the starter tee. The vertical section of pipe can be cleaned from there.

The smokepipe leading from inside to the insulated chimney will have to be dismantled and should be cleaned outdoors. Mark the stovepipe in some way (tiny scratches won't impair its beauty or efficiency) so that you can reassemble it. Then take it apart in sections and carefully carry it outside. A flue brush can be used to clean it, or simply use any long-handled stiff brush that henceforth can be reserved for this task alone. Clean the pipe, inspecting it carefully as you do. Now is the time to replace it if it's showing signs of old age.

The cap will need to be cleaned but this is best left until summer when getting to the roof is a simpler task. A rotating cap will need to be oiled.

Chimneys which need only a yearly cleaning should be done in early summer. Buy a stiff bristled brush to which two pieces of rope, each the length of the stack, are attached. With a person at either end of the pipe, pull the brush back and forth through the pipe. Be prepared with a garbage bag to catch the loosened creosote.

Soot will also gather in the firebox. The walls and baffles should be cleaned with a stiff wire brush.

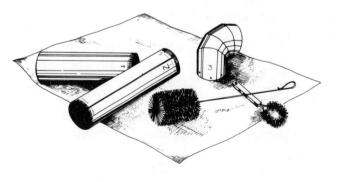

AVOID CHIMNEY FIRES

Chimney fires can be avoided by deliberately setting them when the creosote build-up is small. Once a day with the draft and/or damper wide open, burn a hot fire, preferably in the morning when someone is at home. The intensity of the flame will burn off whatever creosote formed during the night. Calcium chloride (rock salt) is sometimes effective if applied to a vigorous fire. Use two to three cups per application. It should remove the accumulated soot. You can tell when you are burning off the creosote. There will be a whooshing sound as the particles fall into the fire.

After you have burned three cords, clean the chimney. Or clean it every year if you burn less wood than that.

For further protection against creosote build-up, use only well-seasoned wood; include as few 90° angles in the stovepipe as possible and use the shortest possible length of smokepipe; build small, hot fires in the fall and spring; never close the draft completely. Remember that creosote forms when there is insufficient air to the fire; poor draft, cold flues; green or wet wood; too many elbows; unnecessarily long runs of smokepipe; or when the stove is dampened for long periods of time.

Your chances of igniting a chimney fire are even greater if you use the stove for burning trash, newspapers, newspaper logs, Christmas trees, etc. or on sub-zero nights when the stove is pushed beyond its ability.

Fireplaces produce the least creosote; modern wood stoves produce the most, particularly the thermostatically-controlled stoves. The thermostats are activated by the temperature in the firebox, not by the temperature in the stack. A brisk fire will close the damper although the stack may still be cold. Creosote will form rapidly. Exterior chimneys have a similar problem. It may take a half-hour to heat up the masonry. Factory-built stacks are less of a problem because they are insulated. However, all systems develop creosote. You must be continually on the alert.

Fire Extinguishers

You should have a fire extinguisher rated for wood and paper fires. It should be easily accessible.

Smoke Detectors

Every wood-heated home should have at least one smoke detector. There are two kinds on the market, both selling for around $20. They are unobtrusive and easily installed. The ionization type of smoke detector uses a radioactive source to produce electrically charged ions which in turn produce an electric current. When smoke particles enter the smoke detector, they attach themselves to the ions. This impedes the flow of the electric current and the change sets off the alarm. Ionization detectors do not need an electric outlet. As the batteries wear out, they will sound a warning "hiccough." For a considerable period thereafter the smoke detector will be functional, but the batteries should be changed as soon as possible.

Photoelectric detectors employ a light source. When the light beam is scattered by smoke particles, the alarm is set off. For these detectors, an electric outlet is necessary.

Photoelectric detectors will not operate when the power fails because they depend on household current. The need for an electric outlet will limit the number of places a photoelectric detector can be installed. The plugs are made with a cord lock so that they can't be accidentally knocked loose or pulled out by a child.

Photoelectric detectors are more sensitive to smoke from smoldering fires, but slow to detect flaming. Ionization devices have the reverse sensitivity.

116

Detectors have their own little annoyances; a smoky fireplace, a burned hamburger, etc., may trigger the device, but this is a small price.

Smoke detectors should be placed outside the bedroom area or, if it is a two-story house, near the stairs leading to the sleeping quarters. You also should plan escape routes so that, once alerted to the presence of a fire, everyone will know exactly where to go.

STOVE CLEANING AND CARE

In order to keep your stove looking attractive, it should be cleaned regularly. Stove tops rubbed with a wad of waxed paper or with a rag and a bit of fat will look shiny. Give the stove a coat of stove blacking every year. Stove polish comes in liquid or a paste and is easy (though somewhat messy) to apply. Wherever there is scroll work, apply the polish with a toothbrush.

The fireplace facing will discolor, particularly if the brickwork has been painted white. The discoloration can be removed with soap and water. If that doesn't work, try vinegar and water. And if that doesn't help, try muriatic acid (though it may change the color of the stone). Use one part muriatic acid to ten parts of water. Wear rubber gloves. Add the acid to the water, and scrub the bricks with a rag. Rinse immediately in clear water. Avoid spilling the acid.

A yearly inspection should be made of your installation. Sweep the chimney and stove. Check the ash pit. Ashes which fall through the ash dump should be removed. Check the chimney from the roof to be sure that the mortar hasn't deteriorated, and that the flashing is still in place.

Cookstove Cleaning
Periodically apply coatings of grease or oil to prevent a cookstove from rusting. If the stove will be idle a few days, it should be coated to prevent the cast iron from rusting. Before using the stove, remove the grease with a cloth. Once a week the stove should be thoroughly cleaned. Be sure no carbon forms around the oven door opening. It will allow heat to escape and cause uneven heat distribution. Stoves with porcelain enamel, which is essentially glass fused to a metal surface, can be easily damaged. Never wipe the hot enamel with a cold cloth because it may cause crazing or hair lining. The metal and enamel do not contract at the same temperature. Watch out for spilling acids (fruit juices, vegetables), strong soaps, sour milk etc. on the enamel. The stove should be treated with care. Clean with soap and water, or baking soda and water.

Insurance

So far most homeowners' insurance policies still cover homes heated with wood. However, the insurance companies are concerned. Some are sending their policyholders copies of the NFPA publication, "Suggested Procedure for Installation of Wood Burning Stoves" and offering a premium credit for people with smoke and heat detectors. They may soon send questionnaires to discover those who use wood heat. This could lead to a rise in insurance rates or to a close review of your installation. To be safe, check with your insurance company to find out what its current policy is. Soon these companies will require that all installations meet minimum safety standards.

Beyond the Wood Stove

Wood heating has grown in popularity in recent years, and now new techniques and equipment are being devised to make wood heat more efficient and less work for the homeowner.

Wood furnaces, common in many homes until displaced by coal and oil furnaces, are back on the market. Combination units, using wood and another fuel, are popular. The outlook is for both of these to be improved, as manufacturers are spurred by growing sales opportunities.

Research is continuing, too, in methods of storing heat from wood, and in heating the family water supply, with equipment for doing both of these already on the market.

Ahead for us are easier methods for burning wood. Wood chips and chopped up wood waste may soon be available for the homeowner as they now are for larger commercial installations, and with them will come the equipment to automatically feed the fuel into the furnace.

Let's look at some of these methods, and take a look, too, at what may lie ahead if there's an even greater swing toward heating with wood.

FURNACES

Probably sometime in late March while you're still splitting wood to get through the winter, you'll begin dreaming of easier, cheaper methods to keep warm—a beach-side residence in Florida, perhaps, or the good old days of fuel oil at eleven or so cents a gallon, or a wood furnace.

A wood furnace. Is that for you?

Let's summarize quickly the **advantages** and disadvantages of this furnace when compared with a wood stove or another central heating system.

1. Your house will be cleaner than with a wood stove. There'll be no more tracking of sawdust, snow, and dirt through the house; no ashes being spilled on their way out. The house will be warmer, too, with less heat escaping due to those many trips into the house with armfuls of wood.

2. You can have heat in all the rooms of your home, not warmth in one room, gradually dwindling as you move from that room.

3. Wood can be burned in longer, fatter chunks, as large in diameter as the ample door of the furnace, as long as the large firebox. This means less sawing and less splitting as you cut your wood. It also means less time spent in keeping the fire going.

4. If yours is a combination furnace, you get the money-saving qualities of wood heat, plus the back-up of gas or oil, should you run out of wood, or wish to leave your home for more than overnight.

5. You won't be faced with the seasonal tasks of setting up and tearing down the wood stove installation in the fall and spring.

6. Furnaces tend to be safer than stoves. Generally they're installed by professionals who avoid creating safety problems; they're in the cellar where children don't bump into them and get burned; and flammable materials aren't placed too close to them.

7. In some situations, the operation of stoves on the first floor of a home means a much cooler cellar, and the chance for frozen pipes. A furnace in the cellar usually will eliminate this problem.

8. If you have an inexpensive wood supply, there's the advantage of saving money (as with a wood stove) coupled with the advantages of the central heating system.

And the **disadvantages:**

1. The units are more expensive than conventional furnaces. The wood furnace will cost $1100 or more, while the combination furnace prices will start at about double that amount.

2. You'll probably burn more wood than with a stove. You'll probably heat more of your home, with that heat available in the central system. Too, some of those BTU's will stay down cellar, keeping the pipes from freezing, but perhaps also heating crawlspaces, the garage or the outdoors.

3. You will be buying a unit at a time when the industry is striving for technological advancement.

4. Your work will be less, but you still will have to get a supply of wood (and if you're ambitious this means felling trees, cutting and splitting and drying the wood, moving it from the woods and piling it, and moving it into the home).

5. The wood furnace demands more attention than the occasional glance at the thermostat called for by the oil furnace. Wood must be fed into it at least twice daily; ashes must be removed periodically. The combination furnace with its thermostat operating the wood-furnace controls as well as the on-off switch of the alternate system does much to eliminate the periodic nursing many wood stoves demand.

Summing up: We've talked with many wood furnace and combination furnace owners. They are the type who strive for self-sufficiency. They have vegetable gardens, do their own home repairs, are concerned about environmental and energy problems, cut and haul their own firewood. They like their furnaces.

A note of caution: Before investing in any equipment, study your geographic location, the construction of your house, and your own needs. Some houses, particularly newly constructed, well-insulated homes, may not need central heating. In such cases, a stove or two may be more efficient. Homes with excessive heat loss due to age or minimal insulation will always be costly to heat, but the money would be better spent in weatherstripping and insulation than in a change in heating systems.

An unobstructed southerly exposure gives the homeowner the option of active solar systems, or passive systems such as a solar greenhouse addition with water barrels or a masonry wall which will absorb the heat during the day, then radiate it at night. (The sun is the biggest and brightest hope of the future, but the technology is further outside the reach of the average homeowner than that of wood.) Review all your options (and your pocketbook) before increasing your investment.

Furnaces are a must if you want central heat for the entire house. Some furnaces burn only wood; others are for wood, oil, coal, or gas in combination. If you have forced hot air heat, you will want a wood-burning warm air furnace; if you have hot water heat, you will want a wood-burning boiler. The pipes or ducts of your present system can usually be fitted to accommodate a wood-burning appliance. Sometimes the blower of your hot air furnace can be adapted to work with the wood-burning furnace.

It's best to talk to someone knowledgeable in the heating business about your specific furnace before you make any decisions.

So far none of the multi-fuel furnaces is U.L. approved. Since approval is required in only a few states, most manufacturers are unwilling to spend the money to go through the approval process. This means the wood-burner must rely on the recommendations of friends or a trusted dealer.

Wood-stove owners have become smarter and more discriminating in their choice of stoves through experience. The same will be true of furnace owners.

Get answers to these questions before buying a furnace:

1. If you are buying a wood-burning boiler, is the boiler made of rugged material and does it have water cut-offs and pressure relief valves?

2. Is a multi-fuel boiler legal in your area?

3. What length log does the furnace accept? Two feet is ideal; some furnaces hold logs of well over three feet, which means less time spent cutting, but less efficiency in burning.

4. Can ashes be removed while the fire is burning? It is inconvenient if the fire must be out before this can be done.

5. If it is a hot-air unit, does it have a humidifier? Hot air heat is drier than steam heat or hot water heat. This is not desirable, since the dry air dries out your furniture as well as your skin and nasal passages. Too, the human body wants higher temperatures if the air is drier.

6. Does the quoted price include all the items required for installation, such as blowers, thermostats, and pressure relief valves?

7. Finally, is there a qualified installer available?

Installation of an add-on unit to your present furnace may mean a new chimney, also, since fumes from two different fuels should be vented separately. This could add $700-$1,000 to your costs.

1. Multi-fuel systems

Multi-fuel systems operate like conventional furnaces except that the heating device can burn wood, coal, gas, or oil separately or in certain combinations. They all are built with blowers, heat exchangers, automatic dampers, and thermostat controls plus a conventional gas/oil burner. They have the convenience of providing heat whenever it is needed whether or not you forget to stoke the fire. Like the present systems, they give the homeowner the freedom of leaving on vacation without facing the horror of frozen pipes. Multi-fuel units also can function on wood alone should the day come when fossil fuels are gone or prohibitively expensive.

The multiple fuels are burned in one firebox, in separate fireboxes, or in separate fireboxes with some kind of mixing chamber. Two fuels burning in a single firebox is not as simple as it might sound because each fuel must be considered. Gas and oil are fired from a pressure nozzle into a firebox which must be sized for optimum efficiency. Both gas and oil must be kept free of fly ash and soot, and both of these are produced in abundance by wood fuel. Coal demands a particularly durable firebox because of the intensity of its heat.

In some units two thermostats will be needed. One is set for the wood burner, the second for the gas or oil. The higher thermostatic reading is for the wood burner. When the wood fire can no longer maintain that level, the temperature drops until it reaches the lower setting for oil/gas. The oil/gas burner will then kick on.

Check the instructions for what to do in the event of a power failure. In some cases the wood fire must be extinguished immediately or the heat exchanger removed if you wish to use the stove for emergency heating.

The wood firebox should have three to ten times the heat capabilities of a wood stove and should require stoking no more than twice a day. This will reduce your work load appreciably as well as insuring that your home is warm even if you are away or busy.

For multi-fuel burners, consider their smoothness of operation, noise level, ease of adjustment, amount of draft, combustion efficiency, and availability of parts. Efficiency in a furnace is important. A furnace should emit little if any smoke and extract the maximum amount of heat possible.

2. Add-On Units

"Add-on" units are wood burners incorporated into your existing system. They are larger-than-normal wood-burning stoves which can be hooked up to the ducts of your present oil/gas furnace. They sell for between $300 and $800; have a low aesthetic profile; and like furnaces lack the atmosphere and comfort of a wood stove.

The blower in the add-on unit goes on only if there is a wood fire. It moves the heated air from the woodburning unit into the plenum of the forced-air furnace where the hot air is then forced through the rooms by the furnace blower. The blowers are thermostatically controlled. Should there be a power failure, the heat from the wood furnace will rise through the house by gravity.

Lumberjack—*Here's an add-on wood-burning furnace with a blower to pump hot air into an existing hot-air system. Has a plate steel firebox lined with firebrick.*

Installation

The add-on furnace must be vented into a Class "A" all-fuel chimney. Factory-built stacks are expensive but they are safe. The connection from the wood furnace to the chimney should be made with 24 gauge or heavier stovepipe with the crimped end of the pipe facing towards the stove so that should the pipe develop creosote, it will run back into the wood furnace. A damper may be required. The length of pipe to the chimney should include as few elbows as possible (two at the most), and every foot of horizontal pipe should have a vertical rise of at least a quarter-inch. See page 49 for NFPA instructions on safety clearances. Check with your local building codes, building inspector, or fire marshal for further safety instructions.

Add-on furnaces can be installed by the homeowner. Once delivered, check to be sure no damage has occurred in transport. Call your dealer immediately if parts are missing or need to be replaced.

All furnaces operate differently. Read the instructions carefully before you begin assembly. Improper installations are the greatest cause of fires. Watch particularly for proper clearance distances to the ceiling joists.

Wood boilers are best left to a qualified home heating specialist who has had some experience with woodburning equipment.

Sizing a Furnace

Wood furnaces as well as wood stoves should be sized according to your needs. If a stove or furnace is sized too small, you will be tempted to run it beyond its capacity on one of those bitter cold nights. This will create an immediate fire hazard. Oversizing is just as undesirable. The furnace will operate at a low, less efficient level. When the furnace is operated at this level, the stack temperature falls, and conditions are created for fast collection of creosote. Here's a place where the professional advice of a heating engineer can be worth the cost.

Maintenance

All furnaces should have instructions for care and maintenance. You will probably have to clean the furnace once a month, and at the end of the season. Boilers can be damaged from potash corrosion. Creosote is acidic and will corrode pipes. How often you should clean the furnace will depend on the wood you burn and the way you operate the furnace. For the first year monitor the furnace carefully until you know where and how fast your unit collects creosote. In the spring, you also may wish to paint the inside of the firebox with SAE 10 through 50 motor oil.

Riteway

123

This will prevent moisture from the chimney and other condensates from rusting out the chamber.

At current prices furnaces are too expensive an investment for a small home or cabin. If you want a total heating system or are building a new home, the extra expense is worth it.

The following table will give you some idea of the relative initial and operating costs for various home heating systems. The information in this table was provided by the State of Maine Office of Energy Resources.

Annual Costs of Home Heating Systems					
	Furnace Initial Cost	Annual Cost	Fuel Efficiency	Annual Cost	System Annual Cost
Oil (New Installation)	$ 800	$110	0.50	$475	$585
Gas (New)	650	90	0.60	350	440
Electric (New)	400	55	1.00	720	775
Wood Stove (New)	800	110	0.45	435	545
Wood Furnace (New)	1100	150	0.60	325	475
Wood-Chip Furnace	2500	340	0.60	230	560
Oil (Existing)	0	0	0.50	475	475
Wood Furnace (Add-on)	300	40	0.60	325	365

FOR DO-IT-YOURSELFERS

During World War II the Connecticut Agricultural Experiment Station published a bulletin entitled "A Wood Burning Conversion Unit for Household Furnaces."[1] In the pamphlet the authors explore the possibility of adapting oil-burning equipment so that wood or coal could be burned instead. Bill White of the Fire Builders recently experimented further with the Connecticut design. In his booklet entitled "Convert Your Oil Furnace to Wood," White tells how for approximately $230 various heating units can be converted to combination furnaces.[2] He discusses the conversion of five systems: gravity air, gravity water, steam, forced hot air, and pumped hot water.

Although the designs differ slightly, all involve building a brick-lined firebox to the side of the existing unit, relocating the original burner so that the wood gases can pass to a chamber into which the oil/gas burner

[1] "A Wood Burning Conversion Unit for Household Furnaces," Henry Hicock, A. Richard Olson, and Lauren E. Seeley, Sept. 1942, Connecticut Agricultural Experiment Station Bulletin #463.
[2] "Convert Your Oil Furnace to Wood." For a copy write Bill White, The FireBuilders, 352 Stetson Road, Brooklyn, CT 06234. Copies cost $3.00.

fires, with hot gases from both systems then passing into the original firebox. Not all furnaces are adaptable to this system; gravity air, gravity water and steam are the easiest.

UTILIZING EXCESS HEAT

Burning wood in stoves or furnaces does not provide the best combustion efficiency. This is particularly true in furnaces with small combustion chambers because the door is frequently opened to stoke the fire. This creates an irregular draft pattern. Stoking a large furnace with sizeable logs makes it difficult to maintain uniform combustion. Large spaces in the fuel bed reduce the efficiency. These inherent difficulties are always compounded by the wishes of the homeowner who may let the fire go way down during the day, then stoke it up at night. To run a wood-burning appliance consistently at maximum efficiency is almost impossible.

It is also difficult to maintain a steady heat. To control heat output, the wood burner has two choices. He can control combustion by controlling the amount of fuel. This means frequently reloading the stove or furnace with small sticks and with the draft left wide open to maintain high combustion temperatures. The other alternative is to control the rate of burn by controlling the air intake to the fire. Some stoves and furnaces will do this automatically; others require constant readjustment of the damper. Both approaches will create creosote.

Stoves and furnaces to be efficient burners should maintain a constant firebox temperature of at least 3000°F. At this temperature you can be sure all the flue gases are being burned. However, this may make the living quarters uncomfortably hot. In order to have only the amount of heat needed and the highest combustion efficiency possible, some kind of heat storage is necessary for the excess heat. Cast iron, soapstone, firebrick or large masonry walls behind the stove will all retain heat, but heat storage can

be made even more extensive by using either rocks (gravel) or water as a storage medium. When heat is needed, it is carried to the rooms. The excess heat is ducted or piped into storage. This allows the stove or furnace to be operated at high efficiencies with no pollution or creosote build-up and little heat loss up the stack. Gone is the burden of regulating the fire by adjusting the draft.

Rock Storage

The Maine Audubon Society Headquarters in Falmouth, Maine, is a good example of rock-storage technology. Professor R.C. Hill, who developed the system, believes that wood should be burned as in a kiln—plenty of dry wood and plenty of air. If temperatures are in any way lowered in the firebox as happens when the draft is partially closed, the chances of complete combustion are severely lessened. To be sure the volatiles burn completely, the Audubon furnace was designed and tested for firebox temperatures of 10,000°F. At this temperature there are no air pollution problems, complete combustion is certain to occur, and water and a little carbon dioxide are the only by-products.

The building is designed so that there is no need to regulate the heat output of the furnace. Excess heat is ducted to a rock storage area of 105 tons of crushed granite. The stones are roughly one inch in diameter and are piled three feet high on a ten- by seventy-foot grate.

The rock storage also stores heat from the air-type, flat plate solar collectors mounted on the roof. During the night when the building needs heat, a forced air system blows the air from the rock storage throughout the building.

For northern climates November, December and January are impossible months to depend on solar collectors, yet on a yearly basis, solar heat can provide about 40 percent of the domestic heat needs. Wood makes a perfect companion fuel to fill in the gaps. By interfacing the two systems, the Maine Audubon building has been able to reduce its heating costs from $1902 to $435 a year.

Wood-Fired Hot Water

Water is another heat storage medium. Domestic hot water can be heated by solar collectors or by wood stoves and furnaces. More and more stoves and furnaces are providing the option of hot water coils.

Water flows by gravity from the bottom of the existing hot water tank to the stove or furnace, enters the heating coils and is heated by the hot gases rising through either the firebox or the stovepipe, depending where the coils are located. The heated water then flows to the top of the storage tank. The principle is simple. The rising column of hot water sucks cold water from the bottom of the tank into the heating coil. To facilitate this process, resistance must be minimal. Curves and bends may encourage the collection of air bubbles in the system.

Gas- or oil-fired hot water systems turn themselves off once the water has reached the thermostatic setting. But with wood, as long as there is a fire in the stove, the water will continue to heat. With an extremely hot fire, the pressure will build in the pipes and may cause an explosion unless there are sufficient pressure and temperature controls.

Copper tubing should be used because it will not rust. The ¾-inch tubing is connected to the bottom of the storage tank with a drain valve located somewhere near the tank. At the appropriate point there is a union between the tubing and the copper coil.

Location of the Coils
The coils theoretically can be located almost anywhere in the heating unit. They can curve around the inside or outside of the stove; enter a water jacket (as on old cookstoves); wrap around the outside of the smokepipe; pass into and out of the smokepipe; or pass into the smokepipe and form a serpentine coil before exiting. Hot water systems can even be built into fireplace chimneys. The best location depends to some extent on the kind of stove you have.

There will be the most heat transfer inside the firebox, and more heat transfer inside the smokepipe than outside. The more inefficient your stove (i.e. the more heat lost up the stack), the better able you will be to heat your domestic water. Stovepipe temperatures are too low in airtight stoves for locating hot water coils in the pipe. Therefore they should be located inside the firebox, but this means marring the stove by cutting holes for the pipes. A skilled metal worker should do this for you.

Blazing Showers provides a booklet[1] on how to install a water coil in the first section of smokepipe. If you decide to mount it there, check frequently. Because the surface of the inlet pipe will be cool, creosote will accumulate quickly and begin cutting down on the heat transfer.

To avoid creosote deposits, the coil can be mounted inside the combustion chamber if you are willing to cut two holes in your stove.

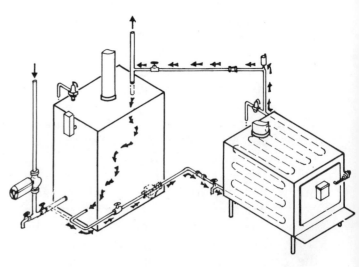

---

[1] "Blazing Showers: Hot Water From Your Wood Stove," 1975. Available for $2.50 from Blazing Showers, P.O. Box 327, Point Arena, California 95468.

Other options include an exterior coil (to avoid both the above problems), mounted on the side of the stove in a box filled with stones or water. This way the pipe is never in contact with stove gases nor must the stove be altered. Tanks of either rock or water in which the pipe is mounted provide a heat storage medium and give you easier access to the pipes should anything go wrong.

There should be a pressure temperature relief valve (usually 150 pounds) located in the run of copper tubing before it re-enters the tank, as well as a pressure temperature relief valve on the tank itself. There should be **no** valves or restrictions between the stove and the relief valve.

Coils must be bent or fabricated and joined either silver soldered or with threaded fittings. Do not use low temperature solder in any joints adjacent to the heat source. You'd best leave the connections to a licensed plumber.

Location of the Tank

The best location for the storage tank is as close to the stove or furnace as possible and at the same level or above the stove or furnace. The tank should be within twenty-five feet to insure that with gravity flow, the water does not cool too much en route to storage. The coils also must not exceed the height of the tank. The water travels through the coils on the principle that hot water rises. If the pipe comes directly into the top of your storage tank, air bubbles may become trapped in the system and impair the convection-driven circulation. With an electric water circulating pump, there is no limit on the distance or height between the tank and the stove.

In one to two hours you should be able to heat ten to twenty gallons of water, but if your tank is set at 110°F. and you have a consistently hot fire, the water may overheat and "pop" the pressure temperature relief valve. This will indicate that you need a larger or second tank.

The following stoves have hot water hookups: All Nighter, Sunshine, DownDrafter, and Hydrostove.

THE BIG PICTURE: INDUSTRIAL INSTALLATIONS

Large-scale wastefulness in the lumber industry; wholesale neglect of our forests; and the fear, particularly in the northern parts of the United States, that it will feel the brunt of the next energy crisis, have led to a great deal of exciting thinking and experimentation with other fuels and other methods of burning. We are now looking not only to fuels the land can grow but also to water-grown fuels, and municipal wastes as possibilities to fill in the energy gap until nuclear, solar, perhaps even coal are safely established as the energy sources of the future.

The federal, state and municipal governments are involved, as well as private individuals, all who in their own way hope to solve the energy dilemma. They are struggling with better forms into which wood can be broken down and more efficient types of burners.

DIFFERENT FORMS OF WOOD

For the homeowner with his own woodlot and a 100,000 BTU or furnace-sized stove, wood as he cuts it is the most convenient, most economical fuel, but wood in this form means controlling the fuel load and draft. Besides this, it is inefficient, provides uneven heat, and leaves the ever-present danger of chimney fires.

For larger installations (apartment buildings, industrial or municipal buildings), use of cut wood is prohibitively time-consuming; an automatic feed system is essential, but for this the wood must be reduced to small, relatively uniform sizes. The smallest size is sawdust, the byproduct of the saw.

There are not many **sawdust** or **sander dust burners** in use because explosions can occur under certain conditions. The dust is blown into the firebox where the density of the dust is measured by an electric eye. If too much air is present, it is possible for all the particles to combust at once. Therefore either the sawdust has to be burned at relatively low oxygen levels or it must be diluted with coarser material such as shavings.

Hogged fuel is a byproduct of the lumber industry. It is much larger, coarser, bulkier wood (from the bark residue and slabs). This is put into a machine which has rotating knives. The knives cut the residue into pieces of approximately ½-1 inch in diameter. Since the machine is called a "hog," the fuel it produces is called "hogged" fuel. The machine is placed in front of and connected to a furnace.

Chips are all kinds of wood (the bark, any waste, branches and/or the bole of the tree) which are reduced to a two-inch uniform product. Chips are usually produced at the logging site. Their uniform size means they can be loaded and transported and conveyed in automatic feed systems much more easily than other forms of wood. Since chips have a large surface area, they dry more quickly and ignite easily, and the rate of burn can be controlled by the rate at which the fuel is fed into the burner. In addition they are cheaper than wood cut for burning.

The interest in utilizing forest waste and the positive results from burning chips may soon revolutionize logging operations. Wood will still be felled with a **chain saw** or the more modern feller-buncher. The **feller-buncher** utilizes a hydraulic system to grasp the standing tree while severing it near ground level with mechanical shears. The tree is then lifted and held by an **accumulator** which gathers, then dumps the cut trees in a bunch.

A **grapple skidder** has a claw which can be operated to pick up or drop a bunch of trees. By moving trees in bunches through the forest, less damage is done to the forest floor, and lifting the trees (grapple skidder) does less damage than cable skidders.

The skidders take the trees to a **yard** where they are sorted, graded, piled, cut, and loaded. Whatever the lumberyards don't use is cut off and fed into the chippers which are on location.

The **chippers** are capable of "digesting" whole trees. An arm with a claw feeds one of the trees into a motorized roller system which moves the tree towards a high-speed set of rotating knives which produce chips of matchbook size. The chips can then be blown directly into a trailer van. A van of forty-five feet can be filled in less than one-half hour. Chippers can handle trees up to twenty-two inches in diameter. A seventy-foot tree is chipped in forty seconds. The chips are then delivered to the customer. With an increase in demand, many of the present problems will be overcome.

Soon chips will be going to a central distribution point where they will be removed and sorted so as to remove the larger chips. They will then be dried and stored for delivery. Deliveries will be periodic, much the way the fuel companies deliver oil today. Instead of an oil tank or coal bin, customers will have a bin or silo into which the chips will be blown. Or perhaps the chips will be delivered in large boxes which, like the tanks for natural gas, will be removed when empty. Chips presently cost approximately $14 per dry ton delivered.

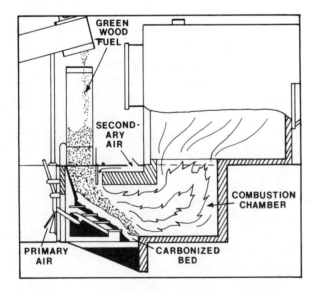

GREEN WOOD FUEL

SECONDARY AIR

COMBUSTION CHAMBER

PRIMARY AIR

CARBONIZED BED

The following table gives some idea of the savings possible from burning wood chips.

Table I

Annual Savings in Fuel Costs Using Wood Chips for a House that Burns 1500 Gallons of Oil Per Year

Wood cost $/ton	Cost/year to heat house	Cost/year to heat with oil	20¢/ gal	30¢/ gal	40¢/ gal	50¢/ gal	60¢/ gal
			300	450	600	750	900
20	250		50	200	350	500	650
30	375		−75	75	225	375	525
40	500		−200	−50	100	250	400

* E. R. Huff, "Wood Chip Furnace: Progress Report," Dec. 1974, Agricultural Engineering Department, University of Maine, Orono, Maine.

The University of Maine has done extensive experiments with chip-burning furnaces. Its present furnace has a storage bin for chips which is located outside. The chips are fed into the furnace via a screw auger. When the thermostat calls for heat, the chips begin to move. Meanwhile the stack blower and gas igniter turn on. When the firebox is hot enough, the igniter turns off and the furnace operates as long as necessary. The chip feed turns off when the thermostat is satisfied.

The system is still being perfected. The augers have caused trouble when the chips are uneven in size. Tracks and chain belts have been tried. The bin which feeds the auger has a V-bottom. Small pieces will jam in the hopper. Other problems include the "fines" (sand, dust, small stones) which don't get sifted out before they enter the firebox. They substantially increase the accumulation of ashes. The chips may have to pass over a perforated plate or some other means to extract the fines before the chips enter the firebox.

Chips will freeze and if they are not pro-tected from the rain, their moisture content will increase. Spontaneous combustion also can occur in the pile which means the chips must be turned periodically. All these problems plus the vast storage area they require has led to burning the chips green. All pre-drying goes on in the chip burner itself.

Methods of Burning

Gasifiers operate by first burning the fuel without sufficient oxygen. The volatile gases which result are blown through a nozzle where secondary air is added. The oxygen produces a gas-like flame. The heat going up the stack is used to pre-dry the chips as they move into the burner unit.[1]

Other methods of burning which achieve better efficiencies than can be had with roundwood include **fluidized bed combustion** in which hogged or chipped fuel is burned in suspension. The incoming fuel drops through the hot gases and is progressively dried, distilled, and burned. Sand or other inert particles as well as the fuel are

---

[1] If secondary air isn't introduced into the furnace, charcoal and a combustible gas are left. This gas can be collected at the top of the furnace. It has a low heat content (150-200 BTU/cu. ft. vs. natural gas with 1000 BTU/cu. ft.) but could be pipelined moderate distances and burned in the equipment now using natural gas.

kept in suspension by the upward movement of forced air. Most of the fuel is burned before reaching the bottom. Larger particles fall to the base of the furnace where they maintain the hot radiating surface. No grates are required; less space is used. This method results in more complete combustion and higher heat transfer rates.

Moran Generating Plant

The experimentation at the Moran Electric Generating Plant in Burlington, Vermont, has now proven that electric power generation from wood fuel is practical. In 1977 the Burlington Electric Department, pressured by rising fuel costs and its northerly location at the end of the many fuel lines, decided to experiment with burning wood chips. The 10-megawatt wood chip unit burned a mixture of 75 percent chips (at a cost of $12/dry ton) and 25 percent oil. In two months the plant was producing electricity at 2.1 cents per kilowatt hour (the previous mixture of coal and oil was generating electricity at a cost of 3 cents per kilowatt hour).

The success of this experiment led to a proposal for a 50-megawatt wood-fired plant which would burn only cull wood, and a plant to incinerate solid waste (refuse) to produce steam for the University of Vermont. The heat from both these plants will be used, it is planned, to maintain year-round growth in an aquaculture facility, producing 100,000 pounds per year of rainbow trout, as well as a one-acre greenhouse for lettuce and tomato production. Construction is scheduled to begin in 1982.

The project is based on the co-generation of electricity and heat which is the most efficient use of fuel. Recycling waste heat from electric generation will be an essential component in any system of the future. In addition, the plant's annual consumption of 470,000 tons of wood chips should result in an improvement in the quality of Vermont forests.

There will be other benefits. Vermont will be able to meet part of her future energy demands for electricity; employment will increase; the forests will be improved; and there will be an increased sense of energy self-sufficiency.

But there are problems with chips. They deteriorate rapidly, and if stoked green they have to be dried in the combustion chamber, with a loss in energy. In the meantime, moisture has been transported. It has provided weight and taken space and lowered the BTU content of the chips. This may justify the cost of pre-drying at a central distribution area rather than in the furnace.

FUEL PELLETS

Pellets are made by compressing wood chips into a product ¾ inch in length and of pencil-size diameter. Their BTU content can be twice that of wood chips because much of their moisture content has been pressed out. They burn efficiently, and can be transported, stored, and handled with great ease.

Pellets are presently produced in Brownsville, Oregon. A Vermont plant is planned in the White River Junction area.

For large-scale heating systems, chips will continue to be cheaper than other fuels, but pellets burn better. Once a market has been established, pellets will be more readily available, and with that eventuality will come the real possibility of automatically stoked furnaces for the homeowner.

Caution

Renewed interest in wood or densified wood fuel has led to the following alarming figures which are frequently quoted. Two hundred years ago the United States was 95 percent forest; by 1870 only 42 percent forest; now in the 1970's it's 76 percent forest. If we've denuded the land once, will we do it again?

Much of the new equipment has large rubber tires which damage the forest floor. There has been talk of flotation tires which will do less damage. Horses do the least.

With increased tree cutting will come increased water and stream pollution. Decomposing organic matter raises the water temperatures and this may endanger aquatic life.

Skidding always increases erosion, some of which will be prevented with total tree harvesting. Since the whole tree is skidded out of the woods on its branches, gouging will be lessened. However, the branches and foliage contain 40 percent of the potassium and 85 percent of the nitrogen of the tree. In conventional logging operations the tops were always left behind. In whole tree harvesting, these nutrients will be removed and thereby increase the nutrient loss to the forest by two to three times. How will this be replaced?

Theoretically the forest can be refertilized after every logging operation with ash from urban and industrial waste and from the plants that burn the wood as a source of energy. Who will insure that the refertilization is conscientiously carried out?

Proponents of wood as a fuel quite rightly point out that wood has a low sulphur content; its ash is reusable; burning wood will not interfere with the carbon dioxide balance of the earth or alter the heat balance; no long distance transportation is necessary; the horrors of spills, leaks, and black lung disease are avoided, but many still remain skeptical. "The whole question of complete-tree utilization today stands in much the same position as the automative industry stood 50 years ago; the potential is high, the ramifications are many and complex, and a large number of unknown variables will affect future development."[1]

The cull wood is certainly available; there is no reason why it can't be removed in such a way to preserve the land, the wildlife, and the productivity of the forest, but forest management is essential. Soil erosion, reforestation, methods of harvesting, transporting, chipping and the nutrient flow must be monitored; areas should be chosen which are fairly level and fertile, and the clear cuts should be small enough to permit rapid reseeding.

FUEL FARMING

If there are so many potential pitfalls to utilizing our forests, perhaps we should grow our fuel under ideal conditions. This thinking has led to the concept of plantation crops grown specifically for their fuel value. Such a plan would provide an endlessly renewable, available, and relatively inexpensive replacement for fossil fuels.

To power a 1000 megawatt station, approximately 245 square miles would be needed for a fuel farm. The land with the greatest fuel farm capability is probably in the Southwest (southwestern Arizona or southeastern California). Here the government already owns a fair supply of acreage and the solar insolation is high enough, summer and winter, to provide a long growing season with little danger of frost. The availability of water is the only limitation. To utilize the Southwest would mean a water storage capacity sufficient to provide some 700 million gallons of water per day.

A number of crops have been mentioned; some approach 10,000 BTU/dry pound (2000 BTU's more per pound than wood). Sugarcane, selected sorghums, sunflower, kenaf, and forage grasses; of the trees, eucalyptus, poplar, sycamore, ash, sweet gum, and red alder; and if plantations are to be cultivated on water, single-celled algae, water hyacinth, and giant kelps are all possible.

There are advantages to growing wood rather than other biomass crops on short rotation cycles. Many trees will regenerate

---

[1] "Complete-Tree Utilization: An Analysis of the Literature, Part I: Unmerchantable Top of Bole," J.L. Keays, Feb. 1971. Forest Products Laboratory, Canadian Forestry Service, Department of Fisheries and Forestry, Vancouver, B.C., Information Report VP-X-69, p. 2.

themselves rapidly when cut from the stump. This permits reuse of the established root system. Unlike other biomass crops, trees can be harvested anytime, and can survive adverse weather. The paper and pulp industries are already practicing short-rotation tree farming; other faster growing, hybridized hardwoods may produce even better, faster crops.

Plantations solve some problems; they create others. Plantations of young trees would be more susceptible to wind-throws, and if of a single species, more susceptible to disease or insect infestation. The irrigation, transportation, use of farm chemicals, etc. which plantations would require may be too energy-expensive to be practical.

THE FUTURE

Wood is suited to space and water heating, but the sun is thermodynamically even better suited. And we must not forget the unique properties of wood which we are wasting when we use it for a fuel. Wood is a good building material because it has both high tensile and compression strength. It is easy to work and to process. Sawdust and shavings can be glued together to make wood substitutes (paper, particle board) which eliminate the grain problem. Resins and turpentine are wood derivatives. And even as an energy source wood may be much more valuable in the form of methanol than as heat. Methanol is a liquid fuel derived from either soft or hardwoods which can be used to power internal combustion engines, gas turbines, boilers, fuel cells, etc. It can be added to gas as a "fuel extender." It has a higher octane than gas and does not pollute. Of the fuels, wood is the least valuable:

natural gas	22,000 BTU/pound
oil	20,000-21,000 BTU/pound
ethyl alcohol	12,800 BTU/pound
coal	8300-14,000 BTU/pound
wood	8000-9000 BTU/pound

However, it is also true that there are burdensome piles of wood and waste riddling our environment. Just the lumbering waste in Maine would be enough to meet the state's home heating needs. There is no use for the "cull," rough and rotten trees, or the bark, saplings, dead wood, branches, and trees killed by disease or fire or for the acres of pucker-brush which abound. One-half of the forest growth is unmerchantable. It is this part of the forest ONLY which we should be talking about as an energy resource.

Indiscriminate use of the forests will be disasterous. Federal and State forests are more easily controlled but in states such as Vermont two-thirds of the land is in private hands in parcels of 100 acres or less. In addition, two-thirds of the firewood harvested to date is harvested by the individuals using it. This means there are a lot of weekend woodsmen. The homeowner caught in the energy crunch and having his own woodlot when left to his own devices is likely to cut what is easiest to fell and closest to home. He may be cutting yellow birch, hard maple, and ash which are much more valuable as sawlogs. Careless felling, steam pollution, and general wastefulness may do as much or more damage to the forests than controlled clear cutting.

Licenses may have to be instituted for large-scale wood removal and some kind of tax incentive to make it worth while for logging operators to remove the residue. Minerals must be restored, the land refertilized. (It takes 60-80 years to fully restore nutrients and biomass loss after whole tree harvesting.) If we are to use wood on any sustaining basis, the environment must be protected.

Pollution

Pollution at the burning site is also of increasing concern. Air quality where wood is burned must be measured. Particulate matter and photo-chemical oxidants are emitted from wood-burning units. A further environmental hazard comes from incomplete combustion. Fireplaces, stoves, and furnaces operated with the damper partially or totally closed cause the fire to release chemicals which may be carcinogenic, and increase heart disease or other illnesses.

Home locations in valleys where there is the possibility of atmospheric inversion are even more risky. Local weather warnings might have to be issued to homeowners so that under certain weather conditions they would be forbidden to operate a wood unit or fireplace.

Other ways this can be at least partially controlled is for much stricter testing of stoves so that stoves which burn fuel incompletely are banned from the market. Further education of the public will be necessary. Safety regulations and operating instructions should be mandatory with every stove sold.

Airborne ash is another contaminant. Twenty-five pounds of ash is released in a fireplace with each ton of wood burned. In densely populated areas this soot may become a serious problem.

"Whether or not it is economically or politically expedient [to use wood] is dependent upon alternative sources of power available in the present or near future, upon long-range availability of fossil fuels, upon sources of atomic energy and pollution loads, upon the total need for power in a given location, together with legal restrictions upon the expansion of certain types of power generation because of a number of pollution effects, and upon the marketability of the by-products."[1]

The future of wood as a fuel is uncertain. As a major source of fuel it could be environmentally harmful and impractical, but as an interim solution to fill an "energy gap" it may be a reasonable choice. For areas of the country where wood abounds, it would provide a local industry, employing local people, paying taxes to local governments. Forced to be regionally self-reliant, we may handle our environment with greater care and respect than we have in the past.

[1] "Complete-Tree Utilization, Part IV: Crown and Slash," Forest Products Laboratory, Canadian Forestry Service, Information Report VP-X-77, March 1971, p. 50.

Catalog

SMALL STOVES

Manufacturer	Stove	Dimensions	Door Opening	Firebox Size	Wood Length	Flue Size	Flue Location	Materials	Weight (lbs.)
Atlanta Stove Works, Inc.	Box Heater Model #27	26″ H × 12½″ W × 14½″ L	9″ × 9″	20″ × 9″ × 13″	24″	6″	Top	Cast iron	115 s.w.
Features Cooking Surface									
Atlanta Stove Works, Inc.	Box Heater Model #32	27″ H × 13½″ W × 15½″ L	10″ × 10″	22″ × 11″ × 14″	27″	6″	Top	Cast iron	125 s.w.
Features Cooking Surface									
Atlanta Stove Works, Inc.	Model #2502	35½″ H × 17½″ W × 22″ L	7″ × 9″	22″ × 17″ × 23¼″	20″	6″	Top	Steel with cast iron top, bottom and door	147 s.w.
Features Thermostat									
Bow and Arrow Stove Co.	Chappee 8008	20¼″ H × 21″ W × 12½″ L			16″	5″	Back	Cast iron	141 s.w.
Features Front window; cooking top; side loader; firebrick lined									
Bow and Arrow Stove Co.	Petit Godin #3720	32¼″ H × 16″ W × 21″ L		470 cu. in.	16″-18″	4″	Back	Steel and cast iron	121 s.w.
Features Front window; firebrick lined; burns wood or coal									
Cawley/LeMay Stove Co., Inc.	Model 400	35½″ H × 18″ W × 36″ L	9½″ × 10½″		16″	5″	Back	Cast iron	300
Features Cooking surface; rotating cast iron flue fitting; ash lip; top and side baffles									

Le Petit Godin 3720—*Delightfully designed, this stove has been listed as "highly efficient" by the British Coal Board. Burns wood and coal.*

Cawley/LeMay 400—*Features you'll like: Large cooking surface with two lids, plus raised rounded edges; sculptured sides; sweep shelf in front of door.*

Manufacturer	Stove	Dimensions	Door Opening	Firebox Size	Wood Length	Flue Size	Flue Location	Materials	Weight (lbs.)
Damsite Dynamite Stove Company	Dynamite Box Stove	27″ H × 18″ W × 34″ L		17″ × 25″ × 19″	24″	6″	Top	10 ga. steel	100
	Features Hollow legs to draw cool air from floor level								
Damsite Dynamite Stove Company	Greenwood Dynamite Stove	38″ H × 18″ W × 34″ L		17″ × 25″ × 21″	24″	6″	Back	10 ga. steel	200
	Features Hollow legs to draw cool air from floor level								
Damsite Dynamite Stove Company	Double Dynamite Stove	38″ H × 34½″ W × 26″ L		17″ × 25″ × 19″	24″	6″	Back	10 ga. steel	200
	Features Hollow legs to draw cool air from floor level								
Enterprise Sales	Enterprise Box Stove No. 25	21¾″ H × 15½″ W × 33½″ L	8⅝″ × 9¼″	9¾″ × 33″		6″	Top	Cast iron	135 s.w.
	Features Cooking surface; top swings to one side								
Enterprise Sales	Enterprise Box Stove No. 18	19″ H × 13″ W × 23½″ L	6¾″ × 6¾″	8″ × 23″	15″	6″	Top	Cast iron	75 s.w.
	Features Cook top with removable cover for faster cooking by placing pot directly over fire								
Free Flow Stove Works	Circulator	33″ H × 23″ W × 13″ L		3.5 cu. ft.	20″	6″	Back	¼″ steel	200
	Features Heavy steel tubing bent to form rib cage								
General Engineering and Manufacturing Corp.	Earth Stove Model 101	32″ H × 30″ W × 23″ L	12″ × 20″		24″	8″	Top	10 and 12 ga. steel	250
	Features Firebrick lined; thermostatic draft								
J and J Enterprises	Frontier S-26-6	27½″ H × 26″ W × 16½″ L			20″	8″	Top/back	¼″ steel	330 s.w.
	Features Firebrick lined; fire screen								
Kristia Associates	Jøtul No. 602	25¼″ H × 12¾″ W × 19¼″ L			16″	5″	Top/back	Cast iron	117 s.w.
	Features Side and top baffles								

Free Flow Circulator—_Curved steel tubes form structure. Cold air flows into bottom of pipes, is warmed and flows out. Has big door that's safe and fits tightly._

Jøtul 602—_Black or green enamel. Cooking surface. Beautiful lines make this attractive when heat for a single room is needed._

Manufacturer	Stove	Dimensions	Door Opening	Firebox Size	Wood Length	Flue Size	Flue Location	Materials	Weight (lbs.)
Martin Industries	Merit Heater No. 520	32″H × 16″W × 21½″L	17½″ × 8½″	19″ × 11¾″		6″	Back	Cast iron front	130 s.w.
	Features Grates; cast liners; burns coal or wood								
Martin Industries	Box Heater #624	23¼″H			23″	6″	Top		102
	Features Swing top; 7″ cover plates								
Martin Industries	Box Heater #628	24¼″H			26″	6″	Top		123
	Features Swing top; 7″ cover plates								
Martin Industries	Box Heater #632	25¼″H			30″	6″	Top		132
	Features Swing top; 7″ cover plates								
The Merry Music Box	Styria- "Excelsior"	39″H × 15″D × 18″L	7¼″ × 7¼″	19″H × 10½″D × 13″W			Back		289
	Features Firebrick lined; humidification chamber								
Monarch Ranges and Heaters	Model FR26C	32″H × 39″W × 14½″L	20″ × 27″	14½″L × 27″W	27″	8″	Top/back	Cast iron	320 s.w.
	Features Franklin-style fireplace; cast-iron, porcelain enameled models available. Also fire screen, grate, cooking pot and adjustable swing-out bracket, brass ball ornaments, barbeque grill.								
Monarch Ranges and Heaters	Model RHR24B	31″H × 30½″W × 17½″L	10″ × 20″	27″ × 27″ × 11″		7″	Top		180 s.w.
	Features Coal or wood; porcelain colors; grates; ash drawer. Glass doors option.								
Portland Stove Foundry	Trolla No. 102	24½″H × 17½″L	6½″ × 9″	11″ × 14″	12″	4″	Top/back	Cast iron	76
	Features Cast bottom liner plate; baffles								
Portland Stove Foundry	Trolla No. 105	25½″H × 24¼″L	6½″ × 9″	13″ × 21″	18″	5″	Top/back	Cast iron	178
	Features Firebrick lined; baffles. Decorative top is option.								
Scandinavian Stoves Inc.	Lange #6303A	23½″H × 16″W × 25″L		20½″L		5″	Top	Cast iron	145 s.w.
	Features Cooking option								
Scandinavian Stoves Inc.	Lange #6203BR	41″H × 13¼″W × 20″L		16″L		5″		Cast iron	213
	Features Tile-like design; decorated cooking plate; baffles; side and bottom liner plates								
Self Sufficiency Products	Gibralter II	24⁷⁄₁₆″H × 13⅞ × 24″L			20″	6″	Top	³⁄₁₆″ and ¼″ steel	240
	Features 6½″ × 15½″ window; 13″ × 7″ cooking surface								

Styria Excelsior—*Look this one over, particularly inside, to see the firebricked heat accumulator chamber (upper third of stove), heat circulation tunnel (center third of stove, and put a pan of water in there for humidification), locking knobs on fuel door, steel damper in place on the six-inch flue connection pipe.*

Lange 6203 BR—*A pleasing parlor stove; has horizontal baffle system, large radiating system for a small stove.*

Manufacturer	Stove	Dimensions	Door Opening	Firebox Size	Wood Length	Flue Size	Flue Location	Materials	Weight (lbs.)
Self Sufficiency Products	Gibralter III	27⅝" H × 15¾" W × 27³⁄₁₆" L			24"	6"	Back	³⁄₁₆" and ¼" steel	272 (includes firebrick)

Features 8" × 17¾" window; 17¾" × 8" cooking surface

| Shenandoah Mfg. Co., Inc. | Model R-77 | 33" H × 18½" W × 32" L | 12" × 13" | 23" H × 15½" W × 26" L | 26" | | Top | Steel | 210 |

Features Firebrick lined; ash pan; thermostatic draft; grate. Cast iron coal grate is option.

| Southport Stoves | Morsø #2B | 28" H × 13" W × 27½" L | | | 20" | 4¾" | Top | Cast iron | 124 |

Features Stove poker; baffle

| Southport Stoves | Morsø #6B | 24" H × 14" W × 24" L | | | 16"-18" | 4¾" | Top | Cast iron | 146 |

Features Ash scoop

| Southport Stoves | Morsø 1122 | 32" H × 27" W × 19" L | | | 20" | 5½" | Back | Cast iron | 158 |

Features Free-standing fireplace; firebrick lined; spark screen

| Thulman Eastern Corp | Reginald 101 | 25" H × 12⁹⁄₁₆" W × 20⅛" L | | | 16" | 5" | Top/back | Cast iron | 120 s.w. |

Features Cooking option; do-it-yourself stove assembly kit; baffles

| Timberline Stoves | Timberline T-18 | 14" W × 21" L | | | 18" | | Top/ sides/ back | ¼" steel | 285 |

Features Screen; baffle; cooking surface; cast iron door; firebrick lined

| Washington Stove Works | Cannonball Olympic #213 | 41" H × 13" D | | | | 6" | Top | Cast iron | 124 |

Features Cooking surface

| Washington Stove Works | Cannonball Olympic #117 | 47" H × 17" D | | | | 7" | Top | Cast iron | 220 |

Features Cooking surface

| Washington Stove Works | Cannonball Martin #S-50 | 30¾" H × 14" D | | | | 6" | Top | Cast iron | 86 |

Features Cooking surface

| Washington Stove Works | Basic Parlor Stove | 31¼" H × 25½" W × 22½" L | | | | 6" | | Cast iron | 180 |

Features Front, top, side openings

Washington Stove Works	Arctic #1-25	23¼" H × 14½" W × 33" L				6"	Top	Cast iron	110
Washington Stove Works	Arctic #30	26½" H × 16½" W × 37¼" L				6"	Top	Cast iron	140
Washington Stove Works	Olympic Franklin #18	25¼" H × 20½" W × 30" L		18" L	18"	7"	Top	Cast iron	175

Features Fireplace stove. Options include spark screen, cooking pot, barbeque grill, brass rail, brass balls, log holders.

| Washington Stove Works | Olympic Franklin #22 | 29⅛" H × 23" W × 33¾" L | | 22" L | 22" | 8" | Top | Cast iron | 225 |

Features Fireplace stove. Options include spark screen, cooking pot, barbeque grill, brass rail, brass balls, log holders

MEDIUM STOVES

Manufacturer	Stove	Dimensions	Door Opening	Firebox Size	Wood Length	Flue Size	Flue Location	Materials	Weight
All Nighter Stove Works, Inc.	Tiny Mo'	26¾" H × 17¼" W × 28½" L			16"	6"	Back	¼" and ⁵⁄₁₆" plate steel	241
	Features	Adjustable legs; firebrick lined; cooking top surface. Options: Blower, door screen, hot water extraction cylinder to heat domestic hot water.							
All Nighter Stove Works, Inc.	Little Mo'	28" H × 19½" W × 31½" L			20"	6"	Back	¼" and ⁵⁄₁₆" plate steel	314
	Features	Adjustable legs; firebrick lined; cooking top surface. Options: Blower, door screen, hot water extraction cylinder to heat domestic hot water.							
All Nighter Stove Works, Inc.	Mid Mo'	31" H × 21½" W × 36" L			24"	6"	Rear	¼" and ⁵⁄₁₆" plate steel	408
	Features	Adjustable legs; firebrick lined; cooking top surface. Options: Blower, door screen, hot water extraction cylinder to heat domestic hot water.							
Ashley Products Division	Columbian 25-HF	34" H × 20" W × 30" D	13¼" × 15" (top) 10¾" × 12" (front)	23" H × 17½" W × 25" L			Top	Steel	
	Features	Double wall body construction; thermostatic draft control; cast iron top and fuel doors							
Ashley Products Division	Carolinian 23-HF	30" H × 18" W × 28½" D	12" × 13" (top) 10¾" × 12" (front)	21" H × 16" W × 22¼" L			Top	Steel	
	Features	Double wall body construction; thermostatic draft control; cast iron top and fuel doors							
Ashley Products Division	Carolina 23-H	30" H × 18" W × 30½" D	12" × 13"	21" H × 16" W × 22¼" L			Top	Steel	101 s.w.
	Features	Double wall body construction; thermostatic draft control; cast iron top and fuel doors							

All Nighter—*Offers Tiny Mo' in small stove category, Little Mo' and Mid Mo' in this category, and Big Mo' among the large stoves. All feature two cooking surfaces, separated by directional air outlets (air enters tubes near floor, is heated, expelled; power blower is optional). Also optional is hot water extraction cylinder for domestic water system. A sturdy workhorse.*

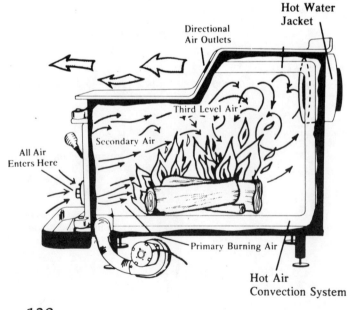

Hot Water Jacket

Directional Air Outlets

Third Level Air

Secondary Air

All Air Enters Here

Primary Burning Air

Hot Air Convection System

Manufacturer	Stove	Dimensions	Door Opening	Firebox Size	Wood Length	Flue Size	Flue Location	Materials	Weight (lbs.)
Atlanta Stove Works, Inc.	Model #24 Woodsman	31½″ H × 13¾″ W × 32⅝″ L	9″ × 9⅞″	11¾″ × 26½″ × 11⅝″	26″	6″	Back	Cast iron	235 s.w.
	Features	Top and side baffles; secondary heat chamber							
Atlanta Stove Works, Inc.	Model #241 Huntsman	33½″ H × 18½″ W × 34⅛″ L	10″ × 11⅛″	14″ × 24⅛″ × 16½″	24″	6″	Back	Steel	380 s.w.
	Features	Firebrick liners; cast iron door; secondary heat chamber							
Bow and Arrow Stove Co.	Fyrtønden Model C	37¾″ H × 19″ D		4000 cu. in.	14″-16″	6″	Top/back	4 mm steel	221
	Features	Screen; grates; tongs; shovel; firebrick lined; secondary combustion chamber							
Bow and Arrow Stove Co.	Fyrtønden Model D	27½″ H × 19″ D		2700 cu. in.	14″	6″	Top/back	4 mm steel	118
	Features	Screen; grates; tongs; shovel; firebrick lined; secondary combustion chamber							
Bow and Arrow Stove Co.	Petit Godin #3721	40″ H × 21″ W × 27″ D		1700 cu. in.	20″	4″	Back	Steel, cast iron	223 s.w.
	Features	Firebrick lined; burns wood or coal							
Cawley/LeMay Stove Co., Inc.	Model 600	35½″ H × 18″ W × 44″ L	9½″ × 10½″		24″-27″	5″	Back	Cast iron	
	Features	Cooking surface; rotating cast iron flue fitting; ash lip; top and side baffles							
Fire-View Distributors	Fire-View #270	25″ H × 27¼″ W × 27⅜″ L	10″ × 14″	20″ D	24″	7″	Top/back	12 ga. steel for firebox, ³⁄₁₆″ for end portions	199
	Features	10″ × 20″ tempered glass window; cooking surface; firebrick lined; tubular design; side loader. Blower is option.							

Left:
Cawley/LeMay Model 600—*Large door, rotating cast iron flue fitting, sweep shelf any housewife will cherish, cook tops are only some of the plus features of this beauty.*

Below:
Fire-View 270—*a compromise between a fireplace and a stove, with tempered glass window, roomy side door, and optional blower.*

Manufacturer	Stove	Dimensions	Door Opening	Firebox Size	Wood Length	Flue Size	Flue Location	Materials	Weight (lbs.)
Fisher Stoves Inc.	Baby Bear	26¼″ H × 15½″ W × 28″ L	8″ × 9″		18″	6″	Back	¼″ and ⁵⁄₁₆″ plate steel	245
	Features Cooking surface; firebrick lined; cast iron door; flue extends into firebox. Hot water coil is option.								
J and J Enterprises	Frontier M-28-8	29″ H × 28″ W × 18½″ L			22″	8″	Top/back	¼″ and ⁵⁄₁₆″ steel	380 s.w.
	Features Firebrick lined; fire screen								
Kickapoo Stove Works Ltd.	Cabin Model BBR-C	34″ H × 20″ W × 27″ L	8⅝″ × 11⅝″ × 11⅝″	4.2 cu. ft.	16″	6″	Top	12 ga. steel/ cast iron	235
	Features Ash compartment, cooking surface, firebrick lined								
Kristia Associates	Jøtul No. 118	30¼″ H × 14¼″ W × 29½″ L			24″	5″	Side/ back	Cast iron	231 s.w.
	Features Secondary combustion chamber; baffles in firebox								
Kristia Associates	Jøtul No. 606	40½″ H × 11¾″ W × 18¾″ L			12″	5″	Side/ back	Cast iron	175 s.w.
	Features Arch design								
Martin Industries	6600 Automatic Wood Heater	44″ H		19″ × 25″			Top		170 s.w.
	Features Cast-iron swing top and bottom; thermostatic draft; heavy-duty steel liner. Blower is option.								
Martin Industries	Wood King 2600-3	35″ H		19″ × 25″			Top		147
	Features Cast iron top, bottom, doors, and door frames; thermostatic draft								
The Merry Music Box	Styria- "Reliable"	42½″ H × 15″ D × 18″ L	7¼″ × 7¼″	22″ × 10½″ × 13″			Back		349
	Features Firebrick lined; humidification chamber								
Mohawk Industries	Tempwood V	24¼″ H × 24″ W × 14″ L	11″ D		12″-14″	5″	Back	⅛″ and ¼″ steel	133
	Features Firebrick lined; downdraft principle								

Jøtul 118—*Satisfying design, a proven heater. Black or glossy green enamel.*

Jøtul 606—*With arch, this little beauty stands 41″ high, has efficiently large surface for heat radiation. Cast iron firebox lining.*

Manufacturer	Stove	Dimensions	Door Opening	Firebox Size	Wood Length	Flue Size	Flue Location	Materials	Weight (lbs.)
New Hampshire Wood Stoves, Inc.	Home Warmers II	29″ H × 16″ W × 24″ L	10″		23″	6″	Back	⅛″ and ¼″ steel	
	Features Cast iron door; baffles; thermostatic draft								
Portland Stove Foundry	Trolla No. 107	28¼″ H × 31″ L	6½″ × 9″	13″ × 25¼″	24″	5″	Top/back	Cast iron	253
	Features Cooking plate; baffles								
Portland Stove Foundry	Trolla No. 800	41½″ H × 25½″ W × 20″ L	6″ × 10″			8″	Top	Cast iron	300
	Features Fireplace options; firebrick lined; grate								
Quaker Stove Co.	Fawn	34″ H × 14″ W × 21″ L		17″ × 11″	15″	6″	Top	¼″ and ⁵⁄₁₆″ steel	380
	Features Firebrick lined; 16″ × 20″ cooking surface								
Scandinavian Stoves Inc.	Lange #6203BR	41″ H × 13¼″ W × 20″ L		16″ L		5″	Top	Cast iron	213 s.w.
	Features Baffles; European tile pattern								
Scandinavian Stoves Inc.	Lange #6303	37½″ H × 16″ W × 25″ L		20½″ L		5″	Side	Cast iron	220 s.w.
	Features Heat chamber; cooking option; cast iron liner in bottom; baffles								
Scandinavian Stoves Inc.	Lange #6302A	34″ H × 16″ W × 34″ L		26″ L		5″	Top	Cast iron	272 s.w.
	Features Cooking option; baffles								
Scandinavian Stoves Inc.	Lange #6204	41″ H × 13¼″ W × 25″ L		20″ L		5″	Top	Cast iron	250 s.w.
	Features Baffles; European tile pattern								
Self Sufficiency Products	Sierra #150	29″ H × 16″ W × 24″ L			22″	6″	Back	¼″ and ⁵⁄₁₆″ steel	335
	Features Firebrick lining								
Self Sufficiency Products	Gilbralter IV	32½″ H × 18½″ W × 32″ L			28″	6″	Back	³⁄₁₆″ and ¼″ steel	320 (with firebrick)
	Features 9″ × 21″ Racon window; 17½″ × 20″ cooking surface; firebrick lined								

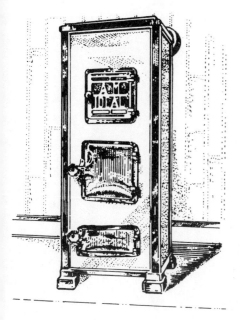

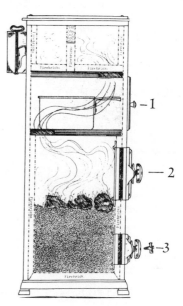

Styria Reliable—*Three doors lead to (1), heat circulation tunnel (put in a pan of water, for humidity) at top, (2), cast iron fuel door in center, and (3), ash-emptying door at bottom. Lots of heat is stored in the many firebricks of the top heat accumulation chamber.*

Manufacturer	Stove	Dimensions	Door Opening	Firebox Size	Wood Length	Flue Size	Flue Location	Materials	Weight (lbs.)
Shenandoah Mfg. Co., Inc.	Model #R65	35¾″ H × 21″ D	12″ × 13″	23″ H × 18″ D	18″		Top	Steel	162 s.w.
	Features	Firebrick lined; thermostatic draft; ash removal pan; grate. Options: Coal or coke cast iron grate ring.							
Southport Stoves	Mørso 2BO	40″ H × 13″ W × 27″ L			20″	4¾″	Top	Cast iron	164
	Features	Heat exchanger arch; cooking top							
Southport Stoves	Mørso 1B	34″ H × 14″ W × 30″ L		5,186 cu. in.	22″	4¾″	Top	Cast iron	254
	Features	Baffles; poker							
Sunshine Stove Works	Sunshine Stove	28″ H × 14″ W × 34″ L			24″	6″		⅛″ and ¼″ steel	300
	Features	Firebrick lined; cast iron door and frame; cooking option							
Thermo-Control Wood Stoves	Thermo-Control 200	27″ H × 18″ W × 30″ L	12″ × 15″	18″ H × 18″ W × 27″ L		6″	Top	¼″ and 10 ga. steel	170 s.w.
	Features	Firebrick lined; thermostatic draft. Hot water heat piping is option.							
Thulman Eastern Corp.	Reginald 102	30″ H × 13″ W × 29″ L	9¼″ × 10¼″	13″ H × 13″ W × 29″ L	24″	5″	Top/ back/ sides	Cast iron	300 s.w.
	Features	Heat exchanger; baffles, cook top; do-it-yourself stove assembly kit							
Timberline Stoves	Timberline T-24	16″ H × 27″ L			24″		Top/ sides/ back	¼″ steel	418
	Features	Screen; baffle; cooking surface; cast iron door; firebrick lined							
Timberline Stoves	Timberline T-SF	26″ W × 26″ L			20″		Top/ sides/ back	¼″ steel	480
	Features	Screen; baffle; cooking surface; cast iron door; firebrick lined							
Vermont Castings, Inc.	Vigilant	30″ H × 24″ W × 32″ L	17½″ × 8¾″		18″	8″	Top/back	Cast iron	245
	Features	Thermostatic draft; baffles, spark screen, shovel; fireplace-cooking option; secondary combustion chamber							
Vermont Iron Stove Works	The Elm	26″ H × 23″ W × 33″ L	15″ D	19″ D × 24″ L.	24″	6″	Back	¼″ steel	250
	Features	Firebrick lined; 9″ window. Cooking top is option.							
Vermont Woodstove Co.	DownDrafter II	28″ H × 22″ W × 25″ L	11″ × 11″	18″ H × 16″ W × 20″ L	18″	6″	Back	Steel plate stainless steel	250
	Features	Firebrick lined, cooking option; thermostatic draft.							
Vermont Woodstove Co.	Canadian Stepstove	30¼″ H × 17⅝″ W × 33⅛″ L			24″	6″	Back	¼″ and ⁵⁄₁₆″ steel	350
	Features	Cooking option; two-step construction							
Warmglow Products, Inc.	Maxi-Heat II				24″	7″	Sides/ back	Cast iron	
	Features	Baffles; firebrick lined							
Washington Stove Works	Olympic Franklin #26	31¼″ H × 25″ W × 38⅛″ L	26″ L		26″	8″	Top	Cast iron	310
	Features	Fireplace stove. Options: Spark screen, cooking pot, barbeque grill, brass rail, brass balls, log holders.							
Washington Stove Works	Olympic Franklin #30	32½″ H × 26½″ W × 42¼″ L	30″ L		30″	10″	Top	Cast iron	375
	Features	Fireplace stove. Options: Spark screen, cooking pot, barbeque grill, brass rail, brass balls, log holders.							

Manufacturer	Stove	Dimensions	Door Opening	Firebox Size	Wood Length	Flue Size	Flue Location	Materials	Weight (lbs.)
Washington Stove Works	Olympic Creast	32½″ H × 36″ W × 24½″ L				8″	Top	Cast iron	355 s.w.
	Features	Thermostatic draft; baffles; heat shield. Option: Spark screen.							

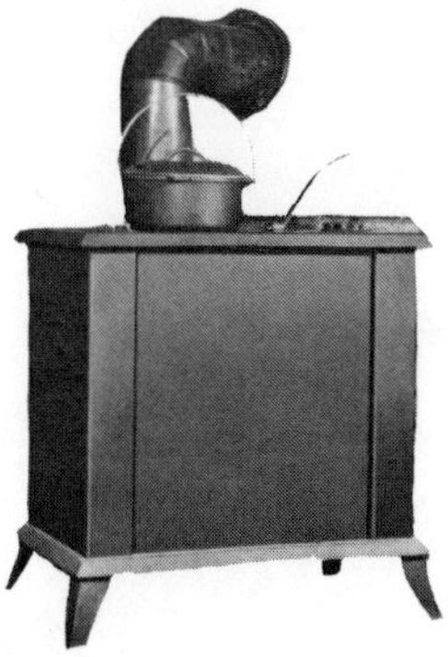

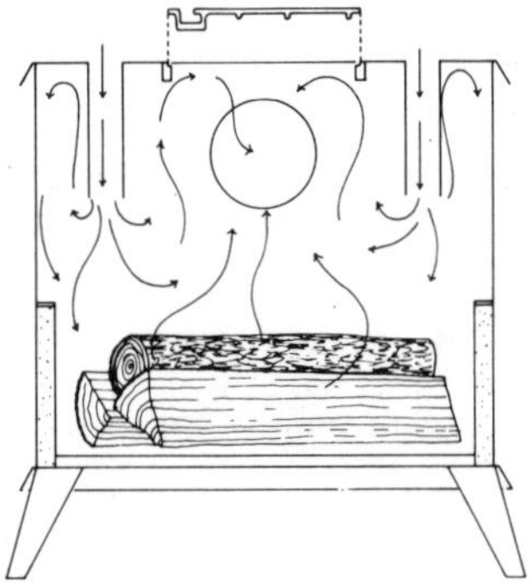

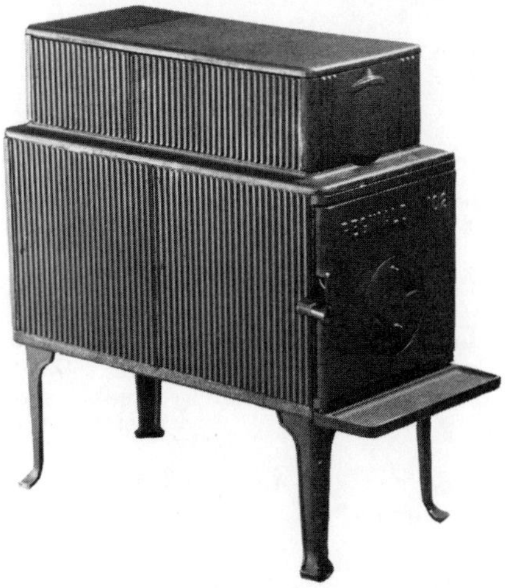

Tempwood V—*Action is on the top of this plate steel stove. Two downdraft vents are there, and so is 11″ circular lid. Remove it for adding wood, removing ashes. (Shovel just for the latter job is provided.)*

Reginald 102—*Here's the 300-pound big brother of the 101, longer, less than one inch wider, and much higher, thanks to the heat exchanger that increases heat radiation area by 36 percent. Three cast iron plates in baffle system.*

VIGILANT

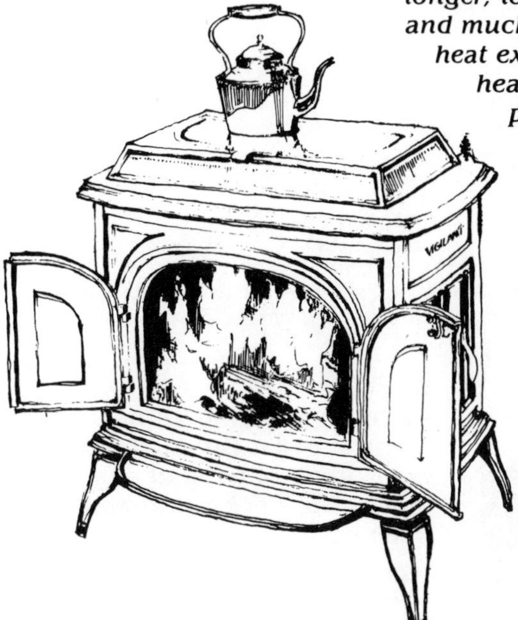

Vigilant—*A small Defiant, with the same features, such as cast-iron construction, three air systems delivering air to the fire, "fireplace" operation when desired, and thermostat control. All the family will appreciate those two folding drying racks that can be tucked out of sight. Great for drying mittens.*

VERMONT IRON STOVE WORKS
WARREN VERMONT

STOVE WORKS
WARREN VERMONT

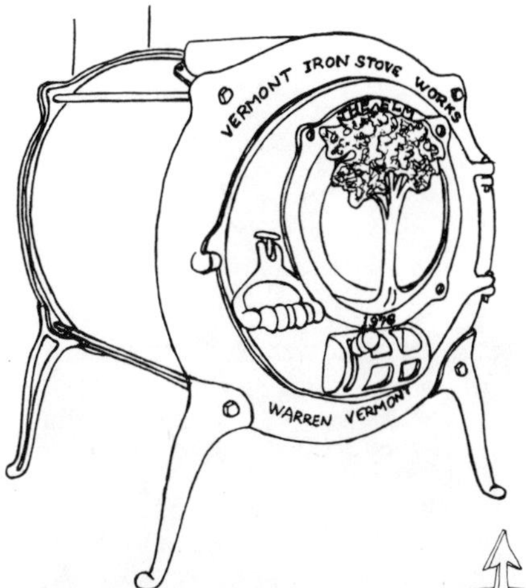

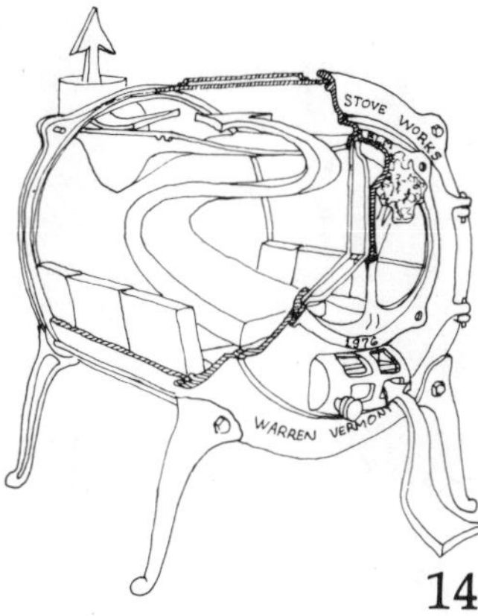

The Elm—*Combine a quarter-inch steel cylinder with a cast-iron back and a cast-iron door with a heat-resistant glass window, line all of this with firebrick and you have an Elm, one of the newer stoves manufactured in Vermont.*

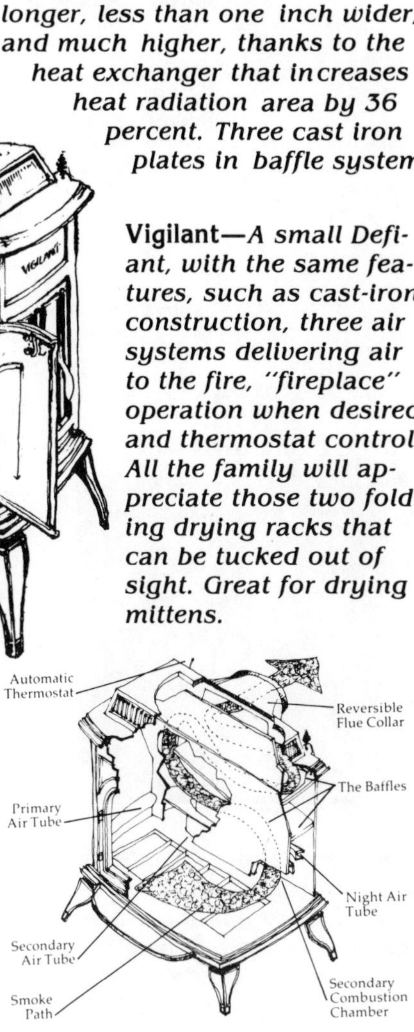

Automatic Thermostat
Reversible Flue Collar
The Baffles
Primary Air Tube
Night Air Tube
Secondary Air Tube
Smoke Path
Secondary Combustion Chamber

LARGE STOVES

Manufacturer	Stove	Dimensions	Door Opening	Firebox Size	Wood Length	Flue Size	Flue Location	Materials	Weight
Abundant Life Farm	Comforter	26″H × 24″W × 20″L	8″ × 12″	21½″L	20″	6″	Back	¼″ cast iron	275 s.w.
Features	Cook top; baffles								
All Nighter Stove Works, Inc.	Big Mo'	41½″L × 31″H × 23½″W			30″	6″	Back	¼″ and 5/16″ plate steel	510
Features	Adjustable legs; firebrick lined; cooking top surface. Options: Blower; spark screen; hot water extraction cylinder to heat domestic hot water.								
Autocrat Corporation	Americana Model 76 FH	36¼″H × 42¾″W × 29″L	26¼″W ×13¼″H	25⅜″W ×17⅛″W	24″	8″	Top		400 s.w.
Features	Franklin-style stove; log grate; ash pan; heat emitting louvers; spark arresting screen; cast iron door and linings; thermostat. Blower is option.								
Autocrat Corporation	Americana 2000	34¾″H × 33½″W × 24″L	13½″H ×26¼″W	25⅜″W ×17⅛″L	25⅜″	8″	Top		390 s.w.
Features	Franklin-style stove; log grate; ash pan; heat emitting louvers; spark arresting screen; cast iron door and linings; thermostat. Blower is option.								
Bow and Arrow Stove Co.	Fyrtønden Model A	34¼″H × 23½″D		4600 cu. in.	18″	7″	Top/back	4mm steel	287
Features	Screen; grates; tongs; shovel; firebrick lined; secondary combustion chamber								
Bow and Arrow Stove Co.	Fyrtønden Model B	31½″H × 21¾″D		4100 cu. in.	16″	6″	Top/back	4mm steel	265
Features	Screen; grates; tongs; shovel; firebrick lined; secondary combustion chamber.								
C & D Distributors, Inc.	Better 'N Ben's	Standard back panel: 34½″H × 42″W; three other sizes available	9″ × 13″	18″H × 18″W × 24″L	18″	6″	Back	11-gauge black iron	150 s.w.
Features	Adjustable legs; stove vents into fireplace flue with fireplace cover panel; heat deflector; cooking surface. Screen is option.								

Americana 2000—*What you'll like about this stove: Use it as a fireplace or a wood-burning heater, has big ash pan, optional blower, thermostat control and heat exchanger.*

Below:
Better 'N Ben's—*Here's a steel box stove that can be linked to your fireplace without any stovepipe. Blocks off fireplace opening. Legs adjustable.*

Americana 76 FH—*Same construction as the 2000 but more traditional appearance.*

Manufacturer	Stove	Dimensions	Door Opening	Firebox Size	Wood Length	Flue Size	Flue Location	Materials	Weight (lbs.)
Fire-View Distributors	Fire-View #360	26½" H × 36⅜"W × 22" L	10" × 14"		36"	7"	Top/back	12 gauge steel for firebox, ³⁄₁₆" for end portions	279

Features Tempered glass; firebrick lined; tubular design; cooking surface. Blower is option.

Manufacturer	Stove	Dimensions	Door Opening	Firebox Size	Wood Length	Flue Size	Flue Location	Materials	Weight (lbs.)
Fisher Stoves Inc.	Grandpa Bear	33" H × 29½" W × 29¾" L	21¾" × 11"	26" W × 21" L	24"	8"	Top	¼" and ⁵⁄₁₆" plate steel	475

Features Cooking surface; firebrick lined; cast iron door; flue extends into firebox

Manufacturer	Stove	Dimensions	Door Opening	Firebox Size	Wood Length	Flue Size	Flue Location	Materials	Weight (lbs.)
Fisher Stoves Inc.	Grandma Bear	33" H × 25½" W × 28" L	17½" × 11"		18"	8"	Top	¼" and ⁵⁄₁₆" plate steel	425

Features Cooking surface; firebrick lined; cast iron door; flue extends into firebox.

Manufacturer	Stove	Dimensions	Door Opening	Firebox Size	Wood Length	Flue Size	Flue Location	Materials	Weight (lbs.)
Fisher Stoves Inc.	Papa Bear	30⅜" H × 18⅜" W × 34" L	10" × 11"		30"	6"	Back	¼" and ⁵⁄₁₆" plate steel	410

Features Cooking surface; firebrick lined; cast iron door; flue extends into firebox.

Manufacturer	Stove	Dimensions	Door Opening	Firebox Size	Wood Length	Flue Size	Flue Location	Materials	Weight (lbs.)
Heathdelle Associates	Nashua #18	29⅜" H × 20¼" W × 39" L	8¾" × 10¾"	3.5 cu. ft.	18"	6"	Back	¼" steel	350

Features Firebrick lined; cooking surface; blower with 265 cfm capacity. Fireviewing screen is option.

Manufacturer	Stove	Dimensions	Door Opening	Firebox Size	Wood Length	Flue Size	Flue Location	Materials	Weight (lbs.)
Heathdelle Associates	Nashua #24	32⅜" H × 24⅞" W × 45½" L	12¾" × 11¾"	5.5 cu. ft.	24"	6"	Back	¼" steel	500

Features Firebrick lined; cooking surface; blower with 465 cfm capacity. Fireviewing screen is option.

Manufacturer	Stove	Dimensions	Door Opening	Firebox Size	Wood Length	Flue Size	Flue Location	Materials	Weight (lbs.)
Heathdelle Associates	Nashua #30	40½" H × 31⅜" W × 62" L	13¾" × 13¾"	15 cu. ft.	30"	8"	Back	¼" steel	850

Features Firebrick lined; cooking surface; blower with 865 cfm capacity. Fireviewing screen is option.

Manufacturer	Stove	Dimensions	Door Opening	Firebox Size	Wood Length	Flue Size	Flue Location	Materials	Weight (lbs.)
Hydraform Products Corp.	Larger Eagle	37" H × 36" W × 28" L	13½" × 33½"		32"	6"	Back	³⁄₁₆" steel	500

Features Firebrick liners. Humidifiers, ovens, grille, water heater. Glass doors are option.

Nashua 18—(and the larger 24 and even-larger 30)—*built of steel, with firebrick lining. Its plus: a manifold system with blower that sucks in cooler air, expels hot air. Screen to replace door is option.*

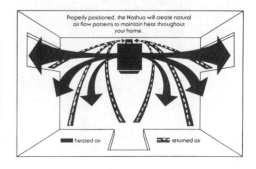

Manufacturer	Stove	Dimensions	Door Opening	Firebox Size	Wood Length	Flue Size	Flue Location	Materials	Weight (lbs.)
Hydroheat	Hydrostove	38″ H × 21″ W × 35″ L	13″ × 15″	13″ × 14″ × 27″	16″-26″	8″	Back	$\frac{3}{16}$″ steel	405 s.w.
Features		Cast iron front frame, door, damper, and legs; asbestos board provided to protect walls and floors; cooking surface; water circulating baffle to distribute heat to your existing central heating system.							
J and J Enterprises	Frontier XL-32-8	35½″ H × 32″ W × 22½″ L			26″	8″	Top/ back	¼″ steel	520 s.w.
Features		Doors of $\frac{5}{16}$″ steel; firebrick lined; fire screen; two levels for cooking. Chrome balls for legs; warming plates are options.							
J and J Enterprises	Frontier L-30-8	32½″ H × 30″ W × 20½″ L			24″	8″	Top/ back	¼″ steel	440 s.w.
Features		Doors of $\frac{5}{16}$″ steel; firebrick lined; fire screen; two levels for cooking. Chrome balls for legs; warming plates are options.							
Kickapoo Stove Works, Ltd.	Standard Model BBR-B	34″ H × 20″ W × 27″ L	$8\frac{5}{8}$″ × $11\frac{5}{8}$″ ×	5.8 cu. ft.	24″	6″	Top	12 ga. steel, cast iron	260
Features		Ash compartment; cooking surface, firebrick lined.							
Kickapoo Stove Works, Ltd.	Kickapoo Fireplace/Stove	50″ H × 24½″ W × 17″ L			18″	7″	Back	10 ga. steel	325
Features		Cast iron grates; recessed flue; foot rest; food warming surface; fireplace screen.							
Kristia Associates	Jøtul No. 4 Combi-fire	41¼″ H × 23½″ W × 22¾″ L			20″	7″	Top or back	Cast iron	286 s.w.
Features		Fireplace option.							
The Merry Music Box	Styria "Imperial"	48½″ H × 18½″ D × 21¾″ L	7¼″ × 7¼″	26″ × 13¾″ × 15″			Back		533
Features		Firebrick lined, humidification chamber.							
Mohawk Industries	Tempwood II	28″ H × 28″ W × 18″ L	11″		16″-18″	6″	Back	⅛″ and ¼″ steel	200
Features		Firebrick lined; downdraft principle.							
New Hampshire Stoves, Inc.	Home Warmers I	34″ H × 18″ W × 30″ L	10″		29″	6″	Back	⅛″ and ¼″ steel	
Features		Thermostatic draft.							

Papa Bear—*One of a family of Bears of various sizes to meet different heating needs. Like the others, papa is constructed of boiler plate, has two cooking surfaces, firebrick lining.*

Kickapoo Fireplace/ Stove—*Take your choice, an open fireplace or a stylish stove, you have both in this model. Ten-gauge steel construction, cast-iron grate, ash compartment and door, built-in damper.*

Manufacturer	Stove	Dimensions	Door Opening	Firebox Size	Wood Length	Flue Size	Flue Location	Materials	Weight (lbs.)
Quaker Stove Co.	Buck	34" H × 17" W × 35" L		30" × 13½"	28"	6"	Top	¼" and ⁵⁄₁₆" plate steel	510
	Features Firebrick lined; 18½" × 33" cooking surface.								
Quaker Stove Co.	Doe	34" H × 15" W × 32" L		27" × 11"	25"	6"	Top	¼" and ⁵⁄₁₆" plate steel	480
	Features Firebrick lined; 16½" × 30" cooking surface.								
Ram Forge	Ram Wood Stove	30" H × 15" W × 38" L	10" × 10"	3.5 cu. ft.	28"	5"	Back	¼" steel	
Ram Forge	Ram Tile Stove	30" H × 15" W × 38" L	10 × 10"	3.5 cu. ft.	28"	5"	Back		300
	Features Hand-painted earthen tiles fitted to top and sides.								
Riteway Manufacturing Co.	Riteway #2000	33" H × 17" W × 28" L	12" × 12"	4 cu. ft.	24"	6"	Side	14 ga. steel	225
	Features Liners, ash pan; thermostatic draft. Cabinets available.								
Riteway Manufacturing Co.	Riteway #37	40" H × 24" W × 33" L	12" × 12"	7½ cu. ft.	24"	6"	Side	10 and 14 ga. steel	400 s.w.
	Features Cast iron grates; firebrick lining; ash pan, thermostatic draft. Cabinets available.								
Scandinavian Stoves Inc.	Lange #6302K	50½" H × 16" W × 34" L	26" L			5"	Side	Cast iron	370 s.w.
	Features Heat chamber; baffles; cook plate; baking option.								
Self Sufficiency Products	Sierra #300	30" H × 18" W × 32" L			30"	6"	Back	¼" and ⁵⁄₁₆" steel	400
	Features Firebrick lined.								
Shenandoah Mfg. Co.	Model #R-75	35¾" H × 24" D	12" × 13"	21" × 23"		6"	Top	11 and 18 ga. steel	178 s.w.
	Features Firebrick lined; thermostatic draft; ash removal tray.								
Southeastern Vermont Community Action	SEVCA	41¾" H × 29½" W × 22¾" D		22" W	18"	8"	Top/ back	³⁄₁₆" steel	
	Features Secondary combustion chamber; cooking surface.								

Tempwood II—*Big brother of the Tempwood V (see Medium Stoves), and four inches larger in all dimensions. Heat output half again as much as smaller model.*

Ram Tile Stove—*Here's the Ram woodstove with fifty pounds of decorative, heat-holding tiles on its top and sides. Slip one or two off for bedwarmers. Quarter-inch steel stove.*

Manufacturer	Stove	Dimensions	Door Opening	Firebox Size	Wood Length	Flue Size	Flue Location	Materials	Weight (lbs.)
Southport Stoves	Morsø #1125	41¾" H × 29½" W × 22¾" L	20" W	22" W × 17" L	18"	8"	Top/back	Cast iron	310
	Features Fireplace option; firebrick lined; baffles; fire screen.								
Southport Stoves	Morsø #1BO	51¼" H × 14¼"W × 30¼" L		5,186 cu. in.	22"	4¾"	Top	Cast iron	365 s.w.
	Features Arch; stove poker.								
The Stoveworks	Culvert Queen	32" H × 22" D	15"	5 cu. ft.	15"	6"	Top	Steel	140
	Features Downdraft design.								
The Stoveworks	Independence	30" H × 16" W × 36" L	12" × 12"	30" L	30"	6"	Top/back	3⁄16" steel	
	Features Ash tray; baffle. Soapstone slabs are options.								
Thermo-Control Wood Stoves	Thermo-Control 500	30" H × 24" W × 40" L	18" × 21"	24" H × 24" W × 34" L		8"	Top	¼" and 3⁄16" steel	390 s.w.
	Features Firebrick lined; baffles. Hot water piping is option.								
Timberline Stoves	Timberline T-33	18" W × 33" L			30"				502
Timberline Stoves	Timberline T-LF	29½" W × 29" D			24"				568
	Features Spark screen.								
Vermont Castings, Inc.	Defiant	32" H × 22" W × 36" L	14¼" × 10¼"		24"	8"	Top/back	Cast iron	340
	Features Thermostatic draft; spark screen; shovel; secondary combustion chamber; fireplace-cooking option.								
Vermont Woodstove Co.	DownDrafter I	32" H × 26" W × 34" L	11" × 11"	22" H × 16" W × 26" L		8"	Back	Steelplate stainless steel	500
	Features Firebrick lined; cooking option; blower; heat exchange chamber. Hot water coils are option.								
Warmglow Products, Inc.	Maxi-Heat I					7"	Top/back	Cast iron	
	Features Fireplace stove; firebrick lined.								

Morsø 1125—*Fireplace-stove combination. Two doors swing out, can be taken off and screen substituted. Firebrick lining. Top or back-vented. Damper a part of collar. Fireplace owners can take off this stove's legs to make it fit within the fireplace.*

Defiant—*Run this one inefficiently and open, like a fireplace, or close it for an airtight with thermostat controls, primary and secondary air systems. A husky worker.*

CIRCULATOR STOVES

Circulators allow the heat to pass between an exterior cabinet and the radiant heater.

Manufacturer	Stove	Dimensions	Door Opening	Firebox Size	Wood Length	Flue Size	Flue Location	Materials	Weight
Ashley Products Division	C-60 Imperial	36″ H × 35¼″ W × 24¼″ L	13⅜″ × 9¾″	23″ H × 14″ W × 27″ L	24″	6″	Back	Steel	267 s.w.
	Features	Thermostatic draft; ash pan; draft equalizer. Blower is option.							
Atlanta Stove Works, Inc.	Homesteader 240	33⅜″ H × 32¼″ W × 19¼″ L				6″	Back	Cast iron; bonder-ized enamel cabinet	240 s.w.
	Features	Thermostatic draft; grate; ash pan. Blower is option.							
Autocrat Corporation	Model #6724	33″ H × 31″ W × 20½″ L	11⅜″ × 12″	22⅞″ H × 25¼″ W × 14½″ L	24″	6″	Back	Cast iron and 18 ga. steel with enamel cabinet	215 s.w.
	Features	Thermostatic draft; grate; ash pan. Blower is option.							
Autocrat Corporation	Model #FF 76	34¼″ H × 32⅜″ W × 21¾″ L	25″ W × 10″ H	20½″ H × 25″ W × 14½″ L	25″	6″	Back	Cast iron and 18 ga. steel with enamel cabinet	245 s.w.
	Features	Thermostatic draft; grate; ash pan; hinged smoke curtain; flue baffle. Blower is option.							
Bow and Arrow Stove Company	Supra 402	26″ H × 21″ W × 12″ L		1500 cu. in.		12″-14″	5″	Back	Steel and cast iron with enamel cabinet	117 s.w.
	Features	Grate; ash pan; cooking option; heat proof window for fireviewing; baffles; burns wood or coal briquets; firebrick lined.							

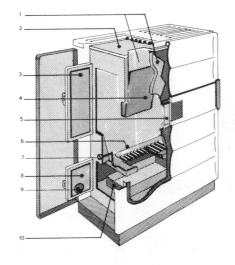

1. Firebrick lining
2. Cast iron top plate
3. Cast iron side-loading door with gasket
4. Cast iron smoke baffle
5. Heatproof window
6. Cast iron ash grate
7. Grate shaker
8. Cast iron ash door with gasket
9. Rotary damper
10. Large ash drawer

Supra 402—*Here's a steel firebox with cast-iron doors, a grate and ash pan, plus a heatproof window centered in a steel cabinet. Cast iron top plate can be used for cooking.*

Manufacturer	Stove	Dimensions	Door Opening	Firebox Size	Wood Length	Flue Size	Flue Location	Materials	Weight (lbs.)
Greenbriar Products, Inc.	The Greenbriar		30″	30″ H × 20″ W × 44″ L	40″	8″	Top	14 ga. steel	
Features	Fireplace-stove unit. Glass window door, grate, water coils are options.								
Hunter	Heater #C-26	35″ H × 28″ W × 22¼″ L	10″ × 11″	4½ cu. ft.	18″	6″			170 s.w.
Features	Baffles; thermostatic draft.								
Hunter	Heater #C-31	35″ H × 34½″ W × 22¼″ L	10″ × 11″	6 cu. ft.	24″	6″		Enamel cabinet	195 s.w.
Features	Thermostatic draft; baffles.								
Kerr Controls Ltd.	Princess	36″ H × 23¼″ W × 36⅝″ L	11″ × 11″	23½″ H × 15¾″ W × 26″ L	26″	6″	Top/ back	Steel cabinet with urethane enamel finish	200 s.w.
Features	Cooking option; thermostatic draft. Blower is optional.								
Kerr Controls Ltd.	Brooklyn	39″ H × 24″ D	12″ × 12″		22″	7″	Top	Steel plate	300
Features	Tubular heat exchanger; fan-forced air.								
KNT, Inc.	The Impression	31″ H × 31″ W × 30″ L			24″	8″	Top	Firebrick and ⅛″ steel	
Features	Grate; ash pan; heat shield; cooking surface. Blower is option.								
Locke Stove Company	Warm Morning Model 701	33¼″ H × 36″ W × 18″ L	10″ × 14″		26″	6″	Back	Porcelain enamel cabinet; cast iron liner plates with firebrick lining	287 s.w.
Features	Thermostatic draft; grate; hinged smoke curtain; ash drawer. Blower is option.								
Martin Industries	Wood Circulator #7801-B	32″ H × 31″ W × 33″ L		18¾″ H × 14⅝″ W × 25¼″ L	25½″	6″	Back	Cast iron and 18 ga. steel with porcelain enamel cabinet	215 s.w.
Features	Thermostatic draft; grate; firebrick lined; cast iron liners; ash drawer; Options: blower; barometric damper.								

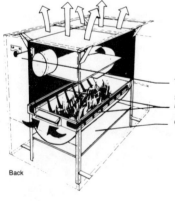

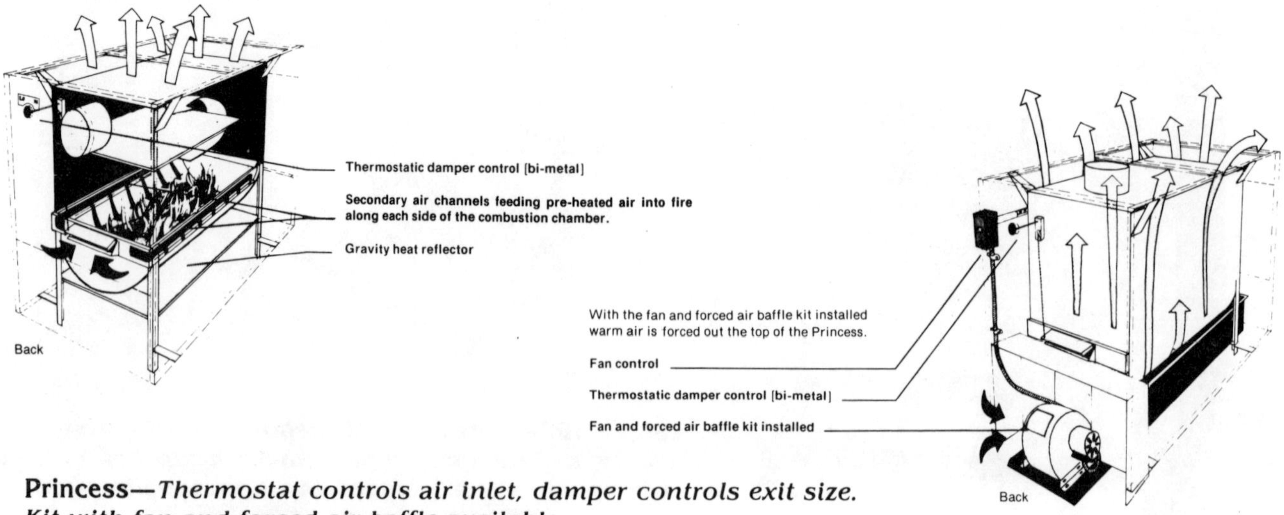

Back

Thermostatic damper control (bi-metal)

Secondary air channels feeding pre-heated air into fire along each side of the combustion chamber.

Gravity heat reflector

With the fan and forced air baffle kit installed warm air is forced out the top of the Princess.

Fan control

Thermostatic damper control (bi-metal)

Fan and forced air baffle kit installed

Back

Princess—*Thermostat controls air inlet, damper controls exit size. Kit with fan and forced air baffle available.*

Manufacturer	Stove	Dimensions	Door Opening	Firebox Size	Wood Length	Flue Size	Flue Location	Materials	Weight (lbs.)
Monarch Kitchen Appliances	Model CR24D	35½ " H × 32 " W × 20½ " L	9¾ " H × 21¼ " W	19⅝ " × × 10 " × 20¼ "		6 "	Back	Steel with cast iron linings; enamel cabinet	260 s.w.

Features Thermostatic draft; spark shield; ash pan; smoke shield. Blower is optional.

| Monarch Kitchen Appliances | Model CR24E | 35½ " H × 32¼ " W × 20¼ " L | 15¼ " × 10¹⁄₁₆ " | 20¼ " × 11¾ " × 22 " | | 6 " | Back | 16 ga. steel; firebrick lined; enamel cabinet | 235 s.w. |

Features Smoke shield; thermostatic draft; ash pan. Blower, shaker grate are optional.

| Monarch Kitchen Appliances | Model CR24F | 35½ " H × 32 " W × 20½ " L | 9¾ " × 21¼ " | 19⅝ " × 10 " × 20¼ " | | 6 " | Back | 16 ga. steel; enamel cabinet | 260 s.w. |

Features Smoke shield; thermostatic draft; ash pan; spark shield. Blower; shaker grate are optional.

| Portland Stove Foundry | Trolla No. 530 | 37½ " H × 26 " W × 16½ " L | | 14 " × 8 " × 8 " | | 5 " | Back | Enamel cabinet; firebrick lined; cast iron | |

Features Grate; ash pan; thermostatic draft.

| Riteway Manufacturing Co. | Wood Heater #2000 | 33 " H × 21 " W × 33 " L | 12 " × 12 " | 4 cu. ft. | 24 " | 6 " | | 14 ga. steel | 200 s.w. |

Features Thermostatic draft; grate; ash pan.

| Riteway Manufacturing Co. | Model #37 | 40 " H × 24 " W × 33 " L | 12 " × 12 " | 7½ cu. ft. | 24 " | 6 " | Back | 14 ga. steel | 400 s.w. |

Features Firebrick lined; thermostatic draft; grate; ash pan.

| Shenandoah Mfg. Co. | Model R-76 | 36 " H × 24 " W × 35½ " L | 13 " × 12 " | 23 " × 15½ " × 26 " | | 6 " | Back | Porcelain cabinet | 280 s.w. |

Features Firebrick lined; thermostatic draft; grate; ash pan.

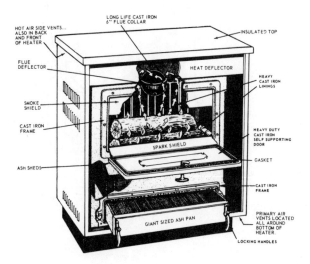

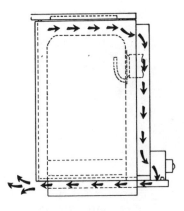

The Impression—*Fireplace design with double steel walls, standing grate, bottom lined with firebrick. Has ash pan; aluminum surface plate for cooking.*

Manufacturer	Stove	Dimensions	Door Opening	Firebox Size	Wood Length	Flue Size	Flue Location	Materials	Weight (lbs.)
Shenandoah Mfg. Co.	Model #R-76L	33″ H × 21″ W × 29″ L	13″ × 12″	23″ × 15½″ × 26″		6″	Back	Porcelain cabinet	215 s.w.
	Features	Firebrick lined; thermostatic draft; grate; ash pan.							
Southport Stoves	Efel	33½″ H × 28½″ W × 15″ L				8″	Back	Cast iron; porcelain cabinet	199 s.w.
	Features	Grate; ash pan; cooktop surface; baffled; glass door.							
U.S. Stove Co.	Wonderwood #726	33″ H × 19″ W × 32½″ L			26″	6″			220 s.w.
	Features	Thermostatic draft; grate; ash pan; firebrick lined. Blower is optional.							
Washington Stove Works	Norwester #38	32″ H × 29″ W × 21″ L	10″ × 13½″	12″ × 24″		6″		Enamel cabinet	270 s.w.
	Features	Blower is optional.							
Washington Stove Works	Norwester #40	31″ H × 29″ W × 19″ L	10″ × 13½″	12″ × 24″		6″		Enamel cabinet	206 s.w.
	Features	Thermostatic draft; cast iron linings.							

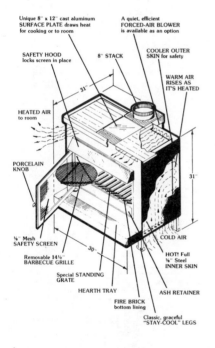

Monarch Model CR 24 D—*Big loading door has smoke shield that keeps smoke from pouring into room when loading wood. Steel cabinet has insulated top, louvers below top and on sides. Optional blower kit takes air from top of combustion chamber, forces it out through heater base.*

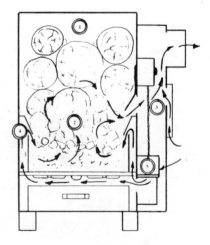

Riteway Model 37—*Big combustion chamber for holding wood. Lined with firebrick. Magnetic damper. Cast-iron grates.*

FURNACES

Manufacturer	Furnace	Dimensions	Door Opening	Firebox Size	Wood Length	Flue Size	Materials	Weight	BTU's/ hour
Arotek Corporation Add-on Unit	Hoval Boiler HK 30	45″ H × 26″ W × 28″ L	12″ × 10″				Firebrick lined	738	80,000- 120,000
Features Combination: oil/gas. Hot water hook-up; automatic draft regulator.									
Arotek Corporation— Add-on Unit	Hoval Boiler HK 45	55″ H × 26″ W × 36″ L	12″ × 13″ (top); 12″ × 10″ (front)				Firebrick lined	1040	128,000- 180,000
Features Combination: oil/gas. Thermostatic draft; hot water hook-up.									
Arotek Corporation— Add-on Unit	Hoval Boiler HK 60	55″ H × 26″ W × 41″ L	15″ × 10″ (top); 12″ × 10″ (front)				Firebrick lined	1250	188,000- 240,000
Features Combination: oil/gas. Thermostatic draft; hot water hook-up.									
Arotek Corporation— Add-on Unit	Hoval Boiler HK 75	55″ H × 34″ W × 41″ L	15″ × 13″ (top); 12″ × 10″ (front)				Firebrick lined	1730	248,000- 300,000
Features Combination: oil/gas. Thermostatic draft; hot water hook-up.									
Arotek Corporation— Multi-fuel Boilers	Hoval ZK 25	66″ H × 33½″ W × 21½″ L		12″ W × 14¼″ L					68,000- 88,000
Features Combination: coal/oil/gas/electricity. Separate combustion chambers and separate flues; hot water tank.									
Arotek Corporation— Multi-fuel Boilers	Hoval ZK 35	70″ H × 33½″ W × 28″ L		12″ W × 21″ L					80,000- 100,000
Features Combination: coal/oil/gas/electricity. Separate combustion chambers and separate flues; hot water tank.									
Arotek Corporation— Multi-fuel Boilers	Hoval ZK 50	70″ H × 42¼″ W × 28″ L		16½″ W × 21″ L					112,000- 144,000
Features Combination: coal/oil/gas/electricity. Separate combustion chambers and separate flues; hot water tank.									
Bellway Manufacturer	Model #F50	48″ H × 30″ W × 44″ L	14″ × 17″		24″	6″	Firebrick lined; steel cabinet		50,000
Features Combination: coal/oil/electricity. Thermostatic draft; grate.									
Bellway Manufacturer	Model #F75	55″ H × 36″ W × 54″ L	15″ × 20″		36″	7″	Firebrick lined; steel cabinet		75,000
Features Combination: coal/oil/electricity. Thermostatic draft; grate.									
Bellway Manufacturer	Model #F125	60″ H × 46″ W × 72″ L	18″ × 23″		48″	8″	Firebrick lined; steel cabinet		125,000
Features Combination: coal/oil/electricity. Thermostatic draft; grate.									

Manufacturer	Furnace	Dimensions	Door Opening	Firebox Size	Wood Length	Flue Size	Materials	Weight (lbs.)	BTU's/ hour
Carlson Mech. Contractors, Inc.	Solid Fuel Boiler Model SF-1	54" H × 23" W × 28" L	14" × 15"	20" × 15" × 26"	20"	8"	¼" steel	700	170,000

Features Thermostatic draft; water heater.

Manufacturer	Furnace	Dimensions	Door Opening	Firebox Size	Wood Length	Flue Size	Materials	Weight (lbs.)	BTU's/ hour
Charmaster Products, Inc.	Charmaster Wood/Oil	54" H × 28" W × 55" L	11" × 13"	22½" W × 30" L	30"		Steel plate; ³⁄₁₆" firebox; 20 ga. steel cabinet	680	

Features Combination: oil. Thermostatic draft; blower.

Manufacturer	Furnace	Dimensions	Door Opening	Firebox Size	Wood Length	Flue Size	Materials	Weight (lbs.)	BTU's/ hour
Charmaster Products, Inc.	Charmaster Wood/Gas	54" H × 28" W × 55" L	11" × 13"	22½" W × 30" L	30"		Steel plate; ³⁄₁₆" firebox; 20 ga. steel cabinet	849	

Features Combination: gas. Thermostatic draft; blower.

Manufacturer	Furnace	Dimensions	Door Opening	Firebox Size	Wood Length	Flue Size	Materials	Weight (lbs.)	BTU's/ hour
Combo Furnace Co.	Forced Air Furnace No. W12-23-0 or No. W12-23-1	53" H × 28½" W × 54" L	12" × 12"	16" × 24"		8"	12 and 7 ga. firebox; 12 ga, heat exchanger; 22 ga. casing	525 s.w.	84,000-95,000

Features Combination: oil. Blower; thermostats; cast iron grate and liners; hook-ups for domestic water.

Manufacturer	Furnace	Dimensions	Door Opening	Firebox Size	Wood Length	Flue Size	Materials	Weight (lbs.)	BTU's/ hour
Combo Furnace Co.	Forced Air Furnace W12-22-8 or W012-22-9	57" H × 30" W × 72" L	12" × 12"	19½" × 36"		9"	12 and 7 ga. firebox; 12 ga. heat exchanger; 22 ga. casing	730 s.w.	140,000-175,000

Features Combination: oil. Thermostats; blower; cast iron grate and liners; hook-ups for domestic water.

Manufacturer	Furnace	Dimensions	Door Opening	Firebox Size	Wood Length	Flue Size	Materials	Weight (lbs.)	BTU's/ hour
Combo Furnace Co.	Model No. WB 22-10 or WOB-22-11 Hot Water Boiler	49½" H × 28½" W × 30½" L	12" × 12"	16" × 24"		8"	12 and 7 ga. firebox; 12 ga. heat exchanger; 22 ga. casing	820 s.w.	84,000-126,000

Features Combination: oil. Thermostats; cast iron grate and liners.

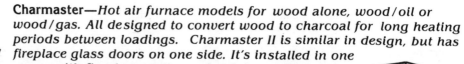

Charmaster—*Hot air furnace models for wood alone, wood/oil or wood/gas. All designed to convert wood to charcoal for long heating periods between loadings. Charmaster II is similar in design, but has fireplace glass doors on one side. It's installed in one room, with fireplace wall opening into another. Fireplace can be opened for putting in wood, or enjoying fire; or wood can be added to furnace through conventional door.*

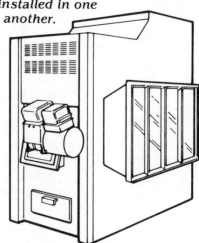

Manufacturer	Furnace	Dimensions	Door Opening	Firebox Size	Wood Length	Flue Size	Materials	Weight (lbs.)	BTU's/hour
Defiance Company	Volcano Add-on Unit	34¼" H × 20½" W × 27" L	11½" × 11½"		24"		¼" plate firebox		
	Features Combination: can be connected to existing hot air system. Ash drawer; baffles; humidifier.								
Defiance Company	Volcano II Add-on Unit	37¼" H × 20¾" W × 27¼" L	11½" × 11½"		24"		¼" plate firebox	485	
	Features Combination: can be connected to existing hot air system. Hollow baffles.								
Dual Fuel Products	Newmac Oil-Wood Furnace #CL-115	51¾" H × 46" W × 54" L	17½" × 17½"	6 cu. ft.	24"	8"	Stainless steel firebox liner	675	113,000
	Features Combination: oil. Thermostatic draft; blowers; separate combustion chambers.								
Dual Fuel Products	Newmac Oil-Wood Furnace #Cl-140	51¾" H × 46" W × 54" L	17½" × 17½"	6 cu. ft.	24"	8"	Stainless steel firebox liner	680	137,000
	Features Combination: oil. Thermostatic draft; blowers; separate combustion chambers.								
Dual Fuel Products	Newmac Oil-Wood Furnace #CL-155	51¾" H × 46" W × 54" L	17½" × 17½"	6 cu. ft.	24"	8"	Stainless steel firebox liner	685	149,000
	Features Combination: oil. Thermostatic draft; blowers; separate combustion chambers.								
Dual Fuel Products	Newmac Oil-Wood Furnace #Cl-170	51¾" H × 46" W × 54" L	17½" × 17½"	6 cu. ft.	24"	8"	Stainless steel firebox liner	690	168,000
	Features Combination: oil. Thermostatic draft; blowers; separate combustion chambers.								
Duo-matic	Duo-matic Combination Furnace	51¼" H × 44" W × 50¾" L	14½" × 12"	20½" × 18¾"	24"	8"	Steel with firebrick	975	
	Features Combination: oil/gas/coal. Separate combustion chambers; thermostatic draft.								
Enwell Corporation	Spaulding Concept Furnace	68" H × 31" W × 56" L	10" × 13"	11 cu. ft.	30"	5"		1000	20,000-100,000
	Features Four-speed blower; automatic thermostatic controls; burns trash, wood, waste; one-piece refractory firebox.								
G & S Mill	Model .5	56" H × 32" W × 72" L	17" × 12"	6.2 cu. ft.	30"	6"	½" steel fire chamber; ⅜" steel heat exchanger	2600	187,652
	Features Thermostatic draft; blower.								
G & S Mill	Model 1	56" H × 32" W × 120" L	17" × 12"	12.5 cu. ft.	54"	8"	½" steel	3100	377,927
	Features Thermostatic draft, blower.								
G & S Mill	Model 2	70" H × 38" W × 100" L	21" × 15"	19.6 cu. ft.	54"	8"	½" steel	4500	595,335
	Features Thermostatic draft; blower.								
G & S Mill	Model 3	82" H × 44" W × 120" L	25.5" × 18"	28.2 cu. ft.	54"	10"	½" steel	6800	860,000
	Features Thermostatic draft; blower.								
G & S Mill	Model 4	94" H × 50" W × 120" L	30" × 21"	38.4 cu. ft.	54"	12"	½" steel	8500	1,171,750
	Features Thermostatic draft; blower.								

Manufacturer	Furnace	Dimensions	Door Opening	Firebox Size	Wood Length	Flue Size	Materials	Weight (lbs.)	BTU's/ hour
G & S Mill	Model 5	106″ H × 56″ W × 120″ L	34″ × 24″	50.2 cu. ft.	54″	12″	½″ steel	10,800	1,548,000
	Features Thermostatic draft; blower.								
Hunter	Valley Comfort #F-51	50″ H × 32½″ W × 65½″ L	12¾″ × 15¾″	36″ L	36″	8″	Steel plate; firebrick lined	860 s.w.	90,000
	Features Thermostatic draft; blower.								
Hunter	Valley Comfort #F-71	50″ H × 32½″ W × 77½″ L	12¾″ × 15¾″	48″ L	48″	8″	Steel plate; firebrick lined	950 s.w.	130,000
	Features Thermostatic draft; blower.								
Hunter	Valley Comfort #RB-3D	46″ H × 30″ W × 45″ L	12¾″ × 15¾″	36″ L × 23″ W	36″	8″	Steel plate	474 s.w.	90,000
	Features Thermostatic draft.								
Hunter	Valley Comfort #RB-4D	46″ H × 30″ W × 57″ L	12¾″ × 15¾″	48″ L × 23″ W	48″	8″	Steel plate	550 s.w.	
	Features Thermostatic draft.								
Integrated Thermal Systems	HS Tarm #OT-35B Multi-fuel Boiler	51″ H × 39½″ W × 30″ L		30″ × 10½″ × 21½″	21½″		⁵⁄₁₆″ plate; enamel cabinet	1089	112,000
	Features Combination: oil/gas/electricity. Hot water heater; thermostatic draft; grate.								
Integrated Thermal Systems	HS Tarm #OT-50B Multi-fuel Boiler	51″ H × 46¾″ W × 30″ L		30″ × 10½″ × 21½″	21½″		⁵⁄₁₆″ plate; enamel cabinet	1444	140,000
	Features Combination: oil/gas/electricity. Hot water heater; thermostatic draft; grate.								
Integrated Thermal Systems	HS Tarm #OT-70B	51″ H × 46¾″ W × 39¾″ L		30″ H × 13¼″ W × 31″ L	31″		⁵⁄₁₆″ plate; enamel cabinet	1800	200,000
	Features Combination: oil/gas/electricity. Hot water heater; thermostatic draft; grate.								
Integrated Thermal	Tasso #A3-9	39½″ H × 18″ W × 27½″ L		24″ × 13″ × 23″		6″	Enamel cabinet	866 s.w.	144,000
	Features Combination: oil/gas. Thermostatic draft; grate.								
Integrated Thermal Systems	HS Tarm MB-Solo #30	50½″ H × 17¾″ W × 25¼″ L	10″ × 12″	12½″ × 15½″			⁵⁄₁₆″ plate; enamel cabinet		72,000
	Features Combination: oil/gas. Water heater; grate; thermostatic draft.								
Integrated Thermal Systems	HS Tarm MB-Solo #45	50½″ H × 17¾″ W × 28¼″ L	10″ × 12″	12½″ × 15½″			⁵⁄₁₆″ plate; enamel cabinet		100,000
	Features Combination: gas/oil. Water heater; thermostatic draft; grate.								
Integrated Thermal Systems	HS Tarm MB-Solo #55	50½″ H × 21″ W × 41½″ L	10″ × 12″	15½″ × 27½″			⁵⁄₁₆″ plate; enamel cabinet		140,000
	Features Combination: oil/gas. Water heater; thermostatic draft; grate.								
Integrated Thermal Systems	HS Tarm MB-Solo #75	50½″ H × 21″ W × 41½″ L	10″ × 12″	15½″ × 27½″			⁵⁄₁₆″ plate; enamel cabinet		180,000
	Features Combination: oil/gas. Water heater; thermostatic draft; grate.								

Manufacturer	Furnace	Dimensions	Door Opening	Firebox Size	Wood Length	Flue Size	Materials	Weight (lbs.)	BTU's/ hour
Jordahl Industries Inc.	Ltd Limited 1000 Series	29″ H × 20″ W × 22″ L			18″	6″	Firebrick lined		75,000-85,000
	Features Combination: oil/gas. Blower.								
Jordahl Industries Inc.	Ltd Limited 2000 Series	36″ H × 22″ W × 28″ L			24″	8″	Firebrick lined		120,000-130,000
	Features Combination: oil/gas. Blower.								
Jordahl Industries Inc.	Ltd Limited 3000 Series	42″ H × 26″ W × 30″ L			26″	8″	Firebrick lined		130,000-150,000
	Features Combination: oil/gas. Blower.								
Kerr Controls Ltd.	Scotsman Wood Furnace	44½″ H × 29″ W × 39″ L		36″ × 23″	36″	7″	⅛″ plate steel	392 s.w.	140,000
	Features Combination: oil. Thermostatic draft; blower.								
Kerr Controls Ltd.	Titan Boiler	43½″ H × 26½″ W × 35½″ L	14½″ × 14½″	16″ × 18¼″ × 25½″		7″	Firebrick lined		
	Features Thermostatic draft.								
Kerr Controls Ltd.	DWO Series	45½″ H × 42¼″ W × 48½″ L				7″	Stainless steel	590 s.w.	114,000-148,000
	Features Combination: oil. Separate combustion chambers.								
Kerr Controls Ltd.	CWO Series	51¼″ H × 44″ W × 50¾″ L				8″		970 s.w.	112,000-170,000
	Features Combination: coal/oil. Separate combustion chambers.								
Kickapoo Stove Works	BBR-D	35¼″ H × 26″ W × 30″ L	8⅝″ × 11⅝″ × 11⅝″ × 11⅝″		24″	6″	Steel; cast iron doors and frames	334	
	Features Combination: gas/oil/electricity/solar. Grate; ash pan; firebrick lined.								
Kickapoo Stove Works	BBR-D5	35¼″ H × 26″ W × 46″ L	8⅝″ × 11⅝″ × 11⅝″ × 11⅝″		24″	6″	Steel; cast iron doors and frames	385	
	Features Blower.								

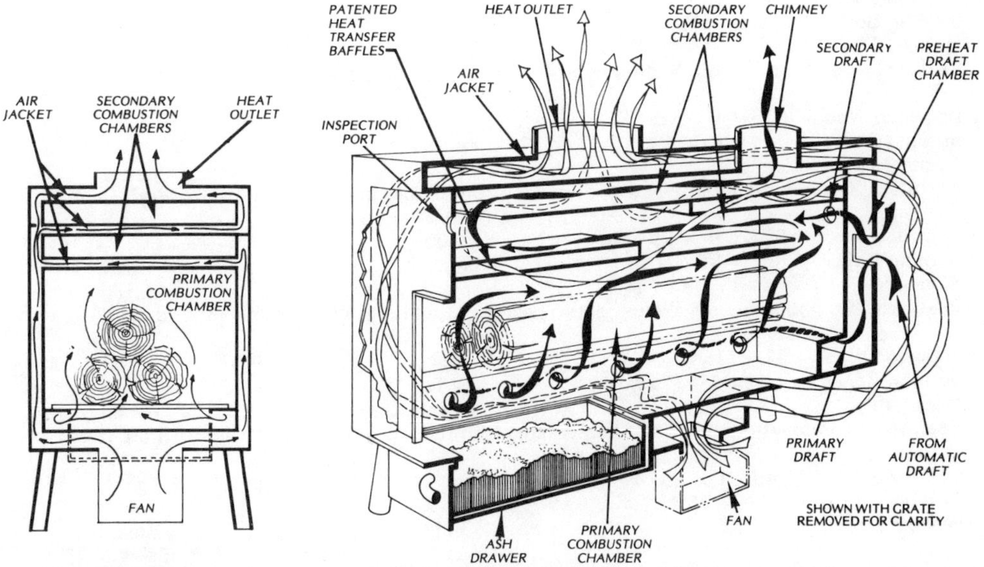

Volcano II—*Here's a square, sturdy steel stove built specifically to add on to a hot air system. It has an ash pan and ash removal system that can't be beat. A blower pumps heat up from the bottom, around the combustion chamber and out through the top and into the hot air system.*

Manufacturer	Furnace	Dimensions	Door Opening	Firebox Size	Wood Length	Flue Size	Materials	Weight (lbs.)	BTU's/hour
Longwood Furnace Corporation	Longwood Dualfuel	40"H × 24"W × 66"L	12" × 12"		60"	6"	Aluminum jacket; stainless steel 14 ga. firebox	550	150,000
Features	Combination: gas/oil. Blower; cast iron grates.								
Lynndale Manufacturing Co.	Furnace #810	51"H × 34"W × 68"L		15 cu. ft.	30"	7"	24 ga. sheet metal jacket; firebrick lined	1200	125,000
Features	Combination: oil/gas/electricity. Thermostatic draft; blower; grate.								
Lynndale Manufacturing Co.	Furnace #910	51"H × 39"W × 73"L		18 cu. ft.	30"	7"	24 ga. sheet metal jacket; firebrick lined	1300	200,000
Features	Combination: oil/gas/electricity. Thermostatic draft; blower; grate.								
Lynndale Manufacturing Co.	Furnace #1007	64"H × 46"W × 96"L		47 cu. ft.		10"		3100	
Features	Thermostatic draft.								
Marathon Heater Company, Inc.	Logwood Lo-Profile	52"H × 32"W × 45"L	16" × 14"		24"	7"	⅛" and 3⁄16" ga. steel	800 s.w.	120,000
Features	Combination: oil/gas. Cast iron tubular grates.								
Marathon Heater Company, Inc.	Logwood Standard	60"H × 32"W × 60"L	16" × 20"		36"	8"	⅛" and 3⁄16" ga. steel	1300 s.w.	245,000
Features	Combination: oil/gas. Cast iron tubular grates.								
Marathon Heater Company, Inc.	Logwood Standard	60"H × 32"W × 72"L	16" × 20"		48"	9"	⅛" and 3⁄16" ga. steel	1800	327,600
Features	Combination: oil/gas. Cast iron tubular grates.								
Marathon Heater Company, Inc.	Logwood Wood-burning Boiler Model 16"	57¾"H × 25"W × 35½"L		4.75 cu. ft.		8"		900	80,000
Features	Combination: oil. Water heater; cast iron tubular grates; thermostatic draft.								
Marathon Heater Company, Inc.	Logwood Wood-burning Boiler Model 24"	57¾"H × 25"W × 47½"L		7.11 cu. ft.		8"		1200	125,000
Features	Combination: oil. Water heater; cast iron tubular grates; thermostatic draft.								
Marathon Heater Company, Inc.	Logwood Wood-burning Boiler Model 36"	57¾"H × 25"W × 59½"L		10.66 cu. ft.		8"		1500	200,000
Features	Combination: oil. Water heater; cast iron tubular grates; thermostatic draft.								
Marathon Heater Company, Inc.	Logwood Wood-burning Boiler Model 48"	57¾"H × 25"W × 71½"L		14.2 cu. ft.		9"		1800	300,000
Features	Combination: oil. Water heater; cast iron tubular grates; thermostatic draft.								
Minnesota Energy Savers Inc.	Lumberjack Add-on Wood Furnace	46"H × 23"W × 43"L	12" × 15"	16" × 18" × 30"	28"	8"	12 ga. steel; firebox of 3⁄16" steel and firebrick lined	550	55,000
Features	Combination: oil/gas. Grate; blower; hinged smoke screen.								

Manufacturer	Furnace	Dimensions	Door Opening	Firebox Size	Wood Length	Flue Size	Materials	Weight (lbs.)	BTU's/ hour
Monarch Kitchen Appliances	Model AF 124	30¾" H × 18" W × 26" L		14" × 24" × 16"	24"	6"	12 ga. steel	160 s.w.	35,000
	Features Combination: oil/gas. Blower; grate.								
Monarch Kitchen Appliances	Model AF 224	36" H × 20" W × 30" L		14" × 26" × 18"	24"	6"	12 ga. steel	225 s.w.	50,000
	Features Combination: oil/gas. Thermostatic draft; blower; grate.								
Monarch Kitchen Appliances	Model AF 324	42" H × 22" W × 32" L		27" × 22" × 14"		6"		300 s.w.	75,000
	Features Combination: oil/gas. Thermostatic draft; blower; grate.								
Powrmatic	Model OW-110 Combination Furnace	51" H ×48½" W × 54" L	17½" × 17½"		24"	8"	Firebrick lined firebox	950	112,000
	Features Combination: oil. Two blowers; thermostatic draft; separate combustion chambers.								
Powrmatic	Model OW-140 Combination Furnace	51" H × 48½" W × 54" L	17½" × 17½"		24"	8"	Firebrick lined firebox	960	140,000
	Features Combination: oil. Two blowers; thermostatic draft; separate combustion chambers.								
Powrmatic	Model OW-150 Combination Furnace	51" H ×48½" W × 54" L	17½" × 17½"		24"	8"	Firebrick lined firebox	965	150,000
	Features Combination: oil. Two blowers; thermostatic draft; separate combustion chambers.								
Powrmatic	Model OW-170 Combination Furnace	51" H × 48½" W × 54" L	17½" × 17½"		24"	8"	Firebrick lined firebox	980	170,000
	Features Combination: oil. Two blowers; thermostatic draft; separate combustion chambers.								

← **G & S Mill Model 1**—*This and four larger models are built for heating large buildings. Homeowners, these aren't for you.*

Valley Comfort—*The four models listed feature separate combustion chambers for use of wood or oil, feeding gases into a common secondary heat exchanger, plus separate thermostats, and twin blowers.* →

Tasso A-3—*This boiler is manufactured in Denmark, can be used alone or combined with an oil or gas-fired boiler in any hot-water heating system. Comes in four sizes, from 126,000 to 180,000 Btu-hour. Cast-iron grates, insulated steel jacket, and designed so that the boiler firebox is surrounded by water.*

159

Manufacturer	Furnace	Dimensions	Door Opening	Firebox Size	Wood Length	Flue Size	Materials	Weight (lbs.)	BTU's/ hour
Ram Forge	Wood Furnace	48″ H × 27″ W × 42″ L	10″ × 10″	14″ × 28½″	28″	5″	24 ga. steel	350 s.w.	75,000
	Features Combination: oil/gas. Blower; baffles.								
Riteway Manufacturing Company	Furnace LF30	65″ H × 36″ W × 73″ L	14″ × 16″	20 cu. ft.	24″	8″	Steel with fire-brick lining	1800 s.w.	160,000
	Features Combination: oil/gas. Thermostatic draft; blower; grate; heat exchanger.								
Riteway Manufacturing Company	Furnace LF50	65″ H × 36″ W × 85″ L	14″ × 16″	30 cu. ft.	36″	8″	Steel with fire-brick lining	2400 s.w.	215,000
	Features Combination: oil/gas. Thermostatic draft; blower; grate; heat exchanger.								
Riteway Manufacturing Company	Furnace LF70	65″ H × 40″ W × 103″ L	16″ × 16″	45 cu. ft.	48″	10″	Steel with fire-brick lining	3050 s.w.	350,000
	Features Combination: oil/gas. Thermostatic draft; blower; grate; heat exchanger.								
Riteway Manufacturing Company	Boiler LB30	66″ H × 36″ W × 56″ L	14″ × 16″	17.5 cu. ft.	24″	8″	Steel with fire-brick lining	2000 s.w.	160,000
	Features Combination: oil/gas. Thermostatic draft; blower; grate.								
Riteway Manufacturing Company	Boiler LB50	66″ H × 36″ W × 68″ L	14″ × 16″	26.2 cu. ft.	36″	8″	Steel casing	2600 s.w.	200,000
	Features Combination: oil/gas. Thermostatic draft; grate; blower.								
Riteway Manufacturing Company	Boiler LB70	66″ H × 40″ W × 84″ L	16″ × 16″	43.4 cu. ft.	48″	10″	Steel casing	3200 s.w.	350,000
	Features Combination: oil/gas. Thermostatic draft; grate; blower.								
Sam Daniels Company	Chunk Furnace R30W	56″ H × 41″ W × 41″ L	15″ × 17″	21½″ × 21⅝″ × 30″	30″	8″	26 ga. steel with stainless steel firebox		100,000
	Features Combination: oil. Thermostatic draft; grate.								
Sam Daniels Company	Furnace R36W	56″ H × 41″ W × 47″ L	15″ × 17″	25½″ × 21⅝″ × 36″	36″	8″	Stainless steel firebox		128,000
	Features Thermostatic draft; grate.								
Sam Daniels Company	Furnace R42W	56″ H × 41″ W × 53″ L	15″ × 17″	25½″ × 21⅝″ × 42″	42″	8″			157,000
	Features Thermostatic draft; grate.								
Sam Daniels Company	Furnace R48W	56″ H × 41″ W × 60″ L	15″ × 17″	25½″ × 21⅝″ × 48″	48″	9″			225,000
	Features Thermostatic draft; grate.								
Sam Daniels Company	Furnace R1-60W	56″ H × 41″ W × 70½″ L	15″ × 17″	25½″ × 21⅝″ × 60″	60″	9″			300,000
	Features Thermostatic draft; grate.								
Sam Daniels Company	R2-60W	65″ H × 53½″ W × 73″ L	15″ × 17″	29″ × 25″ × 60″	60″	10″			400,000
	Features Thermostatic draft; grate.								

Manufacturer	Furnace	Dimensions	Door Opening	Firebox Size	Wood Length	Flue Size	Materials	Weight (lbs.)	BTU's/hour
Solar Wood Energy Corp.	Northeaster 101B	48" H × 36" W × 29" L	13½" × 13½"	24" × 24" × 21"	16"	7"	⅛" steel with steel liners	460 s.w.	100,000
Features Hot water coils; thermostatic draft; grate; blower.									
Solar Wood Energy Corp.	Northeaster 224-B	48" H × 36" W × 35" L	13½" × 13½"	27" L	24"	7"	⅛" steel with steel liners	550 s.w.	125,000
Features Hot water coils; thermostatic draft; grate; blower.									
Thermo-Control Wood Stoves	Model 500A	47" H × 31" W × 44" L	18" × 21"	24" × 24" × 34"		8"	Firebrick lined	480 s.w.	
Features Combination: oil/solar/gas/electric. Thermostatic draft.									
Thermo-Control Wood Stoves	Model 500W	32" H × 24" W × 40" L	18" × 21"	24" × 24" × 34"		8"	Firebrick lined	455 s.w.	
Features Combination: oil/solar/gas/electric. Thermostatic draft.									
Wood Energy Systems Corp.	Wesco Boiler		10" × 14"	17" × 14" × 28"	24"		24 ga. galvanized steel; firebox of ¼" plate	350	70,000
Features Combination: oil/gas. Hot water hook-up.									

HS Tarm MB-Solo—*Here's a wood-burning boiler to link with your oil- or gas-fired central water heating system.*

Kickapoo BBR—*The BBR-D and the BBR-D5 (slightly longer than the first model, and has a blower unit) are wood furnaces that can be linked to your existing system by sharing the existing plenum or the ductwork. Steel construction, cast-iron doors and grate, ash pan. Model shown is the BBR-D.*

Longwood Dualfuel—*Here's a combination furnace (wood and oil or gas) that offers a rustproof aluminum jacket, a stainless steel combustion chamber, large door with a roller for easier loading of big wood chunks, and a flue heat reclaimer.*

COOKSTOVES

The following stoves are designed primarily for cooking.

Manufacturer	Stove	Dimensions	Height to Cooking Surface	Firebox Size	Size of Cooking Surface	Number and Size of Griddles	Size of Oven	Flue Size	Flue Location	Weight/ Materials
Atlanta Stove Works, Inc.	#15-36		29½″	15″ L	35½″ × 21¼″	4 @ 8″; 2 @ 5½″	15″ × 14″ × 11″	7″		285 Cast iron body
Features Warming oven.										
Atlanta Stove Works, Inc.	#8316		28¾″	17½″ L	30¼″ × 20½″	4 @ 8″	13½″ × 13″ × 10″	6″		155 Cast iron body
Atlanta Stove Works, Inc.	#5115LB		31″	15″ L	36″ × 21½″	6 @ 8″	15″ × 14″ × 11″	7″		362 Semi-enameled finish; cast iron body
Features Water reservoir; shelf.										
Autocrat Corporation	Hillcrest		31″		21¼″ × 37½″	6 @ 8″	17″ × 18″ × 11″			240 Porcelain enamel finish; body of 20 ga. steel
Features Water reservoir; shelf.										
Autocrat Corporation	Ridgetop		31″		21¼″ × 34½″	6 @ 8″	17″ × 18″ × 11″			215 Porcelain enamel finish; body of 20 ga. steel
Features Shelf.										
Autocrat Corporation	Kitchenheater	36″ H × 14½″ W × 31″ L	36″	8½″ × 17″ × 8½″	18½″ × 11″	1 @ 8″	6″			160 s.w. Porcelain enamel finish; cast iron firebox linings
Bow and Arrow Stove Co.	Preporod	33½″ H × 28½″ W × 20″L	33½″	5″ H × 6½″ W × 16″ L	20″ × 16½″		10¾″ × 15½″ × 18″	5″	Side	222 Firebrick lining
Features Grates; glass oven door.										
The Merry Music Box	Styria 106	34″ H × 34″ W × 42″ L	34″	5″ × 7½″ × 18½″	29″ × 21″		9″ × 14″ × 23″	5″	Back	611 Enamel finish; firebrick lining
Features Water reservoir; towel rack.										
The Merry Music Box	Styria 119	34″ H × 36″ W × 47″ L	34″	20″ L	30″ × 21″		9″ × 14″ × 24″			800 Enamel finish; firebrick lining
Features Water reservoir; towel rack.										

Manufacturer	Stove	Dimensions	Height to Cooking Surface	Firebox Size	Size of Cooking Surface	Number and Size of Griddles	Size of Oven	Flue Size	Flue Location	Weight/ Materials
The Merry Music Box	Styria 130	34″ H × 40″ W × 51″ L	34″	5″ × 7½″ × 20″	36″ × 24″		9″ × 14″ × 29″	6″	Back	1040 Enamel finish; firebrick lining
Features Water reservoir; towel rack.										
Monarch Kitchen Appliances	Model CE 119Y-1	47¾″ H × 43″ W × 25″ L	34⅝″	8″ × 17½″	18″ × 20″ (coal/ wood); 20″ × 20″ (electric)	2 (coal/ wood), 4 (electric)	15¾″ × 19″ × 21″	7″	Back	537 s.w. Porcelain enamel finish
Features Grates; combination electric/coal/wood stove.										
Monarch Kitchen Appliances	Model R 9 CW	47¾″ H × 25″ W × 43″ L	34⅝″	8″ × 17½″	18″ × 20″		19″ × 15¾″ × 21″	7″	Back	513 s.w. Porcelain enamel finish
Features Coal/wood range; grates; water heater.										
Monarch Kitchen Appliances	Model 24 PY2	36″ H × 14″ W × 23″ L	36″	7″ × 17″		2		6″		Porcelain enamel finish
Features Coal/wood range; grates.										
Old Country Appliances	Salzburg D7N	33½″ H × 35½″ W × 23½″ L	33½″	15¾″ L			8¼″ × 11¾″ × 21¼″	5″	Top/ back/ side	420 Fireclay firebox lining
Features Baking shelf; water reservoir; grates.										
Old Country Appliances	Tirolia DN9	33½″ H × 22½″ W × 21½″L	33½″	16½″ L			9½″ H × 15¾″ W ×21¼″L	6″	Top/ back/ side	540 Enamel finish; fireclay lining
Features Grates; water heater; baking shelf.										
Old Country Appliances	Alpine D6	31½″ H × 33½″ W × 21½″ L	31½″	8″ × 13¾″			8¼″ × 10¼″ × 19″ L	5″	Top/ back/ side	310 Enamel body; fireclay lining
Features Water reservoir; baking shelf.										
Old Country Appliances	Thriftmaster SD4	28¼″ H × 26¾″ W × 20½″ L	28¼″	6¼″ × 11¾″			8″ × 10″ × 17″	5″	Side/ back	245 Enamel finish; fireclay lining
Features Baking shelf.										
Pioneer Lamp & Stove Co.	Victory Jr. 1911 Wood/Coal Range	57″ H × 40″ W × 28″ L	57″	7″ × 9″ × 18½″	30″		15½″ × 15½″ × 10½″	7″	Back	325 Cast iron
Features Wood/coal capacity/hot water coil.										
Portland Stove Foundry Co.	Queen Atlantic 408	32½″ H × 30¾″ W × 52″ L	32½″	9″ × 7″ × 23″		6	20″ × 20″			Porcelain enamel finish; cast iron body; firebox linings
Features Water heater; warming oven; shelf.										

Manufacturer	Stove	Dimensions	Height to Cooking Surface	Firebox Size	Size of Cooking Surface	Number and Size of Griddles	Size of Oven	Flue Size	Flue Location	Weight/ Materials
Portland Stove Foundry Co.	Atlantic 8	28½"H × 38½"	28½"	24"L	30" × 26½"	4 @ 8"	20" × 22"	6"	Top	Cast iron body
	Features Water reservoir.									
Portland Stove Foundry Co.	Trolla #354	25"H × 29"W × 21¼"L	25"	6" × 6" × 12"		2 @ 12½"	7" × 13" × 13"	5"	Top	220 Porcelain finish; cast iron body
	Features Longer legs available.									
Portland Stove Foundry Co.	Trolla #325	15¾"H × 21½"W × 14"L	15¾"	16" × 9½"		2 @ 9½"	None	4"	Top	91½ Enamel finish; cast iron body
	Features Longer legs available.									
S/A Imports Division	Stanley 8B & MK1	28⅜"H × 35⅜"W × 21¾"L	28⅜"				13" × 15¾" × 15"		Top	Enamel finish; cast iron oven
	Features Can be used with wood, coal, anthracite, coke, or peat.									
S/A Imports Division	Stanley 8W	28⅜"H × 35⅜"W × 21¾"L	28⅜"				13" × 15¾" × 15"		Top	Enamel finish; cast iron oven
	Features Can be used with wood, coal, anthracite, coke, or peat.									
Scandinavian Stoves, Inc.	Lange Model 911W	33¼"H × 36¼"W ×24"L	33¼"	17½"L			7½" × 11" × 16"		Top	375 s.w. Cast iron body
	Features Grates.									
Washington Stove Works	Olympic 18 W		32"	8½" × 8" × 16"	32" × 22½"	2	13" × 18" × 18"	7"	Back	320 s.w. Porcelain enamel finish; cast iron firebox lining
	Features Grates; shelf; hot water coils available.									
Washington Stove Works	Olympic 8-15		30¾"	8¾" × 8" × 19¾"	34" × 23½"	2	10" × 18" × 15"	6"	Back	245 s.w. Matte black finish; firebox lining
	Features Iron grates; hot water coils available; shelf.									
Washington Stove Works	Olympic B-18-1 Home Range		31½"	8" × 8¾" × 21"	26½" × 35¼"	2	11¼" × 17¼" × 18½"	7"	Back	490 s.w. Steel body; cast iron lining
	Features Grates; hot water coils available; burns wood or coal.									
Washington Stove Works	Olympic 7-14		30"	7" × 6½" × 18"	26½" × 19½"	2	8½" × 16½" × 13½"	6"	Top	160 s.w. Matte black finish; firebox lining
	Features Grates; hot water coils available.									

The following is a partial list of the many manufacturers, importers or distributors of radiant and circulating wood stoves, free-standing fireplaces, and cookstoves.

Abundant Life Farm
Box 175, Lochmere, NH 03252
Comforter Stove

All Nighter Stove Works, Inc.
80 Commerce St., Glastonbury, CT 06033
All Nighter stoves

Ashley Automatic Heater Co.
1604 17th Avenue, S.W. Box 730, Sheffield, AL 35660
Ashley space heaters

Atlanta Stove Works, Inc.
Box 5254, Atlanta, GA 30307
All types of cast-iron stoves, free-standing fireplaces, fireplace accessories

Autocrat Corporation
New Athens, IL 62264
Cooking ranges and space heaters; Americana stove

Birmingham Stove and Range Co.
Box 2647, Birmingham, AL 35202
Many kinds of ranges, stoves, and heaters

Bow and Arrow Stove Co.
14 Arrow St., Cambridge, MA 02138
Importers of different stoves and ranges

C & D Distributors, Inc.
P.O. Box 766, Old Saybrook, CT 06475
Better 'n Ben's

Cawley/LeMay Stove Co., Inc.
Box 431, R.D. Barto, PA 19504
Box stoves

The Damsite Stove Company
R.D. 3, Montpelier, VT 05602
The Dynamite stove

Dynapac, Inc.
1610 Industrial Road, Salt Lake City, UT 84104
Collapsible stove

Enterprise Sales
R.D. 2, Apple Creek, OH 44606
Ranges, stoves, Franklins

Fireview Distributors
P.O. Box 370, Rogue River, OR 97537
Cylindrical heater with glass door

Fisher Stove Works
504 South Main St., Concord, NH 03301
Fisher stove

Free Flow Stove Works
South Strafford, VT 05070
Free Flow stoves

General Engineering and Manufacturing Corp.
133 S. Snowden St., Andrews, IN 46702
Earth stove

Greenbriar Products
Box 473, Spring Green, WI 63588
Fireplace-stove with glass doors

H.D.I. Importers
Schoolhouse Farm, Etna, NH 03750
Austrian Scandia range, German coal stoves

Heathdelle Associates
RFD 4, Box 153, Laconia, NH 03246
Nashua stove

Hunter Enterprises Orilla, Ltd.
1 Colborne St., W., P.O. Box 400, Orilla, Ontario L3V 6Ki
Stoves, furnaces

Hydraform Products Corp.
P.O. Box 2409, Rochester, NH 03867
Hydrostove, Eagle

J and J Enterprises
4065 W. 11th Ave., Eugene, OR 97402
Frontier stove

Kerr Controls, Ltd.
P.O. Box 744, Truro, Nova Scotia B2N 5G1
Stoves, furnaces

Kickapoo Stove Works, Ltd.
Rt. 1, Main St., La Farge, WI 54639
Kickapoo stoves and furnaces

K.N.T. Inc.
Hayesville, OH 44838
Various stoves and free-standing fireplaces

Kristia Associates
343 Forest Ave., Box 1118, Portland, ME 04104
Jøtul stoves, combis, ranges

Locke Stove Company
114 West 11th St., Kansas City, MO 64105
Drum heater, cabinet heaters

Louisville Tin and Stove Company
Box 1079, Louisville, KY 40201
Airtight heaters

Majestic Co.
Huntington, IN 46750
Free-standing fireplaces

Malm Fireplaces, Inc.
368 Yolanda Ave., Santa Rosa, CA 95404
Free-standing metal fireplaces

Martin Industries
P.O. Box 128, Florence, AL 35630
All kinds of stoves, ranges

Merry Music Box
20 McKown St., Boothbay Harbor, ME 04538
  Stoves, ranges, Styria wood stoves

M & M Mfg. Sales, Inc.
929 S.W. 29th St., Oklahoma City, OK 73109
  Stoves

Mohawk Industries, Inc.
121 Howland Ave., Adams, MA 01220
  Tempwood stove

Monarch Range Company
Beaver Dam, WI 53916
  Fireplace accessories, wood/coal stoves and fireplace heaters

New Hampshire Wood Stoves, Inc.
P.O. Box 310, Plymouth, NH 03264
  Home Warmer stoves

Old Country Appliances
P.O. Box 330, Vacaville, CA 95688
  Stoves, ranges

Pioneer Lamp and Stove Co.
71 Yesler Way, Seattle, WA 98104
  Ranges

Portland Franklin Stove Foundry Co.
57 Kennebec St., Portland, ME 04104
  Cast iron stoves and ranges, Trolla stoves, Franklin stoves

Quaker Stove Co.
200 West 5th St., Lansdale, PA 19446
  Quaker stove

Ram Forge
Brooks, ME 04921
  Box stoves

Riteway Manufacturing Co.
Box 6, Harrisburg, VA 22801
  Riteway stoves, multi-fuel furnaces and boilers

S/A Import Division
730 Midtown Plaza, Dept. 74, Syracuse, NY 13210
  Kitchen ranges, Reginald kitchen stoves

Scandinavian Stoves, Inc.
Box 72, Alstead, NH 03602
  Lange stoves; Tiba ranges

Self Sufficiency Products
One Appletree Square, Minneapolis, MN 55420
  Sierra and Gibralter stoves

SEVCA
Box 396, Bellows Falls, VT 05101
  SEVCA stoves

Shenandoah Mfg. Co., Inc.
P.O. Box 839, Harrisonburg, VA 22801
  Shenandoah stoves

Southport Stoves
248 Tolland St., East Hartford, CT 06108
  Morsø, Imperial, Franklin stoves

The Stoveworks
Marlboro, VT 05344
  Box stoves, Culvert Queen

Sturges Heat Recovery, Inc.
P.O. Box 397, Stone Ridge, NY 12484
  Thriftchanger fireplace heat exchanger

Sunshine Stove Works
Callicoon, NY 12723
  Box stoves

Superior Fireplaces Co.
4325 Artesia Ave., Fullerton, CA 92633
  Zero-clearance fireplaces

Thermo-Control Wood Stoves
Howe Caverns Rd., Cobleskill, NY 12043
  Stoves, add-on furnace units

Thulman Eastern Corporation
3485 Chevrolet Drive, Ellicott City, MD 21043
  Franklin stoves

Timberline Stoves, Ltd.
110 East 1st St., East Syracuse, NY 13057
  Timberline stoves

Union Mfg. Co., Inc.
6th and Washington Sts., Boyertown, PA 19512
  Box stoves

U.S. Stove Company
Box 151, South Pittsburgh, TN 37380
  All kinds of stoves

Vermont Castings, Inc.
Prince Street, Randolph, VT 05060
  Vigilant, Defiant stoves

Vermont Iron Stove Works
Warren, VT 05674
  Elm stove

Vermont Woodstove Company
307 Elm St., Bennington, VT 05201
  DownDraft stoves; importers of Canadian Stepstove

Victorian Woodstoves
1601 Park Avenue South, Minneapolis, MN 55404
  Importers of Jøtul, Ulefos, Reginald; cooking ranges

Warm Glow Products, Inc
625 Century S.W., Grand Rapids, MI 49503
  Warm Glow stoves and accessories

Washington Stove Works
P.O. Box 687, Everett, WA 98201
  Wide variety of stoves and ranges

Jøtul

The following is only a partial listing of manufacturers of wood boilers, wood furnaces, multi-fuel heating systems and add-on units.

Arotek Corporation
1703 East Main St., Torrington, CT 06790
Hoval add-on units and multi-fuel boilers

Bellway Mfg.
Grafton, VT 05146
Bellway boilers, add-on furnaces

Carlson Mechanical Contractors, Inc.
Heating and Boiler Mfg. Division
P.O. Box 242, Prentice, WI 54556
Solid fuel boiler

Charmaster Products
2307 Hwy. 2 West, Grand Rapids, MN 55744
Wood or wood/oil furnaces

Combo Furnace Co.
1707 W. 4th St., Grand Rapids, MN 55744
Furnaces and boilers

The Dam Site Stove Company
R.D. 3, Montpelier, VT 05602
Dynamite furnace

The Defiance Company
Chassell, MI 49916
Volcano add-on furnaces

Dual-fuel Products, Inc.
2775 Pittsburgh Ave., Cleveland, OH 44115
Newmac wood/oil furnace

Duo-Matic
2413 Bond St., Park Forest South, IL 60466
Multi-fuel furnaces

Environ House
Division of Trend Engineering, York Beach, ME 03909
Swedish wood/oil boiler

Enwell Corporation
750 Careswell St., Marshfield, MA 02050
Solid fuel furnace

Frontier Hardware
Box 368, Essex, MA 01929
Warm air furnace

G & S Mill
Otis St., Northborough, MA 01532
Wood furnaces

Hunter Enterprises Orilla, Ltd.
1 Colborne St., W., P.O. Box 400, Orillia, Ontario L3V 6Ki
Wood/oil furnaces

Kerr Controls Ltd.
P.O. Box 744, Truro, Nova Scotia B2N 5G1
Multi-fuel furnaces and boilers

Kickapoo Stove Works, Ltd.
Rt. 1, Main St., La Farge, WI 54639
Wood furnace, add-on unit

Longwood Furnace Corp.
Gallatin, MI 64640
Longwood wood furnace

Lynndale Mfg.
Highway 65 No., Box 1154, Harrison, AR 72601
Wood furnace

Marathon Heater Company, Inc.
Box 165, R.D. 2, Marathon, NY 13803
Logwood wood/oil furnace boilers

Minnesota Energy Savers, Inc.
305 Main, La Crescent, MN 55947
Lumberjack add-on furnace

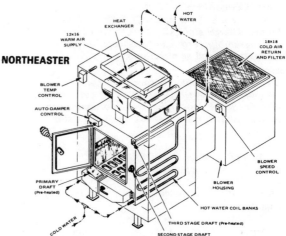

Northeaster—*Model 101-B and the slightly larger Model 224-B is a hot-air furnace with the plus of heating domestic hot water. A compact unit with a cast-iron grate and top-mounted heat exchanger.*

Monarch Range Company
Beaver Dam, WI 53916
Furnaces

Oneida Heater Co.
P.O. Box 148, Oneida, NY 13421
Multi-fuel furnace

Passat, USA, Inc.
Highland Court, Gloucester, MA 01930
Wood/oil boiler

Powrmatic Inc.
2906 Baltimore Blvd., Finksburg, MD 21048
Multi-fuel furnaces

Ram Forge
Brooks, ME 04921
Wood boiler, wood furnace, add-on unit

Riteway Mfg. Co.
Div. of Sarco Corp., P.O. Box 6, Harrisonburg, VA 22801
Multi-fuel furnace

S/A Import Division
Crossroads Park Dr., Liverpool, NY 13088
Surefire add-on wood burning furnace

Sam Daniels Company
Box 868, Montpelier, VT 05602
Wood burning furnaces

Solar Wood Energy Corp.
East Lebanon, ME 04027
Northeaster wood furnace

Thermo-Control
Div. of National Stoves Works Inc., Howe Caverns Rd., Cobleskill, NY 12043
Add-on units

Wilson Industries
2296 Wycliff, St. Paul, MN 55114
Multi-fuel furnaces

Wood Energy Systems Corp.
Box 2, Searsmont, ME 04973
Wesco add-on wood furnace

BARREL STOVES

Country Craftsmen
Wood Burning Stove Kits, Box 333, Santa Rosa, CA 95402
Provides barrel stove kit which includes flue pipe flange, door assembly, three point steel legs, and all the required hardware as well as directions.

Fatsco
251 N. Fair Ave., Benton Harbor, MI 49022
"Woodsman Stove Kit" contains all parts except drum. Includes front door frame and door, ash door, four adjustable legs and leg braces, draft regulator, and door knobs.

Fisher's
Rt. 1, Box 63, Conifer, CO 80433
Kit includes stove pipe collar, top door hardware, bottom door hardware, four legs, and glass assembly. Pyrex glass door for fire-viewing. Barrel stands upright.

Locke Stove Company
114 West 11th St., Kansas City, MO 64105
"Warm-Ever Wood Heaters" are drum-type wood heaters with firebrick-lined firebox and cast iron legs. Parts are also available for do-it-yourself barrel stoves.

Portland Franklin Stove Foundry Co.
57 Kennebec St., Portland, ME 04104
Kit for 55-gallon drum. Parts are of cast iron.

Sotz Corporation
Columbia Station, OH 44028
Double and single drum kits. Cook top available.

Washington Stove Works
P.O. Box 687, Everett, WA 98201
Conversion kits for 55-gallon oil drums. Door, pipe collar and legs come with kit. "The Drummer" is a completely assembled drum stove which includes a grate, insulating back shield and an ash pan.

Yankee Woodstoves
Cross St., Bennington, NH 03442
Preassembled wood-burning stoves which resemble a drum. Available in various sizes.

Country Craftsmen

Thermograte Enterprises, Inc.

TUBE GRATES

Arrowsmith Industries, Inc.
P.O. Box 208, Downingtown, PA 19335
"Arrowsmith Intensi-fire" fireplace grates are 12 inches high, 16 inches wide and 15⅜ inches long. Adjustable to different fireplace openings.

Bassani
3726 East Miraloma, Anaheim, CA 92806
"Eco-hearth heater" is a set of heater tubes with a blower.

Blaze
Industry of Canada Ltd., 50 Electronic Ave., Port Moody, B.C. V3H 2R8
Bar grate with steel tubes

DeForge Industries
Malletts Bay, Colchester, VT 05446
Adjustable tube grates. Double-wall construction, stands 21 inches high, 21 inches wide and 18 inches deep.

Duo-Therm
509 South Poplar, LaGrange, IN 46761
"Hearth Heater" comes in four sizes to fit fireplace openings of 28 to 46 inches

Frahm Fireplace Grate, Inc.
256 S. Pine St., Burlington, WI 53105
Heat circulator grate with blower

The Golden Enterprise
P.O. Box 422, Windsor, VT 05089
Thermal-type grate of two-inch tubing

Heat-N-Glo Fireplaces
1100 Riverwood Dr., Burnsville, MN 55337
Grate heater of 12-gauge steel with blower

Pipe Products Co.
1278 Lincoln Rd., P.O. Box 24, Allegan, MI 49010
Energy grate of six or eight tubes with blower

Texas Fireframe Co.
P.O. Box 3435, Austin, TX 78764
Grate in two sizes: one is 17 inches front width, 14 inches back width, 13 inches deep, 13 inches high, and weighs 21 pounds; the second grate of 30 pounds is 25 inches front width, 21 inches back width, 15 inches in height.

Thermalite Corporation
P.O. Box 658, Brentwood, TN
Grates

Thermograte Enterprises, Inc.
2785 North Fairview Ave., St. Paul, MN 55113
C-shaped tubular steel grates with blower. Thirty-four models, tubes of 14-gauge steel, shipping weight varies between 30-123 pounds. Optional blower. Two-year warranty.

PRE-FAB INSULATED STOVEPIPE

Dura-Vent Corporation
2525 El Camino Real, Redwood City, CA 94064
"Dura-Vent" stovepipe comes in either inch or metric diameters

Enterprise Sales
R.F.D. #2, Apple Creek, OH 44606
"Thor" all-fuel chimneys of triple-wall construction

Oliver-MacLeod Limited
5 Edward St., Gravenhurst, Ontario, Canada POC 1 GO
"Pro-Jet" all fuel, double wall insulated pipe

Wallace Murray Corporation
1820 E. Fargo, P.O. Box 372, Nampa, ID 83651
"Metalbestos" stainless steel insulated pipe

CHIMNEY CLEANERS

Ace Wire Brush Co. Inc.
30 Henry St., Brooklyn, NY 11201
Round and square brushes

Anachron Inc.
Box 8860, Portland, OR 97208
Assortment of chimney brushes

Bow and Arrow Stove Company
14 Arrow St., Cambridge, MA 02138
Chimney brushes (square and round); flexible extension rods in lengths of 3, 4, 5, and 6 feet; and necessary hardware for use with extension rods. Rental service also available.

C & D Distributors, Inc.
Box 766, Old Saybrook, CT 06475
"Jiffy Chimney Cleaner" is designed to be lowered through the chimney from the roof. Adjustable to any chimney flue 7 inches to 12 feet in length. Scrubs flue walls.

Flue-Z Chimney Cleaner
P.O. Box 1102, Cook, MN 55723
Plate mounted on top of flue which can be lowered to clean chimney

Hearth Enterprises, Inc.
508 Shorter Ave., Rome, GA 30161
Chimney cleaning kit of rope, weight, connector, and brush

Kristia Associates
343 Forest Ave., P.O. Box 118, Portland, ME 04104
Five, six, seven and eight-inch brushes

Lite-Wood, Inc.
P.O. Box 267, Flanders, NJ 07836
Round and square chimney brushes in all sizes. Flexible extensions, hardware for adapting brushes to pipe and extensions, and scratch brushes available

Meeco Mfg., Inc.
1137 S. W. Hanford St., Seattle, WA 98134
"Red Devil" is a chemical cleaning agent designed to be thrown on hot fire

Worcester Brush Company
38 Austin St., Worcester, MA 01601
Chimney brushes in all sizes

STOVE POLISH

Rising Sun Stove Polish
P.O. Box 597 Q, Marlborough, MA 01752

FURNACE CEMENT

Do-All Wonder Products
Mt. Vernon, NY 10550

Industrial Gasket and Shim Company
Box 368, Meadow Lands, PA 15347

HEAVY ASBESTOS GLOVES

R.M. Hannawalt Co., Inc.
Box 32, Fort Montgomery, NY 10922
Fireplace and wood stove glove

WOOD SPLITTERS

Albright Welding
Johnson Rd., Jefferson, VT 05464
L.O. Balls Woodsplitter. Powered hydraulic splitters which will take logs between 26 and 48 inches.

Amerind-MacKissic, Inc.
Box 111, Parkerford, PA 19457
Mighty Mac. Hydraulic splitter in 5 HP or 7 HP model.

Arnold Industries, Inc.
Toledo, OH 43606
The Stickler. Twenty-three pound woodscrew that bolts to the hub of car or truck. Log is pulled up the threads. Will split a log up to 24 inches in diameter and 30 inches long.

Bellway Mfg.
Grafton, VT 05146
Roto-Wedge. Screw-type wedge which bolts onto the rear wheel of car or truck without removing the tire. Splits any size and length up to 8 feet.

C & D Distributors, Inc.
Box 766, Old Saybrook, CT 06475
Jiffy Woodsplitter. "Guided Wedge" splitter. Wedge slides on upright steel bar which stabilizes it. Wedge then is hammered into upright log. Weighs 50 pounds.

Chopper Industries
P.O. Box 87, Easton, PA 18042
Chopper 1. Axe with splitting levers which increase the splitting force and keep the blade from sticking in the log. Downward force of axe causes levers to rotate. This creates outward pressure which splits the log.

Wood Splitters (cont.)

Cornell Mfg. Inc.
R.D. No. 2, Box 511, Laceyville, PA 18623
The Cornell Splitter. Log splitter takes 30-inch logs.

Derby Log Splitter Co.
P.O. Box 21, Rumson, NJ 07760
Derby Log Splitter. Homeowner screw or hydraulic units. Derby Bark Buster is self-powered portable screw-type splitter with 3 HP motor. Will take logs 19 inches long and 20 inches wide. Hydraulic unit with 4 HP and 17 second cycle time. Will take logs 19 inches long and 20 inches wide.

Didier Mfg. Co.
P.O. Box 163, 8630 Industrial Dr., Franksville, WI 53126
Hydraulic splitters. Ten models with log capacity between 19 inches and 50 inches.

Energy Associates
P.O. Box 524, Old Saybrook, CT 06475
Woody. Wood-splitting maul with steel handle and "V-shaped" splitting head.

Futura Enterprises
5069 Highway 45 South, West Bend, WI 53095
Powered wood splitters.

FW and Associates, Inc.
1855 Airport Rd., Mansfield, OH 44903
Screw-type splitters.

Knotty Wood Splitter Mfg. Co.
Rt. 66, Hebron, CT 06248
Tractor-driven units.

LaFont Corp.
1319 Town St., Prentice, WI 54556
Hydraulic splitters designed with the professional in mind. Available with 2-, 3-, 4-, and 5-way wedges.

Lindig Splitters
1875 West Country Rd., St. Paul, MN
Hydraulic splitters with tractor mount option.

N.E.H. Corporation
780 Main St., Holsen, MA 01520
The Royal Log Splitter. Hydraulic splitters for truck mount, tractor hitch or independent trailing units. Can take wood up to 27 inches long.

Nortech Corp.
Midland Park, NJ 07432
Portable screw splitters with 8 or 9 HP engine and 12-second cycle time. Also three-point hitch for farm tractors.

Piqua Engineering, Inc.
Box 605, Piqua, OH 45356
Lickity Log Splitter. Hydraulic wedge-type splitter. Thirty-second splitting cycle.

Richard Pokrandt Manufacturing
R.D. 3, Box 182, Tamaqua, PA 18252
Tractor-mounted combination cordwood saw and wood splitter units.

Sotz Corporation
23797 Sprague Rd., Columbia Station, OH 44028
Monster Maul. Mauls with steel handles and heads of twenty-pound hardened steel.

Taos Equipment Mfg. Inc.
Box 1565, Taos, New Mexico 87571
The Stickler. Screw-type splitter, vehicle-driven. Splitter is bolted onto hub after the wheel has been removed. Splits logs from 10 to 30 inches in length and up to 28 inches in diameter. Available in four models.

The Thackeray Co.
2376 Brentwood Rd., Columbus, OH 43209
Unicorn Log Splitter. Wheel-mounted, screw-type splitter.

Thrust Mfg. Inc.
6901 S. Yosemite, Englewood, CO 80110
Thrust Log Splitter. Horizontal wedge splitter, self-contained unit.

Trans America Power Equipment, Inc.
8308 Washington St., Chagrin Falls, OH 44022
Self-powered, screw-type splitter.

United Western Products, Inc.
11295 East 51st Ave., Denver, CO 80239
Dynasplit Log Buster. Splitter attaches to left rear hub with the axle supported by a log. Weighs 28 pounds.

INSTITUTES

Canadian Wood Energy Institute
49 Gloucester St., Toronto, Ontario M4Y 1L8

National Solid Fuel Trades Association, Inc.
P.O. Box 6369, Syracuse, NY 13217
Works to develop codes and standards for safe installation of solid fuel burning devices.

Wood Energy Institute
Box 1, Fiddlers Green, Waitsfield, VT 05673
Wood-related projects, exhibitions and seminars. Publishes "Wood 'N Energy Newsletter."

Index